ATLAS OF
THE NEW WEST

Portrait of a Changing Region

ATLAS OF THE NEW WEST

Portrait of a Changing Region

William E. Riebsame, General Editor
with
Hannah Gosnell
David Theobald

James J. Robb, Director of Cartography
with
Paul Breding
Chris Hanson
Keith Rokoske

**Department of Geography
University of Colorado at Boulder**

Essays by:
Patricia Nelson Limerick
Charles Wilkinson

Photographs by:
Peter Goin

A Project of the

Center *of the* American West
University of Colorado at Boulder

W • W • NORTON & COMPANY • NEW YORK • LONDON

Contact the **Center of the American West** via

E-mail: *centerwest@colorado.edu*

Web page: *http://www.colorado.edu/ArtsSciences/CenterWest/home.htm*

snail mail: *Center of the American West*
             Hellems 373
             Campus Box 234
             Boulder, CO 80309-0234

Atlas of the New West was designed and produced entirely on desktop using the following:

Hardware: IBM RISC 600, Power Macintosh and Power Supercomputing personal computers ethernet connected, SGI Personal Iris, Sun Solaris, and Sneakernet via removable SyQuests and external hard drives

Software: Adobe Illustrator, Adobe Photoshop, ArcInfo, ArcView, Dartmouth College Fetch, EdWare, GRASS, Macromedia Freehand, Microsoft Excel, Microsoft Word, and Quark Xpress

The text of this book is composed in Goudy and Univers 55 and 65

Manufacturing by South China Printing Co. Ltd.

Library of Congress Cataloging-in-Publication Data

Atlas of the new West : portrait of a changing region / William Riebsame, general editor; James
   Robb, director of cartography . . . [et. al.].
       p.   cm.
   Includes bibliographical references and index.
   "A project of the Center of the American West."
   Contents: ch. 1. A region defined — ch. 2. Infrastructure for new West — ch. 3. Water for the
   new West — ch. 4. People in the new West — ch. 5. New West lifestyles — ch. 6. The ugly West —
   ch. 7. Visions for the next West.
   ISBN 0-393-04550-1
   1. West (U.S.)—Social change — Maps. 2. West (U.S.) — Economic conditions — Maps.
   3. Infrastructure (Economics) — West (U.S.) — Maps. I. Riebsame, William E. II. Robb,
   James. III. University of Colorado, Boulder. Center of the American West.
   G1380 .A74 1997 <G&M>
   912.78—DC21   97–18780
                                                                                   CIP
                                                                                   MAPS

W. W. Norton & Company, Inc., 500 Fifth Avenue, New York, N.Y. 10110
       http://www.wwnorton.com

W. W. Norton & Company Ltd., 10 Coptic Street, London WC1A 1PU

1 2 3 4 5 6 7 8 9 0

Contents

Acknowledgments   9
American West Reference Map   11
Preface   12

Paradise Revised by Charles Wilkinson   15

Chapter 1 • *A Region Defined*   46
  (Maps)
    Lay of the Land   48
    Places on the Land   50
    The Bureaucratic West   52
    The Region Compared   54
    A Blank Space   55
    Black Hole   56
    Filling the Void   57
    Public West, Private East   58
    A Wealth of Public Lands   60
    Sovereign Lands   63
    Writing the New West   66

Chapter 2 • *Infrastructure for the New West*   68
  (Maps)
    Flying In and Out of the West   69
    Jet-Setting the West   71
    A Road Runs Through It   73
    Connecting the West   76
    A Corporate Void   78
    Capital for the New West   79

Chapter 3 • *Water for the New West*   80
  (Maps)
    Arid, Extra Dry   80
    Quenching the Thirst   81
    Drenching the Fields   83
    Damming the West   85
    Small Dams, Big Impact   87
    "Jurassic Pork"   90
    Plumbing the Divide   92

Chapter 4 • *People in the New West*   94
  (Maps)
    Peopling the New West   95
    Origins   98
    Tuning into Diversity   100
    Electing Women   102
    Owning a Home on the Range   103
    Ghost Houses   106

Yellowstone's Service Economy   107
Strongholds of the Traditional Economy   108
Retirement Hot Spots   111

Chapter 5 · *New West Lifestyles*   **112**
(Maps)
The Cultured West   113
New Age in the New West   114
Consuming in the New West   116
What's Brewing in the New West   119
The Old West Lives On   121
America's Playground   124
Paying to Play   127
Places Rated, Places Raided   130

Chapter 6 · *The Ugly West*   **132**
(Maps)
A Nuked Landscape   134
Spectacles of the Ugly West   137

Chapter 7 · *Visions for the Next West*   **142**
(Maps)
War and Peace in the West   144
A Wild Future   147

The Shadows of Heaven Itself
by Patricia Nelson Limerick   **151**

Notes   **180**
Sources   **182**
Map Index   **185**
General Index   **189**

Photographs

High Country Log Homes, Buena Vista, Colorado   14
Snowboarder, Squaw Valley, California   16
Anasazi Sign Company, Moab, Utah   20
Cattle in Pasture, Austin, Nevada   24
Owensmouth Cascade,
   Owens Valley–Los Angeles Aqueduct   28
Disc Jockey, KWSO, Warm Springs Reservation, Oregon   36
Carousel, Missoula, Montana   40
Rafters, Arkansas River, Colorado   45
Saguaro, Phoenix, Arizona   150
Shoot–Out, Ponderosa Ranch, Nevada   156
Haywagon Breakfast, Ponderosa Ranch, Nevada   156

Coyote Howls, Old Divide Trading Post, Colorado   *160*
Sagebrush Fire, Colorado.   *164*
Sun Sculpture, Crestone, Colorado   *168*
Nuclear Bomb Blast Debris, Frenchman Flat, Nevada   *173*
"Ground Zero" outsider art, Black Rock Desert, Nevada   *173*
Highway Deconstruction, Las Vegas, Nevada   *174*
Scenic Byway, Las Vegas, Nevada   *176*
Moonrise, Black Rock Desert, Nevada   *179*
Hot springs, The Needles, Pyramid Lake, Nevada   *179*

Acknowledgments

The *Atlas* team owes much to a larger group of advisors and information providers, many of whom are listed in the "Sources" section detailing each major map. Thanks for their advice goes to Rocky Barker, David Getches, Paul Cunningham, Ed Marston, Jeff Limerick, Craig Miller, Peter Morrisette, Ray Ramirez, Elizabeth Rieke, Eric Sandeen and the American Studies students at the University of Wyoming, Don Snow, and Anne Travis. Suzanne Larson and Peggy Jobe, University of Colorado libraries, offered great help.

Charles Wilkinson especially wishes to thank Nancy Nelson, Cynthia Carter, Kristin Howse, and Scott Miller for their research and ideas. Patricia Limerick offers thanks to Shreka Anderson, Tracy Brady, and Lynn Kallos for their research assistance and humorous commentary, and Jeremy Shelton for his visit to the Santa Fe New Age Fair. *Atlas* data grubbers also included Joe Moss, Elizabeth Pike, Tom Perreault, and John Schneider.

Our special thanks for map information go to: Bill Allen, American Rivers; Michael Branson, National Muzzleloaders Association; Margaret Brown, *Southwest Art*; Dick Cameron, Forest Conservation Council; Susan Cherry; Grand Canyon National Park; Marilyn Connely, Northern Colorado Water Conservation District; Betsy Demeny, Opera America; Doug and Dave Dolsen, Carlson Wagonlit Travel; John Echohawk, Marilyn White, Laura West, and Ray Ramirez at the Native American Rights Fund; Glenn Fant, Colorado Motor Vehicle Division; Bill Haskins, Missoula Environmental Center; Nancy Jacques, Colorado Rivers Alliance; Martin Gauthier, Action Cellular; Meg Glaser, Western Folklife Center; Rosalind McClellan, Southern Rockies Ecosystems Project; Bobby Newton, *Ropeburns* magazine; Kathryn Oliver, Allegro Coffee; Larry Jones, Peaberry Coffee; Jerry Ott, Sam Bryan, Khalid Popal, John Roth, and Frank Rabineau, the *New York Times*; Tom Pansky, Bonnevile Power Administration; Ken Rait, Southern Utah Wilderness Alliance; Jeff Richards, Colorado Advanced Technology Institute; and Phyllis and Kevin Stanton.

Peter Goin wishes to thank Dennis Albrecht, Cammy Bauer, Warren "Rudy" Clements, Robert Cree, U.S. Department of Energy, David Geddes and the Ponderosa Ranch, Dana and Kari Goin, Jack and Evelyn Goin, Wanda Hammerbeck, Paul Inchauspe, Renata Lawrence, Michal and Susan Murri, Christine Olsen, Lisa Page, Squaw Valley Ski Corporation, and the University of Nevada at Reno. Everyone involved with the *Atlas* was deeply saddened by the death of Peter's wife, Chelsea Miller Goin, as she returned home to take care of the girls for Peter's first *Atlas* photographic expedition.

Atlas cartographic director James Robb considers most maps one-page books, each deriving from great effort by a number of people. He wishes to thank the folks who made these maps unique and special. Ed Russell, of Computer Terrain Mapping, Inc., provided his considerable expertise on the shaded relief and satellite land cover imagery; thanks also for his contributions to many other mapping projects over the years. Various professional cartographers, graphic artists, photographers, printers, GIS (Geographic Information Systems) and business specialists provided comments, suggestions, and technical problem solving on the *Atlas*, especially Ken Abbott, Todd Ball, James Collins, Heidi Ochis, Bud Shark, Bill Thoen, and Martin Wright. Original page design and illustrations were created by Elizabeth C. Johnston, Art Director. Jean E. Cleavinger, Project

Manger at the University of Colorado Publications Department, offered advice and design suggestions. Allison Fisher assisted in assembling the map index and several graphs. Thanks also to several present and former students in the Geography Department's Cartography and GIS program for their help and comments: Jennifer Eber, Jim Freeman, David Gonzalez, Stephen Huh, Chris Ryan, Brian Silverman, Greg Smith, James Zack, and Craig Willis. We appreciate the support and encouragement of staff and faculty of the Geography Department, especially Marcia Signer, Karen Wiengarten, James Huff (Chair), John O'Loughlin (former Chair), Mark Kumler, and Barbara Buttenfield. James Robb thanks his wife, Gigi, and daughters, Lauren and Zoe, for their love, support, and patience during the long hours in the Cartography Lab.

Tom Precourt at the Center of the American West provided a steadying project management hand; thanks also to Roni Ires at the Center. Ed Barber, our editor at W. W. Norton, took a chance on this unusual and complex book and played an integral role throughout the project.

The American West

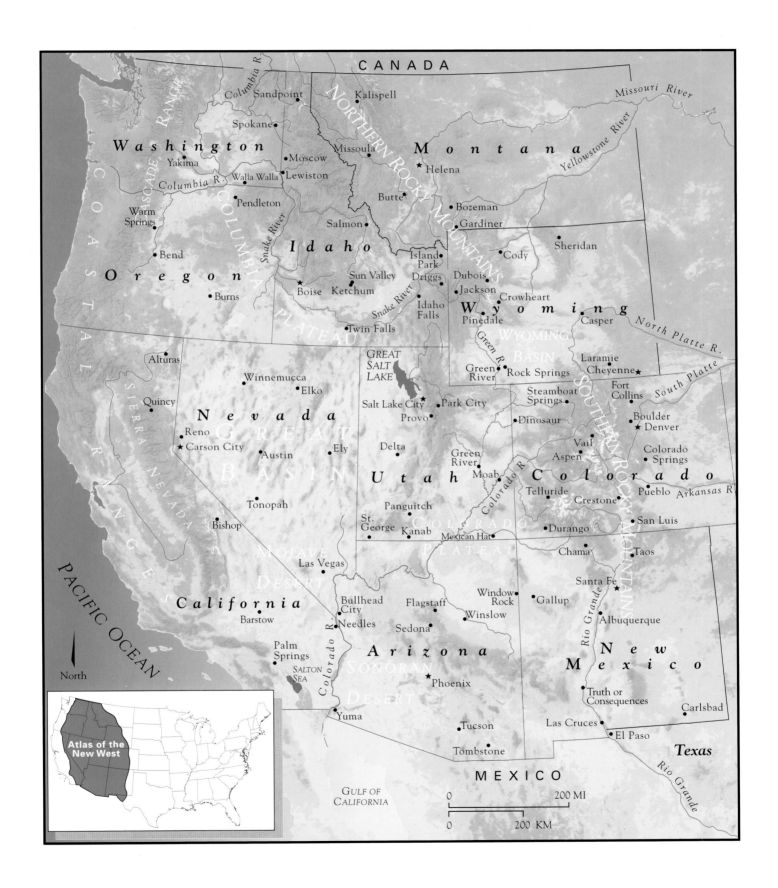

Preface

Do regions matter in a world homogenized by telephone, fax, the World Wide Web, and people who don't stay put? Does regional character or idiosyncracy still separate one part of the country from another? The *Atlas of the New West* expresses our belief that the answer is yes, that Americans still value a sense of regionalism as antidote to globalization and homogenization. They want regions to remain distinctive—the South different from New England, the Midwest different from the mid-Atlantic. They especially hold to notions of differentness in the "West" as a wild place of big spaces, national parks, and cowboys, with something left of the eroding ideal of limitless opportunity.

The American West is partly these things, but the story of the New West is also about a region's transformation into something resembling the rest of the country: a landscape of shopping malls, cookie-cutter subdivisions, and the same old social and economic problems. Our project in the *Atlas*, then, is both to acknowledge the bland American culture that appears to make every place like every other place—a sort of "geography of nowhere" [1]—but also to look beyond it, where we see not so much Old West icons like cowboys and Indians and homesteaders, but rather a postmodern West in which old and new combine to create something different.

The American West, we argue, is the archetypal case of an American region yanked from its historical and myth-based sense of place into hyperdevelopment and plugged-in modernity. Such a transformation forces startling contrasts between image and reality, between old and new. The most obvious contrast runs between a "cowboy economy" built on extracting natural resources and the post–World War II cosmopolitan florescence that, by the 1990s, had thrown the region's economy into the postindustrial, services sector. Traditional life ways—logging, mining, drilling, farming, and ranching—contrast sharply with the new economy of services and information, ostentatious wealth, and tourism. This shift shows on the land, empty, awesome natural spaces now overlain unconformably with a landscape of sprawling cities, greenlawn suburbs, and ranchette estates—conventional American society in an unconventional place.

We tried to capture this fast-paced, place-uprooting, and disquieting transformation of region to make some sense of it to ourselves and others. And, like any group of Westerners contemplating our part of the continent, we wrangled. What to include and what to leave out? Where to bound the West? How to blend the strange and humorous with the familiar and serious? Should we map Indian spiritual sites along with New Age power vortexes? How seriously do we treat the Aspenization of small Western towns? Might we not worsen doleful trends by creating maps of airport commuter zones and rural Internet access? We anguished whether we had embarked upon an enterprise fundamentally optimistic or dour, and how the book's maps, essays, and photographs could convey these conflicting attitudes.

The *Atlas* was partly our droll response to the West's newfound, upscale trappings. We felt loss. Ski resorts, fur shops, and espresso bars have edged out feed stores, cowboy bars, and greasy spoons. Walled estates, golf courses, and factory outlet malls weave through mining and ranching towns. We set out to map the new face of the West, marking microbreweries, mountain biking meccas, and retirement hot spots, to put geographic substance to notions like modem cowboy and amenity migrant. We wanted to map the geographical skeleton on which the New West hung: private-jet ports, water diversions, the few home-grown corporations, and gold medal trout streams. As the book took on a seriousness of purpose well wide of its genesis, we moved also to map enduring threads of Western geography—like Indian reservations and public lands—that surely will go on shaping the West. We then explored the underside of the New West: nuclear bomb factories, chemical dumps, and endangered species—some tottering on the brink, some making a comeback.

Maps, a geographer's customary tool, tell part of the New West's story. And the essays and photographs tie things together, speaking of events and feelings beyond the reach of cartography. These elements tell multiple stories from an orbit of perspectives, but our final message is hopeful. We hope that the New Westerners, from wherever they hail, will pay more attention to their regional home, think more about the consequences of their presence in this extraordinary landscape, and act to make the region a better place. The goal of this book is to lay out the geographical stuff with which they are refashioning and reimagining the West.

William Riebsame
Boulder, Colorado

Paradise Revised

By

Charles Wilkinson

In March, 1959, six businessmen climbed aboard a snowcat and plowed up and through deep powder into the Colorado high country above the Gore Valley. Rising to a ridge, they looked down over five broad mountain bowls. One of the men, Earl Eaton from nearby Eagle, had come upon the bowls five years earlier while prospecting for uranium. An experienced skier, he immediately saw the terrain for what it was—an expanse that offered nearly incomparable skiing. A short while later, Eaton enlisted Pete Siebert, who managed the Loveland Basin ski area, in a quest to establish a ski operation. Siebert was thunderstruck: "I turned my skis loose on three feet of powder and it made me giddy. One way or another, I was going to make this place go." The two men soon bought 1000 acres of ranchland at the foot of the mountain, straddling old Route 6, to serve as a base. Eaton and Siebert had ambitious plans drawn up, then invited in the other four men, all substantial investors.

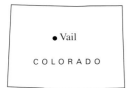

The snowcat tour marked the group's last checkpoint before committing to an expansive undertaking. Their view from the summit that bright spring day erased any remaining doubt. After strapping on their skis and weaving down virgin slopes to the valley floor, they broke open a bottle of wine to celebrate their dream. This was the place to build a world-class ski area and an entire new town to serve it. Less than three years later, in December, 1962, Vail opened for business.

By the end of the 1960s, Vail Associates had spent some $50 million to transform the valley, so recently a place of unpopulated forests and open ranch land, into one of the world's great destination resorts. Yet only one-third of the mountain's potential ski runs had been developed. Vail had just one golf course (the narrow valley could, and would, accommodate eight). The potential for restaurants, shops, condominiums, and luxury homes was enormous. Vail wanted a boost to get to the next level, and so did other Colorado ski areas.

There was a model. Squaw Valley had lured the Winter Olympics to California in 1960, with spectacular results. The ski area boomed after the Games and others nearby blossomed to absorb—and multiply—the enthusiastic demand for mountain recreation. Development erupted at neighboring Lake Tahoe, still a lazy, old-family resort community until the Olympics.

Smart investors saw similar returns in the Colorado Rockies. The Winter Olympics could put Colorado over the top. Vail Associates became a main player, seeking to promote both Vail and the slopes at Beaver Creek, still on the drawing board. By the early 1970s, an aggressive campaign had made Colorado the leading candidate for the 1976 Winter Games.

Other Coloradans weren't so sure. One of them was Dick Lamm, then a state legislator. Colorado's growth rate had been steadily climbing since the end of World War II and, to Lamm's eye, many of the results were bad. Air pollution—"the Brown Cloud"—hung over Denver. Traffic congestion had begun to plague the Front Range towns. Over on the Western Slope, in the Interior West, coal, uranium, oil shale, and oil and gas development were putting money into

(facing page) High Country Log Homes, near Buena Vista, Colorado. These builders specialize in Scandinavian full-scribe and Swedish cope construction; they assemble three to four homes a year.

people's pockets, but there were costs to the land, rivers, aquifers, and air—and to the communities that had to absorb outsiders drawn by the energy rush. Even the ski areas damaged the environment by using scarce water for artificial snow and displacing prime elk habitat with ski runs and construction sites. Besides, in Lamm's view the problems were Colorado's but most profits left the state: Colorado and the other Rocky Mountain states were being treated like colonies. For Lamm, the Olympics would only aggravate the state's growing pains.

Lamm's grassroots anti-Olympic movement garnered enough signatures to force a statewide referendum barring the state from spending any funds on the games. The ballot measure passed in 1972 by a hefty 3–2 margin, effectively ending any chance of Colorado's hosting the games. Two years later, Lamm ran for governor and won, due in good part to his outdoorsman's image enhanced by walking nearly a thousand miles across Colorado.

These events in Colorado, as well as any, mark the beginning of the New West. The creation of Vail, the rise of a high-stakes recreation industry, and the dispute over the Olympics epitomized a new dynamic in the region. Recreationists, most of them newcomers and urban, wanted expanded opportunities in the West's big, magical backcountry but questioned traditional extractive development. Environmentalists doubted both. Businesspeople found that very big money lay not only in minerals and timber but also in powder snow and in the condominiums that could be so neatly blended with it. Locals, caught in the middle, struggled to achieve some measure of prosperity and to preserve their uncluttered way of life. Over time, the changes evidenced in Colorado would be expanded and deepened by such disparate forces as the completion of the interstate highway system and the easy availability of jet travel; the invention of the computer, modem, fax, and satellite dish; the mass production of Winnebagos and Jeep Cherokees; innovations in fly rods, hiking boots, ski equipment, and bicycles; advances in air quality controls, mining methods, water conservation, and forestry and range science; the application, or attempts at such, of ecosystem management and sustainable development; a profusion of splendid books by Western writers; the rise of Indian sovereignty; and the public's deepened passion for mountain terrain coupled with its newfound love of desert and plains. A revolution.

Yet only a revolution of sorts. True, ever since a watershed lying astride the late 1950s, 1960s, and early 1970s, we have seen an upswelling of values that has made for a very different mix at the end of the century than existed, say, in the late 1940s. Most of the ascendant values, however, cannot rightly be called new; all had long preceded "the New West," although they may have been held by a small minority or may have existed in a different form. John Muir, for example, loved and understood the land, as did many others. This included ranchers, farmers, loggers, and plain Westerners who cherished their homeland but happened to prefer exploring the backcountry with a deer rifle rather than a mountain bike. Nor have the "new" ideas replaced the traditional attitudes and interest groups between the Rockies and the Sierra. The influence of water developers, timber and energy companies, and the ranch cattle industry is alive and well. Western county commissioners and United States senators from the dry states vote in patterns strikingly similar to generations past.

The New West also has brought its full supply of irony. Reformers espous-

"A land ethic for tomorrow should be as honest as Thoreau's Walden, and as comprehensive as the sensitive science of ecology. It should stress the oneness of our resources and the live-and-help-live logic of the great chain of life."

— *Stewart Udall*, The Quiet Crisis *(1963)*

(facing page) Snowboarder at a pipeline, Squaw Valley ski resort, Lake Tahoe, California.

ing tourism as an economic alternative to the traditional extractive industries find that hordes of tourists can wreck the land every bit as thoroughly as an open-pit mine. Migrants, fleeing the urban rush, move to the Rockies only to find that their numbers and values have begun to infuse slow-paced mountain towns with the chic and high speed they sought to escape. Recreationists searching for solitude overcrowd the wilderness. Colorado, having once thumbed its nose at the Winter Olympics, now would kill to host the games—as Salt Lake City will in 2002.

Old West, New West, it is hard terrain to read. One prevails this week, the other the next; one typifies this place, the other the place just downvalley. Some changes have been cosmetic, others profound.

So you can say New West—and we do—because it has become common parlance and because it collects a rough set of ideas in a way that is often useful. But use the term gingerly. And mark it down that the New West has given us ample evidence that it is not necessarily better, only different.

Canyonlands Town

A principal reason that Vail and the proposed 1976 Winter Olympics so typify the New West is that those events centered on the federal public lands. The United States owns fully one-half of the Intermountain West and nearly all of the spines—the high country where ski areas might be located. For Earl Eaton, Pete Siebert, and their Vail partners, as with all Western ski developers, this meant a lease of the ski slopes from the Forest Service. The Olympics would have been held mostly on public lands—as they will be in Utah.

So, too, does the new town of Vail owe its existence to the public lands (and to Interstate 70 and Eisenhower Tunnel, which together give travelers from the Front Range and its airports a straight shot to Vail). Vail Mountain—holding the ski area—rises above the town to the south. The high peaks of the Gore Range, which includes the Eagles Nest Wilderness Area, lie to the north.

It turned out that Vail, because of its scenic beauty and the skill and resources of Vail Associates, never needed the games. The mountain town has grown into one of the immensely rich enclaves of the New West. The Vail Board of Realtors, more than 400 strong, lists nearly $400 million in sales annually. Trophy homes sell with regularity at $1 million and up—indeed, some bare lots run into seven figures. The same phenomenon has remade Santa Fe, Taos, Sedona, Telluride, Aspen, Steamboat Springs, Moab, Park City, Jackson, Sun Valley, Coeur d'Alene, and, to lesser degrees, Bozeman, Bend, Durango, and other locales. Beyond their prosperity, they all have one thing in common: they are inlaid in natural splendor.

Moab presents a fascinating and telling example. Long a scruffy ranch and mining town, Moab hit its mineral boom late, with the uranium frenzy on the Colorado Plateau of the 1950s and 1960s. But the bottom soon fell out of the uranium market and the town fell on hard times. Then, in the mid-1980s, Moab burst on the scene as the mountain biking capital of the New West. Today, 1.5 million visitors pass through Moab each year.

During the Fat Tire Festival and the Jeep Safari, 15,000 people or more—triple the permanent population—will stay over in town or in nearby

UTAH

Moab

environs. Land prices don't yet match Vail's, but Main Street lots worth $6000 in 1990 sell for more than $100,000 by the mid-1990s. Many a fancy home is going up in Moab, Spanish Valley, Castle Valley, and other nearby places.

Part of Moab's New West boom can be attributed to its proximity to Arches National Park, just six miles to the north, and to the town's status as gateway to Canyonlands National Park, 60 miles to the south. These world-famous parks annually draw hundreds of thousands of foreign visitors alone. More fundamental, though, are the Bureau of Land Management lands that envelop Moab. Here mountain bikers ride the challenging, spectacular Slickrock Trail and other routes through the sandstone terrain. Most of the backcountry is open for four-wheeling. Hikers head out into Negro Bill Canyon, Mill Creek Canyon, and the vast expanses of the Behind-the-Rocks region.

In Moab we can see attitudes that, at least among the general public, make the New West truly new. When I first went to Moab in the early 1970s, my reaction lay somewhere between boredom and "aarghh." It was just a dusty, grubby mine town. My eyes never saw the drama of Poison Spider Mesa and the Moab Rim, the long, sheer redrock escarpment rising a thousand feet above the southwestern edge of town. I had no idea, no remote comprehension, of the wonders—fins, arches, and petroglyphs —that lay on the other side of the rim in Behind-the-Rocks.

Partly, I had been conditioned to think of BLM lands as leftovers. The national parks of legend—Yellowstone, Yosemite, Grand Canyon, Teton, Rocky Mountain, and others—had the highest status among the public lands. The national forests, fully one-quarter of the Intermountain West and long the most contested ground, held special fascination for me. Just after the turn of the century, Theodore Roosevelt, working hand-in-glove with Gifford Pinchot, set aside nearly 150 million acres as forest reserves to the loud and sustained howls of Western developers. These grand strokes earned TR his place as America's greatest conservation president. The national forests then remained quiescent until after World War II when, to fuel the postwar housing boom, the timber harvest from the forests increased tenfold. The Forest Service, which had gained a white-hat reputation, overdid it, cutting more trees during the postwar era than was sustainable and more than the New West, which had a love affair with the national forests, wanted. Overcutting in the Bitterroot National Forest, near Missoula, led to the Bolle Report of 1972, written by the great conservationist and forestry school dean, Arnold Bolle; the report excoriated the Forest Service for bad timber practices and triggered congressional reform. Much later, in the 1990s, the spotted owl controversy put still more pressure on the Forest Service to throttle the chain saws in the deep backcountry.

In common with most of the general public in the early 1970s, then, I conceived of wild land in terms of the national forests. High alpine country. Streams. Lakes. Aspen. Snowpack. The country around Vail, yes. The country around Moab? What country?

I and millions of others eventually learned about the desert and Utah's BLM lands. Mainly we simply learned how to look and listen and feel. But, as with many facets of the New West, we were mightily aided during the past two generations by the craft and passion of Western writers. Speaking for the desert was Edward Abbey.

"The desert grants each of us our own bundle of understandings, charges us with the preservation of its messages."

— Ann Zwinger, Testimony (1995)

Abbey has been both worshipped and reviled for *The Monkey Wrench Gang* and other calls to arms against the industrial forces of the American Southwest. But, however one may come down on those issues, Abbey was also a first-rate writer and philosopher. Perhaps the best example is *Desert Solitaire*, a book that can fit comfortably in any university philosophy or policy course concerned with the relationship between human beings and the natural world. Abbey proves the worth of time spent in the desert as an intellectual experience as well as an emotional and aesthetic one. Always iconoclastic, he drew this meaning from the world's most-photographed natural arch, not far from Moab:

> The beauty of Delicate Arch explains nothing, for each thing in its way, when true to its own character, is equally beautiful. . . .
>
> A weird, lovely, fantastic object out of nature like Delicate Arch has the curious ability to remind us—like rock and sunlight and wind and wilderness—that out there is a different world, older and greater and deeper by far than ours, a world which surrounds and sustains the little world of men as sea and sky surround and sustain a ship. The shock of the real. For a little while we are again able to see, as the child sees, a world of marvels. For a few moments we discover that nothing can be taken for granted, for if this ring of stone is marvelous then all which shaped it is marvelous, and our journey here on earth, able to see and touch and hear in the midst of tangible and mysterious things-in-themselves, is the most strange and daring of all adventures.

He wrote this of the desert's long, ordinary spaces:

> Strolling on, it seems to me that the strangeness and wonder of existence are emphasized here, in the desert, by the comparative sparsity of the flora and fauna: life not crowded upon life as in other places but scattered abroad in spareness and simplicity, with a generous gift of space for each herb and bush and tree, each stem of grass, so that the living organism stands out bold and brave and vivid against the lifeless sand and barren rock. The extreme clarity of the desert light is equaled by the extreme individuation of desert life-forms. Love flowers best in openness and freedom.

And Abbey loved—loved—the humblest of desert things:

> My favorite juniper stands before me glittering shaggily in the sunrise, ragged roots clutching at the rock on which it feeds, rough dark boughs bedecked with a rash, with a shower of turquoise-colored berries. A female, this ancient grandmother of a tree may be three hundred years old; growing very slowly, the juniper seldom attains a height greater than fifteen or twenty feet even in favorable locations. My juniper, though still fruitful and full of vigor, is at the same time partly dead: one half of the divided trunk holds skyward a sapless claw, a branch without leaf or bark, baked by the sun and scoured by the wind to a silver finish, where magpies and ravens like to roost when I am not too close.

"Please keep in mind that while Moab has been designated the 'Mountain Bike Capitol of the World,' probably less than 10% of Grand County's population actually rides a bicycle. Most of us still ride pickup trucks, dip snuff and spit out the window. Many of our elected officials still think wilderness is a commie trick. And yet, in just such a town as this, on any given day, half the men seen on the street are wearing brightly colored tights."

— Home Page of Jim Stiles, Publisher of The Canyon Country Zephyr *(1997)*

(facing page) Anasazi Sign Company, Moab, Utah.

Thus Abbey, who raged with all of his heart and mind against what he called industrial tourism, helped create it by helping us to understand and love the desert. Abbey, once a park ranger at Arches, grew to love the old, inglorious Moab. He would go into town on Saturday nights to drink beer with the cowboys and miners. Today, he would see industrial tourism close-up just by watching the Winnebagos and four-wheel-drives grind down route 191 into downtown Moab. He would see, too, how the multitudes—the public lands of the Colorado Plateau receive 50 million visitor-days a year—tear up the backcountry, eroding the frail soil, spreading trash, spoiling wildlife habitat, desecrating Anasazi sites, and by their (our) sheer numbers debasing the openness and freedom so dear to Abbey.

But there is more to modern Moab than the evils of industrial tourism.

A recent May—by then I had come to know the canyon country—I travelled over to Moab to do some hiking, and in the warm-air evening ran into a friend, as fierce an environmentalist as I know, on Main Street. She loves the Colorado Plateau also. She's read every word Abbey wrote.

We talked a while on the sidewalk and then a man she knew came by. He grumbled about how Moab had grown so crazy. "The damn bikers and four-wheelers have overrun this place and it's wall-to-wall motels," he said.

He had to leave and my friend and I decided to have a leisurely dinner at Catarina's. Later, as we were finishing up pasta on the open patio, she said slowly, "You know, I just flat don't agree with him. This is such a vital place. You can find any kind of person here, from ranchers to Navajos to river runners to the modern cowboys to the French. You'll hear more languages spoken on the Main Street sidewalk than in any town between San Francisco and Chicago. It's like a big river. All the currents feed into Moab."

And she was right. Lord knows there have been enough jokes about 1990s Moab to plug Landscape Arch, but in truth, this is a dynamic community both blessed and beleaguered by its surrounding glory. Moab's good and creative people are experimenting, working hard to craft a sensible relationship between our species and a jagged, erratic, redrock stretch of land that not long ago we scorned but that we now know is sacred. In that sense, while Moab is far more New West than most places, it represents the essential stresses and dreams that characterize the interior West as the region moves into a new century.

On the Range

Ranchers control more Western land than any other class of property owners. For most ranches, the privately owned land—the base ranch—is a small part of the spread. A ranch will lease most of its land (tens or even hundreds of thousands of acres) from the BLM or the Forest Service, and sometimes from the state. Many ranches will be a conglomerate of all four kinds of land.

Ranching has become a flashpoint in the conflict between the Old and New West. Federal lands under grazing leases remain open to public recreation and these users, many of them from the cities, do not like what they see. Much of the Western range is overgrazed. Notably, cattle tend to gather in the riparian areas, green strips along streams and creeks that nurture wildlife and provide nutritious forage for cattle. As the cattle take out grasses and brush—eating some, pounding some down with their hooves—the riparian soils yield to erosion. When melting snowpacks send down the fierce spring runoff, the churning

"[T]he cattle kingdom spread from Texas and utilized the Plains area, which would otherwise have lain idle and useless. Abilene offered the market; the market offered inducement to Northern money; Texas furnished the base stock, the original supply, and a method of handling cattle on horseback; the Plains offered free grass. From these conditions and from these elements emerged the range and ranch cattle industry, perhaps the most unique and distinctive institution that America has produced."

—Walter Prescott Webb, The Great Plains (1931)

streams—swollen in size many times over—can tear out the soil right down to bedrock. The workings of cattle and water have created many if not most of the cutbanks that characterize western creeks and streams. Concerns about this truly significant land degradation are accompanied by other, perhaps less transcendent, outrages, including cowpie-stained Hi-Tec and Vasque hiking boots.

Traditionally, public lands transactions had been handled as essentially private matters between federal agencies and private users. And so it was in the early sixties, when Earl Eaton and Pete Siebert approached the Forest Service for a lease of ten square miles in the early 1960s to make Vail. Working under the name of the Trans Montane Rod and Gun Club to assure low visibility, they slid easily into a deal without any public scrutiny. Likewise, the public rarely figured in public lands grazing leases.

This closed system began to open up in the early 1970s, with the passage of freedom of information and sunshine laws and statutes requiring a public voice in public lands decision making. The consequences of federal land policy—including environmental impacts, large subsidies, and the fueling of population growth—became highly politicized. Many new environmental groups were founded and older ones, such as the Sierra Club, Audubon, and The Wilderness Society, vastly expanded.

In 1974, the Natural Resources Defense Council, one of the new organizations, obtained an injunction against the BLM. Judge Flannery of the District of Columbia required the agency to prepare 144 environmental impact statements under the National Environmental Policy Act to assess how Western grazing lands should be managed. The opinion documented a need for strict measures: range lands, including riparian areas, were in poor condition compared to their historic potential. Judge Flannery made it clear that this affected antelope, trout, ducks, and other wildlife species, not just domestic stock.

The range litigation ignited the smoldering conflict between environmentalists and ranchers, who had their own story to tell. The ranch cattle industry produced, they argued, many economic benefits. More fundamentally, though, they saw social value in ranching, and they were right. Go around the West—Gunnison, Chama, Baker, scores of other towns—and you will find solid communities built on ranching. Besides, working ranches had clear environmental benefits, especially when compared to the alternative: most of the condominiums the environmentalists decried were going up on good river bottom land sold off by struggling ranchers. Keep the cattle ranchers and sheep growers economically healthy and keep the valleys in open space.

Antagonisms have run high. The Sagebrush Rebellion and the rise of James Watt in the early 1980s came mainly out of the public rangeland controversy. In the 1990s, People for the West! and the Wise Use movement drew heavily on a ranch constituency. Their theme was that city people had no business making decisions in ranch country; local people should control their own destinies. In particular, the public lands ought to be run as they always had been, for ranching, logging, and mining.

Tempers flared in many places, especially Catron County, New Mexico, and Nye County, Nevada. Violence finally broke out in 1995 in Carson City, Nevada. Fortunately, no one was injured when a pipe-bomb went off in a Forest Service office.

"Frederick Jackson Turner was wrong. He said we lost the western frontier in the 1890s, when the urban population of the West first exceeded its rural population. But in Utah we lost the frontier in 1976, with the enactment of FLPMA. Before FLPMA, these people could do virtually anything they wanted on the public lands."

— Utah Commissioner Bill Booker, quoted in Wheeler, Reopening the Western Frontier *(1989)*

But, while there is frustration aplenty on the Western range, violence is far from mainstream conduct on the ranches. In fact, some modern ranchers are carving out distinctive niches in the New West.

Tony and Jerrie Tipton, a husband and wife team, run a ranch near Austin, in central Nevada, just north of the Nye County line and 170 miles east of Reno. Their 26,000-acre Forest Service lease lies the on the west slope of the Toiyabe Range in the heart of the Basin and Range Province. Most people speed through central Nevada on I-80 or US 50, but if you explore the slopes and draws of the Toiyabe or the other numerous north-south ranges, you find deer, sage grouse, clear-running creeks, and, until late spring, snow fields on the mountain crests that rise to 11,000 feet and higher. This is land worth caring for.

The Tiptons realize that cattle have given the Western landscape a hammering, but they also know, from having grown up on ranches, that the oldtimers never had access to modern range science. The Tiptons, like a good number of ranchers, are convinced that creative management practices can both restore the range and improve the bottom line.

I spent a day out on the Tipton's ranch and saw how they had blended range science research with their own experience, instincts, and knowledge of the land. Jerrie, tall and lean like her husband, explained how they had monitored land health by setting up hundreds of transects—randomly located areas, only a few square yards each. Data from each transect is collected each year. Jerrie bounded out to a transect and dropped to her hands and knees. "See this plant? Native Indian ricegrass! It's new to this transect. You've got to think of range management in terms of individual plants."

The Tiptons work hard on strategic herding of their cattle. "Cattle can do a lot of your work for you, breaking up the ground and pruning the plants. But you've got to keep them moving." Their monitoring shows that the Indian ricegrass and native plants have come back. Individual plants grow much closer together, and show less stem and more leaf. Along Big Creek, the sedges and other water-loving vegetation flourish.

The Tiptons took risks, in money and time, to put in place new land management techniques. They also took another kind of risk. In 1987, they hosted a group of more than 200 people interested in the Nevada range. Attendees included environmental groups, cattlemen's organizations, and government offices. The idea was to bring diverse people together in search of common ground on range management in general and on the Tipton ranch in particular. The group now meets four times a year, averaging 10–20 people per meeting, and is chaired by Jerrie's sister, Tommie, a trained conflict resolution facilitator.

At first, the proposal met with plenty of skepticism. This included Tony Tipton, once a deep-dyed Sagebrush Rebel. Several individual environmentalists have participated, but most of the main-line green organizations chose to stay away. Federal employees were chary, too: perhaps their authority would be diminished. But the management team agreed on goals, based on a shared love of the land and a respect for community, and on the means to achieve them. The effort has been mostly successful. The proof is in the transects. Now the management team process is embodied in a memorandum of understanding between the Tiptons and the Forest Service.

"Supreme over all is silence. Discounting the cry of the occasional bird, the wailing of a pack of coyotes, silence—a great spatial silence—is pure in the Basin and Range. It is a soundless immensity with mountains in it. To stand, as we do now, and look up at a high mountain front, and turn your head and look fifty miles down the valley, and there is utter silence."

— *John McPhee,* Basin and Range *(1980)*

(facing page) Cattle in pasture at Silver Creek Ranch, north of Austin, Nevada.

The collaborative experience at the Tipton ranch has a growing number
of analogues across ranch country, described by Dan Dagget in *Beyond the
Rangeland Conflict: Toward a West That Works*. Further, management practices are
steadily improving on most ranches. Ranchers will admit to being hidebound but
they also are pragmatic people. Younger ranchers, back from college, bring with
them innovations in range science. Many in the older generation now accept
that keeping the cattle moving can bring more profits and better wildlife habitat—and the improved hunting and fishing that goes with it.

Open, collaborative processes and progressive range management are
now federal policy. This has been largely the work of Bruce Babbitt who, along
with Dick Lamm, personifies a sort of New West public official. Babbitt became
secretary of the interior in 1993 with a background deeper than anyone ever
appointed to that office, the most important one for the West. Born of a leading
pioneer family, he grew up in Flagstaff, a ranching, mining, and timber town.
Always well read, he began to take a broader view of the West when he encoun-
tered the work of Wallace Stegner: Babbitt, just a teenager at the time, described
Beyond the Hundredth Meridian as "the rock that came through the window." He
went off to Harvard Law School and, after private law practice in Phoenix and a
stint as attorney general of Arizona, served three terms as governor.

Babbitt's antagonists accuse him of launching a "War on the West," but
the charge is unfair. He grew up with, and understands and respects, people in the
traditional industries. As a lawyer, he represented many business interests. As
governor, Babbitt convened the stakeholders to work out a consensus resolution
of Arizona's groundwater crisis. As interior secretary, he spearheaded the 1993
"Timber Summit" in Portland that led to forest reform and helped facilitate an
historic settlement of water and wildlife issues in the Sacramento Bay Delta. He
has found innovative ways to administer the Endangered Species Act more flex-
ibly and reach stable, long-term agreements with private landowners affected by
the ESA.

Babbitt also ventured into the thicket of range grazing. He began by
holding a series of listening forums around the West. Emotions ran high. I
remember attending one of them, a 1993 gathering in Flagstaff. I looked out on
500–600 people—a good three-fourths of them ranch sympathizers, creating a sea
of Stetsons. Soon thereafter, Babbitt issued proposed federal regulations that,
among other things, raised grazing fees and directed BLM land managers to crack
down on poor grazing practices, especially in riparian areas. Ranchers (who might
well have opposed any new regulations) saw this as top-down, command-and-
control federal interference. The Old West mobilized. A legislative initiative
incorporating Babbitt's proposal went down in early 1994, suffering death by
Senate filibuster.

Stung by the setback, Babbitt went back to the drawing board, holding a
remarkable set of eight roundtable meetings, co-chaired by Governor Roy Romer,
in Colorado. The sixteen-person group included a broad mix of interests. Two
influential participants, Ken Spann, a rancher-lawyer, and Gary Sprung, of the
High Country Citizens Alliance, had already cooperated in a consensus venture,
in the spirit of the Tiptons' effort, in the Gunnison River Valley on Colorado's
Western Slope.

In 1995, Babbitt issued new BLM range regulations based on the findings of the Colorado group. The idea is to improve rangeland health while bringing decision making down to a grassroots level. Management plans will be developed by resource advisory councils (RACs), usually composed of fifteen local members equally divided among ranchers, environmentalists, and the general public. The RACs (in most states there will be several, covering separate geographic areas) must meet general environmental objectives set in the regulations; the Interior Department can override their recommendations, but the RACs have wide latitude to work out on-the-ground solutions for meeting the departmental objectives. The working assumption is that normally the RACs' recommendations will be adopted.

Babbitt's approach to range reform reflects the sentiments of growing numbers of Westerners who want collaboration rather than the pitched battles that have marked the New West. Literally hundreds of grassroots efforts, large and small, successful and unsuccessful, have grappled with the problems of public lands logging, wilderness designation, air pollution at the Grand Canyon and elsewhere, watershed management, and new mine start-ups, as well as grazing.

Not everyone likes this trend. In particular, the national environmental groups have raised a large red warning flag about grassroots consensus efforts. Michael McClosky, chairman of the Sierra Club, had this to say:

> A new dogma is emerging as a challenge to us. It embodies the proposition that the best way for the public to determine how to manage its interest in the environment is through collaboration among stakeholders, not through normal governmental processes.
>
> [O]f six case studies examined at [a recent conference on the subject], the Sierra Club was not formally involved in any, nor were most other national environmental groups.
>
> There are reasons for this. Industry thinks its odds are better in these forums. It is ready to train its experts in mastering this process. It believes it can dominate them over time and relieve itself of the burden of tough national rules. It has ways to generate pressures in communities where it is strong, which it doesn't have at the national level.

Well enough said. Still, the rural West is coming of age. New Westerners know more, not just about modern resource management, but also about the region's past and its possibilities. Most critically, a yearning for community now runs through a region long cursed with rootlessness and boom-and-bust cycles. A full place, in other words, needs more than prosperity and a clean, scenic environment. It also needs civility.

City and Country

The Intermountain West, along with its neighbor to the east, the Great Plains, is the most rural area in the continental United States. There are the most low-population counties, the greatest distance between neighbors, the most open space. The rural West also gives the West its most distinctive qualities—Indian

"Instead of attacking Wise Use, environmentalists should sit down and study it, simply to learn why it appeals. It offers something environmentalism has never offered: a cogent focus on both livelihood and equity. The early conservationists were quite keen on both. They wanted to grow 'forests for the home-builder first of all,' and that popular slogan linked them to every American family struggling to make a living.

Livelihood speaks to people, to their sense of both survival and pride. The central problem with environmentalism is that it lacks a cogent, convincing focus on livelihood, and that has made it vulnerable to Wise Use attacks. The grand cause of protecting the environment from humans means that lots of humans now feel unwelcome in what they see as the environmentalists' visionary world. It doesn't take too many thousands of the unwelcome to form a countermovement, if somebody's willing to organize them, and that's precisely what has happened."

— Donald Snow, "The Pristine Science of Leaving It All Alone," in Northern Lights (1994)

country, ranch country, the tidy Hispanic settlements in the Southwest, mining towns, the big sky plains, the high country, the deep canyons, the wilderness. Objectively justified or not, the West is a place where romance is unavoidable fact, a place you cannot talk about, cannot think about, without an overlay of romance. The hinterlands give the West that aura.

Yet the West is at once the most urban region in the country. Eighty percent of its people live in the cities, islands in the big empty. In the Old West, outlying acres had political control—membership in western legislatures was tied largely to counties, not population. Then, in *Baker v. Carr* (1962), the Supreme Court shook the political landscape with "one person, one vote" and reapportionment. Now the statehouse balance, as well as the economic capital, is lodged in the cities.

The relationship between the cities and the country has been characterized by unease on good days, by open combat on the bad. It began with water, which always guarantees a good fight in the West.

The West lies beyond the 100th meridian, the dry line. West of the 100th meridian, nearly all of the terrain receives less than 20 inches of precipitation a year, the amount needed to grow crops without artificially putting water on the land. From the Gold Rush on, a central question for every investment scheme was: "Do you have the water rights?"

By the late nineteenth century, Western settlers, both urban and rural, began to run up against the aridity in earnest. The easy water diversions had been done. Now really large-scale water engineering would be needed. Western farmers and ranchers lacked the necessary capital, so they lobbied Congress for construction money and got the resulting Reclamation Act of 1902, which subsidized a Western irrigation empire. On rivers from the Missouri to the Sacramento, these reclamation dams held back the spring runoff; the impounded water was then released during the summer irrigation season when rivers in their natural condition would run low. Canals, splaying out from every Western river, delivered water to the fields, where it gushed out to make crops bloom from the dry soils. Even today, agriculture accounts for 80–90 percent of water use in Western states.

The cities also needed water—less, to be sure, than agriculture, but plenty nonetheless. In the early 1900s, Salt Lake City began poking around in the Uintah Basin, across the Wasatch Range, and Denver sent its engineers to the other side of the Continental Divide on reconnaissance missions into the Colorado River Basin; both cities had in mind massive reservoir and tunnel projects to make these transbasin diversions work. Los Angeles had even bigger plans: to transport water from the Owens Valley, 200 miles to the north across the Sierra Nevada, and to build an aqueduct from the Colorado River, 268 miles away on the Arizona line. Paranoia and resentment swept across the rural West as these and many another project surged ahead during the first part of the century, and as water development accelerated to meet the urban real estate boom in the decades following World War II. How, people in the country wanted to know, can the cities just steal our water?

The people of the New West asked the same question, and with the same intensity, but for different reasons. To their eyes, a different "they" was stealing the water. How did the consortium of cities, irrigators, industry, and state and fed-

(facing page) The Owensmouth Cascade, Owens Valley-Los Angeles Aqueduct. The water arrives here after a 233-mile journey across the Sierra Nevada. At its 1913 dedication, aqueduct creator William Mulholland pointed to the water and said, simply: "There it is. Take it."

eral bureaucrats get the right to steal water from the West's rivers, even dry them up if they wished, and to flood deep, glorious gorges?

At bottom, the answer is that traditional Western water law amounts to legalized theft or, put more politely, a mechanism to allow private water users to take—for free—as much water as they want from public rivers and aquifers. It was a simple system, developed in Gold Rush mining camps and called "prior appropriation." The keystone of prior appropriation was seniority, "first in time, first in right": the first user had a guaranteed supply (subject always to the vagaries of aridity), the next senior had the second priority, and so on down the line, as long as water still flowed. Only utilitarian, extractive uses—mining, farming, ranching, municipal, industrial, and domestic—that physically took water out of the stream were eligible. If the senior user, or users, took the whole stream or river, so be it. Once water was diverted, even though taken for free, a water user automatically acquired a vested property right, protected by the Constitution. Although water is said to be the West's most precious resource, traditional prior appropriation allowed for profligate waste of water, both in the cities and on the farms.

Prior appropriation rewarded the aggressive, those who got to the water first. This meant that Western water law, as it played out on Western rivers, had a fundamental bias in favor of big interests. Rural areas lost out to cities. Small farmers lost out to large irrigation districts with the clout to lobby Congress for subsidized dam-and-reservoir projects. Indian tribes and Hispanic communities lost out to everyone. Fly-fishers, streamside cabin owners, river runners, hikers, artists, poets, and, for that matter, trout, deer, beaver, willows, sedges, rapids, and canyons were of no account at all.

In time, by the 1990s, some reform measures have been put in place. Instream flow requirements now keep water in some streams. Indian water rights have been vindicated on some reservations. Conservation measures have been adopted or imposed in some urban areas and irrigation districts. But progress is glacial. The large, senior, vested rights still rule the rivers. Prior appropriation is the West's biggest, best-oiled, and most durable machine.

The cities used the water laws to the hilt during the past half-century. Most Americans think of the period of Manifest Destiny, in the nineteenth century, as the time when the West was settled. Not so. The decisive time for peopling the West has been the post–World War II era—the one we are still in. In 1945, the region's population stood at 16 million. By 1996 it had risen to 58 million. In the Interior West, population has shot from 5 to 18 million. Except for increases in the early 1990s, rural population has remained quite constant. Virtually all of the growth has taken place in the cities. This postwar build-up of the West is one of the most colossal exercises of industrial might in world history.

To accomplish that, the urban centers needed vast amounts of water and energy. They had exhausted sources close to home, so they moved out into the rural areas. Whether cities within the Intermountain West (Denver, Albuquerque, Phoenix, Tucson, Las Vegas, Reno, Salt Lake City, Boise, and Spokane) or urban areas on the Pacific coast from the southern California complex to Seattle—they all reached into the empty for their needed resources.

One main target was the Colorado Plateau—the canyon country of the

"Among . . . the most important [rules of custom in the early mining camps] are the rights of miners to be protected in the possession of their selected localities, and the rights of those who, by prior appropriation, have taken the water from their natural beds, and by costly artificial works have conducted them for miles over mountains and ravines, to supply the necessities of gold diggers, and without which the most important interests of the mineral region would remain without development."

— Irwin v. Phillips (California Supreme Court, 1855)

Southwest. The deep canyons, if plugged, would make superb reservoirs. So, too, was the plateau rich in minerals: the ages had laid down some of the best coal, oil, gas, and uranium deposits on Earth. Almost before anyone knew it, between 1955 and 1975, mostly before the days of environmental impact statements and public input, the Colorado Plateau was laced with dams and reservoirs up to 200 miles long, power plants with stacks 70 stories tall, 500- and 345-KV powerlines spanning hundreds of miles, and uranium mines, mills, and waste dumps. The cities have exported their wastes literally hundreds of miles, clouding stunning 120-mile vistas, staining high country lands and wildlife with acid rain, bulldozing or inundating historic Anasazi and Fremont sites, and flooding redrock canyons. The Hopi, Navajo, and other traditional tribes have paid the highest prices, seeing their ancestral lands degraded and receiving in return below-market leases of their coal and water.

In the Pacific Northwest, the Seattle and Portland metropolitan areas accomplished the extraordinary hydroelectric postwar build-up in the Columbia River Basin. Today, of the mainstem Columbia's six hundred miles between Bonneville Dam near Portland and the Canadian border, hydropower dams and reservoirs have left just fifty miles of freeflowing river. Here, too, the cities exported their costs to the interior. Wild salmon once filled streams all over eastern Washington, eastern Oregon, and central Idaho, all the way up into tributaries that flow down from the Continental Divide. Many of these salmon runs have been put on the endangered species list. The tribes have fished that country, living off the big fish, for 11,000 years or more.

The rural West has long felt under the thumb of the cities for reasons other than resource extraction. The urban areas have always been the supply centers. People in the country had to travel to the city or wait for the city to deliver. Mining and timber quickly became corporate, before the nineteenth century ended, and all the corporate headquarters were in the cities. The state capitals have been located in distant urban centers. Rural Westerners have long complained about the heavy hand of Washington, D.C., but Western cities also colonized the rural West.

If anything, the urban-rural conflict deepened as the New West emerged. Ultimate decision making over the extractive resources became ever more remote as multinationals took over mines, timber operations, and even ranches. Chains forced out local clothing, hardware, and grocery stores. Investment money for the new kinds of projects—ski areas, condominiums, motels, and fast-food outlets—came from the outside. And the cities themselves: painful places even to think about, much less go to, what with all the noise and rush and pollution.

Then you have the tourists. To country people, they seem to be everywhere. They're pushy. They don't leave all that much money behind. Something just doesn't exactly ring true about those biking helmets and tight, powder-blue Lycra shorts on the main street of Ely or Pinedale or Twin Falls.

Still and all, even implacable outlanders privately concede that their mandatory treks to The Big City at least hold out options never available before. The press has rightly made much of how the "cow towns" have "got culture" since the 1970s. The Denver Center for the Performing Arts presents a first-rate schedule every season, ranging from Broadway plays in the grand Auditorium Theatre

"Who but Dominy would build a lake in the desert? Look at the country around here! No vegetation. No precipitation. It's just not the setting for a lake under any natural circumstances. Yet it [Lake Powell, created by Glen Canyon Dam] is the most beautiful lake in the world.

. . .

Don't give me the crap that you're the only one who understands these things. I'm a greater conservationist than you [David Brower, former Sierra Club head] are, by far. I do things. I make things available to man.

Unregulated, the Colorado River wouldn't be worth a damn to anybody. You conservationists are phony outdoorsmen. I'm sick and tired of a democracy that's run by a noisy minority. I'm fed up clear to my goddamned gullet!"

— Floyd Dominy, former Commissioner of the Bureau of Reclamation, quoted in John McPhee, Encounters with the Archdruid (1971)

to avant-garde drama in the intimate Ricketson Theatre. The Heard Museum in Phoenix draws 250,000 visitors annually to its world-renowned collection, with an emphasis on indigenous people. Nearly every city has a substantial symphony, and most offer ballet and opera. Fortunately, cities in the Interior West have not taken the "cow town" opprobrium too seriously: many of the best institutions, like the Heard, have distinctly Western emphases, ranging from the Arizona-Sonora Desert Museum in Tucson and its specialty in desert ecology, to the Denver Art Museum's focus on Hispanic, colonial, and Native American art, to the Basque Museum in Boise, and to Santa Fe's seemingly countless Hispanic and Native offerings.

Sports and entertainment, as well as culture, have flourished in the cities. The Denver Broncos, which became the Intermountain West's first major-league sports team in 1960, has a loyal following throughout the Rockies. If the Arizona Cardinals football team has the feel of the carpetbagger about it, the Phoenix Suns, Utah Jazz, and Colorado Rockies have become fixtures. Las Vegas may hold out little in the way of traditional culture (Deke Castleman quipped, "Las Vegas is not renowned as a literary town. In fact, the word 'book' around here, 90 percent of the time is a verb."), but rural Westerners, like people the world over, have been drawn to the crap tables and shows in droves. Besides, the "Wet 'n Wild" waterpark is incomparable and might even salve some of the pain that will likely result from Las Vegas's relentless campaign to acquire rural Nevada water.

The sleeper is Salt Lake City. It is a gracious place of broad tree-lined streets, set at the foot of the Wasatch Range. Temple Square includes the Family History Library, the world's largest collection of genealogical records; gentiles curious about their roots are not only admitted but welcome. The Church has had the wisdom to look the other way when it comes to the sacred emblems of the New West. Salt Lake City has several first-rate brew pubs. The Salt Lake Roasting Company, with its motto, "coffee without compromise," is the best espresso place in the West, Seattle included. If you go to the Roasting Company, perhaps you'll run into the trucker from Vernal who, philosophizing about the New West, told me, "Just because I don't like those damned ugly biking uniforms doesn't mean I'm not going to drink their coffee."

Indian Country

Indian holdings comprise the other large blocs of land that, along with the federal public lands, make the Interior West distinctive. In the continental United States, some 300 tribes have reservations totaling about 57 million acres, most of it located in the West. A central fact about tribes is that they are sovereigns, that is, governments. As such, Indian reservations are political as well as social islands within the larger society. To nearly everyone's surprise, except perhaps the tribes', Indian governments have become creative, assertive, and influential forces in the West.

In the 1950s, when the seeds of the New West began to germinate, Indian societies hit their historic low. The tribes had faced two great waves of settlers and laws. The first, the ravage of European diseases and wars, extinguished whole tribes, especially in the East, and forced the others onto reservations a fraction the size of their ancestral lands. Following that, beginning in 1887, Congress and the developers came after the reservations—guaranteed, of course, to the tribes as permanent homelands—opening large areas of Indian country for settlement by non-Indians. Between 1887 and 1934, Indian land holdings plummeted from 140 million acres to 48 million.

Then, in the 1950s, Congress terminated more than a hundred tribes. Under the termination policy, their lands were either sold off or transferred to a private tribal corporation that lacked sovereign powers and federal protection. This meant, among other things, that any remaining tribal lands became subject to state taxes and that members of terminated tribes lost their treaty-negotiated rights to special programs in health, education, and other areas. Fear gripped those tribes not terminated, which included almost all of the tribes in the Intermountain West; tribal leaders were reluctant to begin progressive programs for fear that any successes would qualify them as self-sufficient—and ready for termination. Many individual tribal members were put on "relocation," that is, given a bus ticket to a big city, a new suit of clothes, and access to a transition program, which usually was poorly run or nonexistent.

Assimilate Indians. Make them Americans. Stamp out their worldview. The sense of despair among Indian people over termination was palpable.

Yet, out in Indian country, a great many Indians, by the force of their will, simply refused to accept all of the official actions designed to eradicate their Indianness. By miscellaneous day-to-day acts they kept the sovereignty and the worldview alive by stacking cord wood next to the hogan, telling the coyote stories over winter fires, fishing the streams, hunting the woods, holding the old ceremonies, teasing out the old humor, and speaking the languages.

An extraordinary series of events began to unfold in the wake of termination. The fears and determination of individual Indian people began to coalesced on the Northern Plains, in the green Northwest, in Navajo land, in red-earth Oklahoma, across all of Indian country. The tribes decided to make a stand together, as sovereigns, as peoples of worth and dignity. And the truth is, it was a last stand.

No longer would the tribes stand passively by while others made their decisions. Tribal governments took over federal programs on the reservations. Bureau of Indian Affairs dominance faded. These changes revitalized Indian societies, governments, and economies. Gradually, in one of the most inspiring social movements of this century, the tribes began to take back their reservations.

No one can say with precision when this movement began. Looking back, however, we can see it gathering steam in the 1970s. The return of Blue Lake to the Taos Pueblo in 1970. The Menominee Restoration Act in 1973, when the termination of the Wisconsin tribe was reversed. The Self-Determination Act in 1975. Health and education reform. The Indian Child Welfare Act of 1978, which recognized tribal court authority over adoptions and stopped state court judges from awarding Indian children to non-Indian families. In time, literally hundreds of other accomplishments in Congress. The tribes, too, blocked the continuing confiscatory proposals. Except for budget cuts, which have inflicted their share of pain, Congress has passed virtually no laws over Indian opposition since 1968.

The modern Indian offensive has also relied heavily on the courts. Since the 1950s, the Supreme Court alone has rendered over 100 Indian law opinions, more than in fields such as international, environmental, antitrust, and securities

"The primary goal of Indians today is not for someone to feel sorry for us and claim descent from Pocahontas to make us feel better. Nor do we need to be classified as semi-white and have programs and policies made to bleach us further. Nor do we need further studies to see if we are feasible. We need a new policy by Congress acknowledging our right to live in peace, free from arbitrary harassment. We need the public at large to drop the myths in which it has clothed us for so long. We need fewer and fewer 'experts' on Indians.

We need a cultural leave-us-alone agreement in spirit and in fact."

—Vine Deloria, Jr., Custer Died for Your Sins: An Indian Manifesto (1969)

law. The Rehnquist Court of the 1990s has been notably less protective of Indian rights, but overall the tribal litigation offensive still has prevailed in a strong majority of the modern cases, large and small. The essential phrase "tribal sovereignty" returned to our constitutional vocabulary. The federal government's trust obligation to tribes was enforced. Tribal natural resource rights were honored.

Court opinions, even those of our highest tribunal, are just paper unless they are put to work. Indian people began to implement those decisions in Indian country. Tribal governments reestablished or expanded their tribal courts, developed natural resource agencies, created tax and land use programs, founded tribal colleges, and assumed responsibilities in areas such as child welfare, law enforcement, road construction, hospital and clinic administration, firefighting, garbage collection, and alcohol treatment.

Deep problems remain in Indian country. Poverty is widespread, which is why so many tribes have turned, reluctantly, to gaming. Although determined progress is being made, alcoholism, the blight that seems to hold enmity for Indian people, remains virulent. Still and all, Indians have remade Indian country. Talk with Indian people and you'll find that virtually every reservation is better off than 30, 20, 10, or 5 years ago.

The Warm Springs Tribe of Oregon presents an example of the kinds of advances that tribes have made in recent years. This is a confederated tribe, composed of three tribes. The United States created these confederated tribes, of which there are many, in the nineteenth century by locating two or more ethnologically distinct tribes on single reservations and recognizing one common government. Although the confederated tribe exercises governmental power, individual members also identify with their ethnological tribe. Thus, depending on the circumstances, as with this discussion of Warm Springs, one may refer both to the confederated tribe or one of the three ethnological tribes as a tribe.

In 1855, the Warm Springs and Wasco, two Columbia River fishing tribes, negotiated a treaty with the United States. Later, the federal government moved the Northern Paiutes onto the reservation. In the treaty, the tribes ceded away most of their land, including their territory on the Columbia River, but the reservation is magnificent nonetheless. Lying 50 miles south of the Columbia, Warm Springs is bounded by the crest of the Cascade Range on the west (10,500-foot Mount Jefferson marks the southwestern boundary). The diverse reservation encompasses thick Douglas fir forests in the high country, then slopes down through high desert terrain to the Deschutes, one of the West's blue-ribbon fishing rivers, which forms the eastern border. All told, the tribe's land base includes nearly 650,000 acres, slightly more than one percent of Oregon.

The tribe managed to fend off termination proposals during the 1950s and then began to carry an assertive agenda. One longstanding issue involved disputed lands called the "McQuinn Strip." The reservation's first official survey dates back to 1871, and tribal people immediately objected, knowing that it did not reflect the boundaries that their chiefs had carefully staked out with federal agent Joel Palmer during the treaty negotiations in 1855. In 1887, a government surveyor named McQuinn made a resurvey, which vindicated the tribal position.

Nothing happened for nearly a century. Tribal members continued to insist that the McQuinn Strip be returned. Finally, in 1972, after a prolonged legislative effort, the tribe succeeded; Congress corrected the surveying error and transferred 61,000 acres of land, about ten percent of the modern reservation, from the Mount Hood and Willamette National Forests to the tribal domain. The tribe also has pursued an aggressive program to buy up lands sold off by various government programs. Such tribal land-acquisition efforts are fairly common across the West: total Indian land holdings have increased by some ten million acres since 1960.

The Warm Springs tribe numbers about 3600. Eighty percent or more of the members live on the reservation. The tribe runs its own timber mill and, in a trend found on many reservations, the tribal government has replaced the Bureau of Indian Affairs as forest manager. The tribe also operates a hydroelectric regulating dam on the Deschutes River and recently opened the elegant Museum at Warm Springs. In the 1970s the tribe established Kah-Nee-Tah, a luxury resort, and in 1995, after a long and difficult debate, began a tribal gaming operation at Kah-Nee-Tah. Indian tribes have the power to regulate liquor sales and most reservations remain dry; at Warm Springs, alcoholic beverages can be purchased only at Kah-Nee-Tah.

Tribal government is strong and stable at Warm Springs. The eleven-member Tribal Council (eight are elected and three are chiefs, one appointed for life by each of the three tribes) holds legislative and executive authority. The tribal court has three judges. The tribal administration, with approximately 400 employees, is divided into branches for natural resources, law enforcement, social services, finance, and other functions. Handsome, well-kept tribal headquarters give the substantial sense of a large, rural county government, but with a strong Indian flavor. Most employees are tribal members and the architecture and decor are unmistakably Indian. A large bronze statue, located in front of the tribal complex, portrays a Warm Springs woman in traditional tribal attire.

Warm Springs is progressive in that it has sound business operations and deals ably with the federal and state governments. Nonetheless, tribal traditions are evident everywhere. The languages are still spoken, most notably at the north end of the reservation, where nearly half of the people speak Sahaptin and all of them sing the old Sahaptin songs and understand the prayers and ceremonies. Spilyay Tymoo, the tribal newspaper, advertises tribal language classes and KWSO-FM, the tribal radio station, has several tribal language programs. The traditional way includes a slower, light-hearted, family-oriented day-to-day life as well as the ceremonies, large and small, that take place week by week: births, funerals, and weddings, and the feasts—for salmon, deer, roots, and berries—that mark the seasons. The annual pow-wow, Pi-Um-Sha, is a summer gathering time for thousands of people—tribal members, Indians from other tribes, and non-Indians.

A few years ago, I went to Warm Springs with my son, Dave, for Huckleberry Feast. We had little advance notice of the exact date because, like most of the ceremonies, the timing depends on the natural cycle: when would the huckleberries be exactly right? But Dave and I managed to match our visit with the appointed day, during the first weekend in August.

Huckleberry Feast is always held at HeHe Longhouse, which sits next to

"[T]he exclusive right of taking fish in the streams running through and bordering said reservation is hereby secured to said Indians; and at all other usual and accustomed stations, in common with the citizens of the United States."

—Treaty between the United States of America and the Warm Springs and Wasco Tribes *(1855)*

"The right to resort to the fishing places in controversy was a part of larger rights possessed by the Indians, upon the exercise of which there was not a shadow of impediment, and which were not much less necessary to the existence of the Indians than the atmosphere they breathed."

—United States v. Winans *(United States Supreme Court, 1905)*

the Warm Springs River in a flat, open ponderosa pine grove. The ceremony, a Washut service conducted in Sahaptin, took place inside the longhouse. It began with the old sound of drums and the rolling, guttural songs. The dancers moved in a circle, counterclockwise.

At the very end of the songs (there had been seven sets of seven songs), the women came in, some clad in buckskin, others wearing wing dresses, all of them with traditional basket-caps, woven from roots. The women bore baskets, filled to overflowing with freshly picked huckleberries. Once again, a season had produced an abundant harvest. The feast followed, the huckleberries complemented by deer meat, salmon, roots, potatoes, bread, cakes, and pies. Then, for hours, people talked and watched the dances. Dave, who was nine, splashed in the coldwater creek, his blonde hair unique among the dark Indian children.

At Warm Springs, as elsewhere in Indian country, humor is at the heart of the Indian way. I talked with Benny Heath outside of the longhouse, the ponderosas filtering the bright mid-afternoon's sun. Benny's father had been a traditional chief on the Tribal Council, and Benny had grown up on the reservation, speaking Sahaptin, before going off to Eastern Oregon State College to get his degree. Then he'd returned home.

Benny explained many of Huckleberry Feast's songs and dances. We talked and joked about fishing on the Deschutes, college football, and the tribe's timber program. Benny, in his early forties, confided in me that he had found his calling: he was an E.I.T. When I asked him what that meant, he feigned surprise, then responded: "elder in training."

We were interrupted fairly regularly because Benny had become a small businessman for the day. He had made T-shirts, emblazoned "Huckleberry Feast, 1991, HeHe, Oregon," in a mellow purple hue. He was selling them for five dollars apiece. I told him the color was exactly on target, and wished him luck. I also kidded him that, given the price tag, this didn't seem like a very promising entrepreneurial venture.

"You know," Benny said, growing serious for a moment, "I love Huckleberry Feast. It's such a wonderful occasion. I remember Huckleberry Feasts all the way back to when I was a little kid. I just want to memorialize it in my own way.

"But you know what else? I see these T-shirts going out into the world, all over Oregon, maybe even farther. And I think of all of the people who are going to look at them and ask: 'Where the hell is HeHe, Oregon?' "

Warm Springs is not somehow typical of Indian tribes. No single place is. The diversity is too great for that. Yet what can be said is that the modern resurgence on the reservations—which has played out in one fashion at Warm Springs, and in other ways for other tribes—has made tribes truly relevant to life in the larger western society to a degree not seen since the nineteenth century.

Indian contributions have become part of the intellectual bloodstream of the New West. Vine Deloria, Jr., Leslie Marmon Silko, Scott Momaday, James Welch, Linda Hogan, Sherman Alexie, the poet Simon Ortiz, and others have written piercingly about Indian life—sometimes elevated, sometimes depressing, always touching deep chords because of the poignancy and dignity of the search to preserve an old way and to fit into a new one not voluntarily chosen. The art—the kachinas, rugs, paintings, jewelry, pottery, and fetishes—has rightly

The circle is made of ourselves. Relatives, friends linger past the comfort of age and sleep. The people are a circle of respect on the floor. East is the sun, a pattern painted over the door frame. Songs gather in motion, in the rustle of drummers. Seven hearts. Seven pairs of hands. Seven parts of the earth. The rumble calls into the echo, the longhouse of our past. In this house shawls rest over shoulders like palms. In this house children in simple lines move around the floor. Oldest to smallest, the floor vibrates with the dancers. A song in one throat draws up the drums. The hand moves. With one heart, we move. The song is in each place, seen and unseen. Shells move as feathers touch air. We send this pulse to the center and outward. The sun over our heads extends hands of warmth. We send out a surge of recognition with one light.

—Elizabeth Woody (Warm Springs), "Longhouse I" in Seven Hands, Seven Hearts (1994)

(facing page) Disc jockey Donna L. Wainanwit, KWSO radio, Warm Springs Reservation, Oregon. Tapes in the foreground hold the station's native language programs.

become a high and favored form. The dances—Huckleberry Feast, Bean Dance at Hopi, Bear Dance at Ute, Crow Fair, many others—are inspiring in their color and rhythm and in the diligence and dedication it takes to put them on. And finally, as the pressures on the West's lands and waters continue to mount, the non-Indian society may be awakening—not out of romanticism but out of simple enlightened self-interest—to the Indian worldview, which teaches that we are one with the natural world and that stability, not acceleration, is the right and necessary way.

The modern sovereignty movement has done something else. It has changed the maps. When the New West began, Indian reservations were either unknown or accepted as a matter of politeness. They were, at most, historical places, soon to be formally assimilated. Indian people refused to stand for that, reasserting—and winning back—a sovereignty that had thrived for millennia. In 1970, the West effectively had two kinds of sovereign governments—federal and state. Today, the maps must show, not as a matter of politeness but of governmental and social reality, a third kind of sovereignty, that of the tribes. That hard-won adjustment of political geography is one of the deepest-running changes we have seen in this New West.

Carousel

On May 27, 1995, twenty-three years after the birth of Vail, a very different kind of venture—a community carousel—opened in Missoula. It was the first hand-carved carousel built in the United States since the Great Depression. That might have been distinction enough, but, beyond that, this undertaking had a spirit unto itself. Missoula's goal was simply to build a carousel but, in so doing, it embodied a maturing of the best impulses of both the New West and the Old.

Chuck Kaparich—dreamer, artisan, and organizer—brought the turning, painted horses into being. In 1989, a ride on the Spokane carousel had rekindled childhood memories. As if under a sort of spell, he began reading everything he could find about carousels and spent $500 telephoning carousel historians.

Kaparich, though a woodworker, had never carved. Still, undaunted, with a birthday gift of woodcarving tools from his wife, he plunged in. In time, carving during his off-hours, he had carved four ponies. He could visualize his ponies, and many others in a herd, doing their colorful work and play for the people of Missoula.

On a summer day in 1991, Kaparich hauled one of his ponies in for a meeting with Dan Kemmis, Mayor of Missoula. The tall, angular Kemmis—a person has to struggle not to call him "Lincolnesque"—has written two well-received books, *Community and the Politics of Place* and *The Good City and the Good Life*. A graduate of Harvard and the University of Montana Law School, Kemmis preaches the politics and philosophy of populism and inclusion, urging disparate community groups to come together and to imagine the future they want for their place. Once people rise above yesterday's grievances and today's hot-button issues, he believes, the larger community interest will emerge. Comfortably knowledgeable among the theories of Thomas Jefferson, Jane Jacobs, and Hannah Arendt, Kemmis might seem to be an unlikely Western mayor. But he likes philosophy that works in the real world, and has managed to become Speaker of the Montana House of Representatives, and, later, Missoula's twice-elected mayor.

Chuck Kaparich laid out his plan to Kemmis. The essence of it was both to-the-point and, in its own way, astonishing. "I want to build a carousel for Missoula. I don't want to get paid for it or anything, but I want to make sure that it's preserved into the future and I want this little spot on the riverfront." "This little spot" was Caras Park, land owned by the city near the Clark Fork River.

In another mayor's office this might have seemed like pie-in-the-sky, or possibly frivolous, but Kemmis saw the potential in Kaparich's idea. He encouraged Kaparich to meet with Geoff Badenoch, over at the Missoula Redevelopment Agency.

This time Kaparich lugged in all four ponies. "I want," he told Badenoch, "to carve a carousel and give it to the community. If I do, will the city give it a good home?" Badenoch was initially skeptical, and both men recall his vigorous head-shaking during the first part of the meeting. The irrepressible Kaparich, however, was nothing if not tenacious. By the end of the session, Badenoch had joined Kemmis as a believer.

Kaparich moved into high gear. With his open, infectious smile, he was, as Badenoch puts it, "a ten-year-old boy trapped in a middle-aged man's body," but Chuck Kaparich also had an organizer's mind and a hellish amount of energy. Eventually the carousel building would cost about $350,000. There was, however, a financial wrinkle, a quite surprising one in this day and age.

The wrinkle was that Kaparich, who had spent about 350 hours on each of the first four ponies, and all the other woodcarvers would volunteer their time. This explained why no hand-carved carousel had been made in America in half a century: the cost of conceiving, carving, painting, and otherwise decorating, all with meticulous and loving care, a full herd of carousel ponies was prohibitively expensive. But not in Missoula, not on Chuck Kaparich's watch.

Work on the carousel surged ahead. Although the city donated the land, and the basic labor was accounted for, the Carousel for Missoula Foundation Board had to raise funds for the carousel structure, a band organ (so that the carousel music would not operate on taped music), the wood and materials for the ponies, and other items. The people of Missoula stepped forward enthusiastically. In the "Adopt a Pony" program, individuals or groups sponsoring a particular pony with a pledge could have a say in the pony's design and even the name. Elementary school classes across town signed up, with many children selling crafts, doing chores, and pledging their allowances.

How truly magical the ponies were. "Prairie Rose," decked out in pale blue, evokes the wild roses of eastern Montana. "Appaloosa" is the strong, charging Indian peace pony. "Pal's Pal," in pastel yellow, blue, and pink, and with carved garden roses on his mane and halter, is the gentle sort: "Since Pal's Pal is not a jumper," his carver observed, "I've noticed that babies, little kids, and older people like to ride on him." "Big Sky Gaiety" is named and designed to preserve the memory of a registered Montana mare owned by a 14-year-old girl. In all, the swirl of colors includes 38 ponies and two chariots for the elderly and the disabled.

I happened to be in Missoula in May 1995, during the week before the carousel opened. It was all the talk. Chuck Kaparich had put grins all over town.

"But this valley of common ground remains hidden because we all inhabit a world in which values are always private, always subjective. Always, that is, except when we are engaged in practices. What barn building and violin playing, softball and steer raising all have fundamentally in common is this: all of them deal with questions of value, with what is good or excellent (a well-built barn; a well-executed double play), but they all do so in an explicitly social setting, wherein purely subjective or individualistic inclinations are flatly irrelevant, if not counterproductive. . . .

If public life needs to be revitalized, if its renewal depends upon more conscious and more confident ways of drawing upon the capacity of practices to make values objective and public, if those practices acquire that power from the efforts of unlike people to live well in specific places, then we need to think about specific places, and the real people who now live in them, and try to imagine ways in which their efforts to live there might become more practiced, more inhabitory, and therefore more public."

—Daniel Kemmis, Community and the Politics of Place (1990)

I thought back twenty years to a time when Missoula captured me with its logging, blue-collar, and university combination that characterizes it still. Great hiking lay right at the edge of town. The Montana writers' movement, so vibrant today, was already in high bloom then. The leader was Richard Hugo, who (since Stegner was of an earlier time, having published as far back as the 1930s) may have been the first modern Western writer. Hugo and his poetry were of this place—the Milltown Union Bar, the Big Blackfoot River, and the plain people and events of Western Montana.

Back then, though, downtown had been neglected. The Clark Fork, such a big river surging down from the Hellgate, seemed separated from town. By the 1990s, downtown Missoula had come back, with renovated buildings, a welcoming riverfront with trails, and—the carousel. These things are all part of the philosophy and practicality of Dan Kemmis, a mayor working hard on managing growth in new housing and, as well, restoring the traditional areas of town. "We have to do a better job," he says, "with our public spaces. Politics is as much about space as people. The two are inseparable."

When the carousel opened, the *New York Times*, Charles Osgood of CBS, Roger Peterson of NBC, and others of the national media had descended on Missoula to memorialize the event. That day, and many to come, however, belonged to the ponies and the people of Missoula, the big-eyed kids and the grown-ups who love their town and are damned proud of it.

Quincy

As I reflect on the New West, I realize ever more that it is the ordinary places that I find most captivating and satisfying. The New West comes on a sliding scale. Every Western town and city has been changed, even if the only difference is the number of pass-through tourists heading for somewhere else. Vail marks one end of the scale. Missoula is more toward the middle. Toward the other end you find Quincy. I'm lucky. I have family there and visit often. It's not much in the way of New West, but I'll tell you true, it's good West.

Quincy, at 3,400 feet in the northern part of California's Sierra Nevada, has always sat in between. During Gold Rush days, miners made fabulous finds on the North Fork of the Feather River (memorialized by Louise Amelia Knapp Smith Clappe's wonderful correspondence back East, The Shirley Letters, written from Rich Bar in the early 1850s) and excellent if not fabulous discoveries on the Middle Fork of the Feather. Quincy was located on higher ground, in between the two canyons and a half-day's wagon ride from each. Today, Quincy holds no

specific allure, no big blue lake, no magnificent river or ski slope. Lake Almanor and its boating and fishing are one hour's drive north, Lake Tahoe and the ski areas an hour and a half to the south. The New West, like the Gold Rush, has influenced Quincy but directed its main force elsewhere.

People in Quincy mostly applaud the anonymity. The 10,000 residents live there because of the relaxed, small-town lifestyle. No McDonalds, Wendy's, or Burger King. One traffic light. High-school sports, and Little League in the summer, are major social events. The outdoors-oriented community rests on the edge of American Valley, a broad mead-

(facing page) Painting a red apple on a new, hand-carved carousel horse, Missoula, Montana, January 1997. Carousel volunteers and adoptive families tuck memorabilia—family photographs, clippings, momentos—into the hollow basswood horses.

ow, a mile and a half or so across, banked on all sides by low mountains.

What a great walking town, up in the residential neighborhoods where there are stone and woodframe historic homes, down Main Street, out on the valley floor. You can see a little New West downtown, where some of the businesses have spruced up for the gradually increasing tourist trade. There's a bed and breakfast now. Morning Thunder, the comfortable breakfast place with good huevos rancheros and local art on the walls, lives up to its name by serving serious coffee, with the appropriate consistency of soil erosion. A few years back Morning Thunder added espresso. A latté aficionado, I nonetheless stick with the original.

The Plumas National Forest surrounds the town. This leaves Quincy, in common with dozens of other Western communities, with the blessings and burdens of being symbiotic with a national forest. The Forest Service has a great deal to say about business, governance, and society. America's biggest timber-producing national forests are found in the Northwest, including western Montana and northern Idaho, down into northern California. The Plumas, with outstanding ponderosa and Douglas fir stands, is the southernmost of these highly productive forests. So Quincy is a timber town, the Forest Service its largest employer and the Sierra Pacific Mill (including logging and trucking contractors) second.

Pressure to reduce the timber harvest—the cut—in the national forests has steadily increased since the early 1970s. It had to. The Forest Service was cutting too much for the New West, and some of the Old, to stomach. By the late 1980s, the cut was coming down fast, especially in the Northwest and especially in northern spotted owl habitat. The Plumas is at the southern end of the owl's range.

This meant even more instability to a community whose economy had always been subject to the whims of the lumber market. Long before the spotted owl, the mill was never reluctant to lay off employees for economic reasons. Down cycles in timber hit the community hard. People don't want to leave, but many are regularly forced out.

There are no Tetons, no Yellowstone near Quincy, but it is arresting, uncrowded country even so. Twenty miles due west is Buck's Lake, rimmed by summer cottages and a few modest lodges. The watershed on the north side of the lake is in Buck's Lake Wilderness Area, the only wilderness in Plumas County. I went to the dedication ceremony. One of the speakers talked about the difficulty of dedicating wilderness designation in this antigovernment county. He referred to an elderly gentleman who loved his view across Buck's Lake to the national forest, a view now spared the chain saw. But the old man opposed wilderness because it meant federal intrusion. "Why can't they," he asked, "just leave it the way it was?" Above Buck's Lake, the Pacific Crest Trail, a hiking corridor from Mexico to Canada, runs through the wilderness area.

Rock Creek is a few miles outside of Quincy. Full of brook trout, this modest slip of a creek makes for joyful springtime fly-fishing with young people. My son, Seth, and I hiked down into a shallow canyon on Rock Creek late one June afternoon. Just seven, he took four or five small, bright brookies. On another day, my niece, Jamie, then eight, caught her first fish from a pool enclosed by skunk cabbage and tall grasses. We laughed at how wet we got from the dew.

The wildest place I've found in Plumas County, even more so than the

"Anything beyond the Missouri was close to home, at least. He was a westerner, whatever that was. The moment he crossed the Big Sioux and got into the brown country where the raw earth showed, the minute the grass got sparser and the air dryer and the service stations less grandiose and towns rattier, the moment he saw his first lonesome shack on the baking flats with a tipsy windmill creaking away at the reluctant underground water, he knew approximately where he belonged."

—Wallace Stegner, The Big Rock Candy Mountain *(1943)*

official wilderness area, is the Middle Fork of the Feather River. A dirt road in the national forest comes to a dead end half an hour outside of town, making an informal trailhead. The canyon at this point is more than 1,500 feet deep and the river corridor has been declared part of the wild and scenic river system.

It's a steep but easy hike down to the river, about two miles. The ponderosa pines grow more scrubby, the groundcover more sparse, as you descend. It's snaky. I've gone down into the canyon four times, and been buzzed on three of them. Three-fourths of the way down (the river sounds are pounding now), you hit a fork in the trail, one branch to Oddie Bar the other to No Ear Bar. The mining country generates the best place names. Both branches sound great, but I can never resist the latter. I've got to track down the story.

The Middle Fork is a big river, a white-water rafter's challenge. It is full of large, handsome boulders, many of them perfect fly-casting platforms. This stretch is good trout water, but all of my trips have been in July or August, past the best fishing time in this hot, low terrain. The fishing in the direct sun is mostly fruitless, although I do it anyway. I've caught some rainbows at dusk, but they have not been many or big.

The swimming is fabulous. This is the native pursuit of my brother-in-law, John Cunningham, who shatters the deep, clear pools like a 190-pound spaniel. I take a bracing dip and return to my fishing, buoyed by John's downstream whoops and splashes.

I love canyons the most. Rather than heading toward an exposed summit, my natural choice is to descend into secrecy. The next bend always brings some surprise, a slick riffle, a hawk on the wing, a rocky outcrop, a different slant of shadows. Canyons are calming, enveloping, parental. Even the melody of the name, cañon, brought north by Hispanics, stirs me so, smooth and vibrant as the living river at the bottom.

So I am fishing the canyon as much as the river, seeking trout and also landscape and solitude. This Middle Fork Canyon is one of the best—green-sided, sheer, remote. I work my rod, getting a rhythm, learning this reach of water and imagining secrets beyond the bend. My eyes play over the canyon walls whenever my fly is off the water, and sometimes when it is on. Later, I round the corner, the shadows find the river and a pair of water ouzels come out, skimming and dipping for bugs. I lose a sturdy rainbow after a silvery, heart-thumping strike, but land two smaller ones.

The hike back out is steep and sweaty. Lots of stops along the way. It is past nightfall and the snakes are down, but you hear rustling, probably deer but maybe bear, back in the brush. I've seen a total of three people, aside from John and my other companions, on these canyon hikes. We celebrate our return to the trailhead with hugs, high-fives, and beer from the cooler.

I've done a respectable amount of exploring in the country around Quincy, but of course locals know the area better than I could dream of. They may say they live in Quincy, but the whole Feather River country is their home.

It is an ambiguous homeland, a hard place to make a living and give due care to the land. Even the angriest loggers and millworkers, with their jobs on the line, love the land and want to do right by it. They also want work.

In response, Quincy has been the base for one of the leading consensus-building efforts in the modern West. A group of people, coming from all parts of

"Though water has been one of the most complex and divisive issues in the West, it is also what draws us together in this place and allows us to stay. Water is the common bond that we as humans share with one another and with all other creatures. It is one of the life-forming gifts that we must have in order to live, and that we all therefore must share. Historically, if there has been any healing in the world, it has come from the rivers. It is 'by the rivers of Babylon that we lay ourselves down, by the cooling waters we lay down.' So water is not only a difficult, complex, and divisive issue; it is one source of our unity, a symbol of rest and health for mind and body, and our great hope."

—Gary Holthaus, "Rivers," in Arrested Rivers (1994)

the community, began talking about ways for the Plumas National Forest to do better by the land and the community. Eventually they called themselves the Quincy Library Group. One unlikely leader is Michael Jackson, an environmental activist who had led the fight to designate the Buck's Lake Wilderness Area when wilderness was still a fighting word in Plumas County. But Jackson—like Nevada rancher Tony Tipton, the former Sagebrush Rebel—mellowed. He's earned the respect, as a union attorney, of the people who work in the woods.

The Quincy Library Group came up with a plan for giving greater protection to the land, especially in headwater areas that drain into spawning areas for the wild, endangered salmon. The Forest Service, however, kept the group at arm's length from the beginning, perhaps fearing a loss of control over forest management. At this writing, it is unclear whether the Forest Service will go with the Quincy Library Group's carefully worked-out consensus view.

I hope the Library Group's approach prevails. Old-style, high-yield logging on the public lands is a thing of the past. Part of Quincy's future is in timber, which can be scaled back and still remain a staple in the economy, but other parts of the economy need to be expanded, as many of the local businesses are doing. There are going to be plenty of tough choices but also plenty of people and businesses drawn to places that never became rich or famous but, having learned from the mistakes of those who did, stayed grounded—good, stable communities inlaid in uncrowded, Western surroundings.

Quincy has its choices intact because it has not been overwhelmed by the New West. It can still make its own future. Maybe Quincy will find its own way. Maybe it will choose aspects of the New West that it wants and reject others. Maybe Quincy will find its own carousel.

(facing page) Rafters apprehensive about approaching storm along the Arkansas River, Colorado.

Chapter 1: A Region Defined

The "West" keeps moving around in time and space. At moments in American history it was everything beyond the Alleghenies, then all lands west of the Mississippi, and, finally, a coastal West of dynamic Pacific cities. It is also a congery of subregional stories: the challenge and tragedy of farming the Great Plains, exploration of the Rocky Mountains and Colorado Plateau, dynamic tension among Natives, Hispanics, and Anglos in the Southwest, and creation of distinctive, cosmopolitan cities like Los Angeles and Seattle, that anchor America's quadrant of the Pacific Rim. We touch on many of these Wests, but focus on a geographical core—the Interior West—stretching from the foothills of the Rocky Mountains to the crests of the Sierra Nevada and Cascade Ranges.

Many Americans still think of the Interior West as the old-style frontier, but in fact over the past forty years a profound transition of landscape and social life has almost completely modernized this geography. The transition continues in the 1990s as millions move to the West—some curling back east from the coast to get there—especially into the small-town and rural Interior. Americans like the New West, and, voting with their feet, moving vans, sport utility vehicles, and plane tickets, have made Colorado, Arizona, Utah, Nevada, and Montana the five fastest growing states in the country in the 1990s. Another great Western land boom is underway.

Mining, logging, and ranching—long the defining Western land uses—still mark the West, but the extractive economy now trails the so-called "services" sector, everything from hamburger flippers to telecommuting professionals now settling into Western places. Lifestyle refugees pour in from other states, building mountainside homes near trout streams and ski runs. Long-term residents also find affluence in the new economy, latching onto a new job or sometimes simply by selling a piece of land worth wildly more than a couple of decades ago.

Grand Tetons, Wyoming   Riebsame

San Luis Valley, Colorado   Riebsame

La Sal foothills area, Utah   Riebsame

Westerners disagree mightily about just what the West is or should be. To some the New West is a postindustrial, high-tech society riding hard in the saddle of a beautiful but fragile landscape. Others see a West still rooted in its natural resources, sporting a facile New West patina of software firms, service workers, and city slicker cattle drives—a thin veneer that will soon erode, they claim, because you've got to produce something physical and concrete—lumber, beef, molybdenum—to be a real and lasting economy.

To gain perspective on this place, we first examine its geography: the landscape of nature, places, bureaucracies, people, public lands, and Indian lands. A region is made of all these things, and held together by ideas, from notions of cultural and personal meaning and identity, to prosaic e-mail among friends comparing the relative advantages of one trout stream over another. We end this chapter with a map of the region's modern writers. They speak not only for Westerners, but also translate the West for others.

Lay of the Land

Great Basin, Grand Canyon, Columbia Plateau, Grand Tetons, Zion Canyon, Mountain of the Holy Cross—names attached to the Western landscape bespeaking grandeur, spiritualism, nationalism. Less optimistic sentiments abound too: Hell's Canyon, River of No Return Wilderness, Devil's Tower, Death Valley, but the dominant theme in perception of the Western landscape is optimism and majesty.

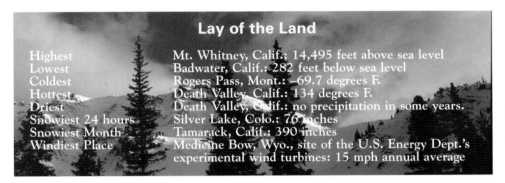

Lay of the Land

Highest	Mt. Whitney, Calif.: 14,495 feet above sea level
Lowest	Badwater, Calif.: 282 feet below sea level
Coldest	Rogers Pass, Mont.: –69.7 degrees F.
Hottest	Death Valley, Calif.: 134 degrees F.
Driest	Death Valley, Calif.: no precipitation in some years.
Snowiest 24 hours	Silver Lake, Colo.: 76 inches
Snowiest Month	Tamarack, Calif.: 390 inches
Windiest Place	Medicine Bow, Wyo., site of the U.S. Energy Dept.'s experimental wind turbines: 15 mph annual average

In *Shane*, the classic Western film, the hero (played by Alan Ladd) rides out of a background of sweeping mountains (the Tetons), his horse framed by a deer's antlers. Shane, and the wilderness behind him, embody majesty and the purity and endurance of uncompromised spirit—but the scene, and subsequent story of how Shane protects the homesteaders from a cattle baron's greed, also speaks of how human spirit can subdue wilderness, making it home.

In a sort of topographic psychoanalysis, American affection for imposing Western landscapes—expressed in paintings, film, pational parks, and the family vacation—is a form of cultural monument envy, a continental inferiority complex born of the nation's lack of the trappings of European culture (cathedrals, grand estates, monumental government buildings); European immigrants could not reinvent, nor readily transfer, the place-rooted culture of their home countries, but they could, especially in the West, revel in landscape drama of wilderness and ruggedness.

The thinly vegetated West reveals its geology to all who will see. The place is more mountainous, convoluted, and incised than any other American region except Alaska. Between the Great Plains and Rocky Mountains lies the nation's sharpest topographic boundary. In many places from Montana to New Mexico one may stand at the mountain front with one foot in the Plains and one in the Rockies. To the east a vast plain stretches to the Mississippi; to the West lie range after range of mountains, deep canyons, and searing deserts. The Rockies on the east and Sierra Nevada on the west create the Great Basin, the nation's largest area lacking a drainage outlet to the sea. John C. Fremont and

Lay of the Land

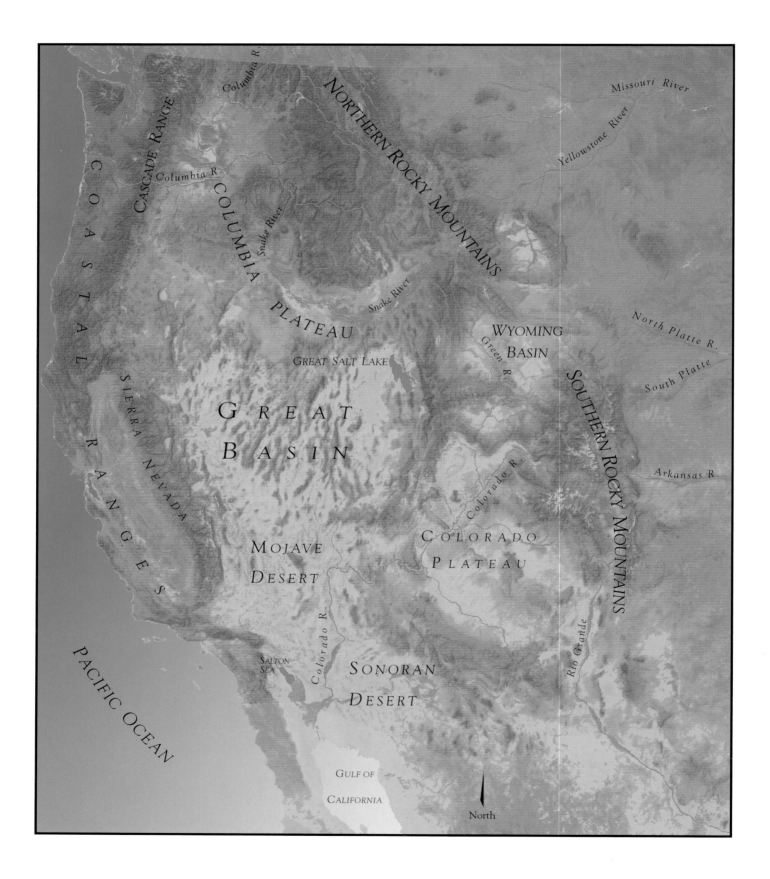

CASCADE RANGE

Columbia R.

NORTHERN ROCKY MOUNTAINS

Missouri River

Yellowstone River

Columbia R.

COLUMBIA

COASTAL

PLATEAU

Snake River

Snake River

WYOMING BASIN

North Platte R.

Green R.

GREAT SALT LAKE

South Platte

SIERRA NEVADA

GREAT
BASIN

SOUTHERN ROCKY MOUNTAINS

RANGES

Arkansas R.

Colorado R.

MOJAVE
DESERT

COLORADO
PLATEAU

PACIFIC OCEAN

Colorado R.

SALTON
SEA

SONORAN
DESERT

Rio Grande

GULF OF
CALIFORNIA

North

other explorers theorized that so much land had to be drained by a great river. But no outlet for the basin's rain and snowmelt was ever found. Water leaves the basin only through evaporation, creating huge salt flats called playas and saline lakes that rise and fall with the seasons. The biggest of these, Great Salt Lake, rose and spread as the exceptional snowpack of 1983 finally melted. It flooded the salt flats where rocket cars had set land speed records, and seeped into Salt Lake City's airport and western suburbs. Flooding of the Bear River Wildlife Refuge on the lake's east shore set the stage for Terry Tempest Williams' book *Refuge*, about family, cancer, and submerged nature.

The alternating basin and range topography common to the Great Basin creates a fragmented landscape of snowy mountains rising above desert basins. One of these basins, Death Valley, sank far enough into the earth's crust to become the continent's lowest and hottest place, 282 feet below sea level at Badwater, California.

The Great Basin is bounded to the north by the Columbia Plateau, a layercake of ancient lava flows. Here great rivers—the Columbia, Snake, Kootenai—carry snowmelt from the Rockies into the Pacific, cutting straight-walled canyons, like the one near Twin Falls, Idaho—not quite spanned by Evil Knievel's rocket-powered motorcycle in 1973. Eroding volcanic cones dot the plateau, clustering in a part of southern Idaho called Mountains of the Moon. South and east of the Great Basin lies the West's most emblematic scenery: the Colorado Plateau, host to dozens of national parks and monuments, from Grand Canyon to Dinosaur. Another layercake, this one made of sediments cemented into massive red sandstone, the plateau was slowly lifted by deep geological forces as the Colorado River and its tributaries eroded through it. The result, a labyrinth of steep canyons—the Canyonlands, hiding place of George Hayduke, mythic hero of Edward Abbey's *The Monkey Wrench Gang*, and the New West's premier sightseeing, hiking, and mountain biking empire.

One cannot eat landscape, the lament goes. But ask Westerners why they live here and many will mention the mountains and deserts right off, perhaps then citing career or family. Landscape appreciation is more than a leisure activity in the work-a-day West, it is big business; but along with this mercantile approach, Westerners take psychic sustenance from the lay of the land.

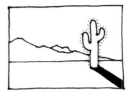

Lay of the Land

A satellite's eye view of the western U.S. reveals a rumpled landscape of mountains and plateaus traversed by a few rivers, like the Colorado and the Columbia. The Great Salt Lake centers this view: to its east lie the Rocky Mountains, including 54 peaks over 14,000 feet in their southern stretch. A swarm of mountain ranges mark the Great Basin west of the Salt Lake, and the Sierra Nevada and Cascade Ranges separate the Interior West from the Pacific Coast. Natives and immigrants named every mountain, canyon, river, and lake of this land, but here we offer the landscape with only a few human labels.

New West Metropolitan Areas, 1994 population

Phoenix	2,473,000
Denver	2,190,000
Salt Lake City	1,178,000
Las Vegas	1,076,000
Tucson	732,000
El Paso	665,000
Albuquerque	646,000
Colorado Springs	452,000
Spokane	396,000
Boise	348,000

Source: U.S. Census Bureau

Places on the Land

The western geopolitical landscape is splashed with names depicting history, political power, heroic individuals, nature, and famous (or infamous) events. Economic and political power is written all over the land: place names resonant with corporate America (Anaconda, Ken-

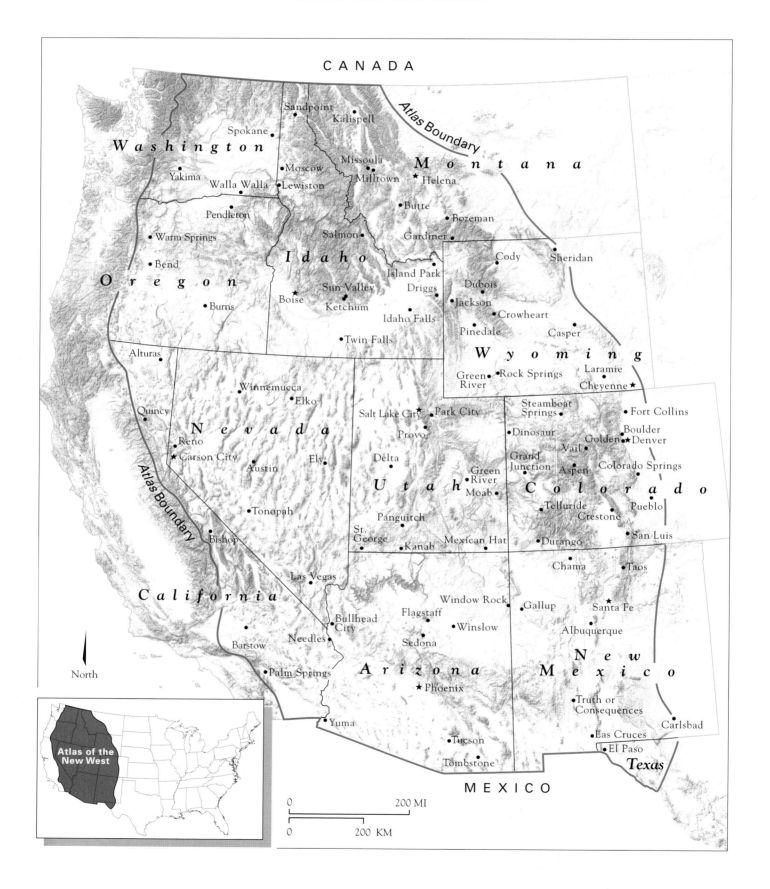

CANADA

Atlas Boundary

Washington

Sandpoint
Kalispell
Spokane
Moscow
Missoula
Montana
Milltown
Yakima
Walla Walla
Lewiston
Helena
Pendleton
Butte
Bozeman
Warm Springs
Salmon
Gardiner
Idaho
Bend
Cody
Sheridan
Island Park
Dubois
Oregon
Sun Valley
Driggs
Boise
Ketchum
Jackson
Burns
Idaho Falls
Crowheart
Pinedale
Casper
Twin Falls
Wyoming
Alturas
Green
Rock Springs
Laramie
River
Cheyenne
Winnemucca
Steamboat
Elko
Springs
Fort Collins
Quincy
Salt Lake City
Park City
Dinosaur
Boulder
Nevada
Provo
Vail
Golden
Denver
Reno
Grand
Aspen
Colorado Springs
Carson City
Junction
Austin
Ely
Delta
Utah
Green
Colorado
River
Tonopah
Moab
Telluride
Pueblo
Panguitch
Crestone
Bishop
St.
San Luis
George
Durango
Kanab
Mexican Hat
Chama
Taos
Las Vegas
California
Window Rock
Gallup
Santa Fe
Bullhead
Flagstaff
City
Albuquerque
Needles
Winslow
Barstow
Sedona
New
North
Arizona
Mexico
Palm Springs
Phoenix
Truth or
Consequences
Yuma
Carlsbad
Tucson
Las Cruces
El Paso
Tombstone
Texas

MEXICO

Atlas of the
New West

0   200 MI

0   200 KM

necott, Sinclair, Butte) or powerful politicians and leaders: Brigham City, Coolidge and Hoover Dams, Billings, Denver.

George Stewart, in his landmark book *Names on the Land*, showed that geographic naming is complicated and nuanced. To be sure, some names are obvious, like, say, Eagle Peak (well, maybe not so obvious: Did an eagle nest there? Was once seen there? Killed there? Found dead there? Or did someone named Eagle climb it first, see it first, or dream it first?), other names are a bit more tricky (is running water a creek, brook, stream, or river?), and some are downright mysterious: Keet Seel, River of No Return, Separation Rapids, or Angel Fire. People can't resist enshrining themselves or others on mountain peaks: Lincoln, Roosevelt, Hayden, Powell, Linnaeus, Cleveland, Sheridan, Custer, Crazy Horse. Anthropomorphic monikers also dot the Western landscape: Heart Lake, Skull Mountain, Bald Pate Peak, Finger Lake, West Thumb. Lacking an explorer, local hero, or elite to supplicate, or resemblance to a body part, the landscape was often named for its Natives, perhaps a Native name retained in some form of awkward Anglicized spelling or pronunciation: Absaroka, Washakie, Togwotee, Batatakin, Tonto, Hualapai, Ishawooa. Often, the Anglo, French, or Spanish term for natives and their places was used: Flathead, Nez Perce, Jemez.

Early Euro-American explorers and settlers dominate Western geographic naming: Lewis and Clark are enshrined on towns, rivers, and highways along their transcontinental route. Likewise, they paid homage to their supporters, especially Jefferson and Gallatin; the latter, as Secretary of Treasury at the time, held their purse strings and got his name on a river and other physical features.

Some names reek of the Old West: Tombstone, Arizona; Truth or Consequences, New Mexico; Big Timber, Montana; Santa Fe, New Mexico; Durango, Colorado; Laramie, Wyoming. Others are simply practical and descrip-

Places on the Land

Most Westerners live in cities and towns, not out on the open range. Even so, only four Interior West cities—Phoenix, Denver, Salt Lake City, and Las Vegas—contain more than a million souls. Wyoming and Montana boast no place over 100,000 people, and the entire area of California, Oregon and Washington east of the Sierra Nevada and Cascade Ranges includes only one: Spokane at 396,000.

Heaven and Hell on Earth

Mountain of the Holy Cross: Snow patches on the north face of this Colorado mountain appear to form a thousand-foot-high cross.

Hell's Half Acre: badlands near Casper, Wyo.

Devil's Thumb: lone rock spires all over the West, like the one above Boulder, Colo.

Sangre de Cristos (Blood of Christ): Colorado-New Mexico mountain range that catches the blood-red light of the setting sun.

Bright Angel: various features in the Grand Canyon, Ariz.

Devil's Punchbowl: hot spring near Thermopolis, Wyo.

Devil's Kitchen: redrock outcrops in Southern Utah; name common to several mountain and desert sites in the West (three in Wyoming alone).

Devil's Garden: redrock outcrops in Arches National Park, Utah.

Devil's Playground: sandunes in California's Mojave desert.

Hell's Canyon: Snake River Canyon in Oregon and Idaho.

Angel Peak and Lake: above Wells, Nev.

Jacob's Ladder: rock outcrops on Lone Peak near Salt Lake City, Utah.

Dante's View: overlook into Death Valley, Calif.

Devil's Golf Course: fractured salt bed in Death Valley, Calif.

Devil's Slide: steep rock outcrop along the Yellowstone River, Mont.

Angel's Landing: sandstone shelf in Zion National Park, Utah.

The Bureaucratic West

CANADA

Washington

Montana

Oregon

Boise

Idaho

Wyoming

Nevada

Salt Lake City

Utah

Denver

Colorado

California

Las Vegas

Arizona

Albuquerque

New Mexico

Phoenix

El Paso

Texas

MEXICO

County Boundary
State Boundary
Bureau of Reclamation
EPA
U.S. Forest Service

tive: Colstrip, Smelterville, Leadville, Encampment, Old Faithful. Finally, natural attributes sometimes called forth reasonably natural names: Wind River, Beartooth Peak, Snowmass Mountain, Aspen, Great Salt Lake, Pinedale, and hundreds of Cottonwood Creeks, Dry Creeks, and Sandy Creeks announce the obvious on the Western map.

Names on the land are also implicated in business competition and realpolitik. The Colorado River was named by Spanish explorers in its lower reaches, which ran red with iron-rich sediments from the canyonlands it traversed. Up in the Utah desert the Colorado's two main tributaries were separately named by white explorers: the Green River, heading up in Wyoming's Wind River Range (called Seedkeedee by the Indians), and the Grand River, headwatered on the west side of Colorado's Front Range. Rules of riverine nomenclature are a bit ambiguous, but when history gives a river multiple names, the earliest (in this case: Colorado) usually takes precedence, and is applied upstream to the biggest tributary at each stream junction. But historical circumstance gave the Colorado an identity crisis: it simply ceased to exist above the confluence of the Green and Grand. Until, that is, the Utah legislature considered renaming the Green River as the Colorado in 1921, wishing to have more of the famous Colorado in their state. The measure failed, but gave Colorado legislators a similar idea, and, with President Harding's help, they decreed—before the Utahns could gather back in session—that the Grand River was actually the Colorado, reasoning that the Colorado River should flow from the state of the same name and that tourists to Colorado deserved to see the Colorado River.

Many places with innocent names became infamous through dark events: on Sand Creek in eastern Colorado soldiers massacred 150 Cheyennes who had exchanged their weapons for a peace treaty; at Donner Pass in the Sierra Nevada, the well-known troop of settlers succumbed to cannibalism; Trinity Site, New Mexico, was ground zero for the decidedly unholy first atomic bomb; and the Little Bighorn River provided the stage for Sitting Bull's defeat of Custer. At least one well-known Western place name is now also a verb. Planners and community leaders in booming resort towns, weary of real estate inflation, movie-star invasion, and worker homelessness, have added Aspenization to the development lingo of the New West.

The Bureaucratic West

Most attempts to make sensible political boundaries in the West have failed in the face of an implacable grid laid out by the first land surveys. Some early scholars and political leaders—John Wesley Powell was one—wanted the West divided up differently than the East. Had Powell won out, everything from house lots to county and state lines would have matched watersheds or other natural boundaries. As it is, the geography of bureaucracy is a tangle of boundaries, some drawn straight across the most convoluted landscape in the nation, others meandering to accommodate topography or politics. Though water matters a great deal to Westerners, few political boundaries recognize watersheds. Wyoming and Colorado are almost perfect squares, aligned to the national grid; the boundaries of New Mexico, Utah, Nevada, and Arizona are mostly straight-

The Bureaucratic West

A tangled mess of overlapping jurisdictions, the Interior West, as elsewhere in the U.S., is carved up politically by counties and states; but the region is also riven by federal agencies: the U.S. Forest Service and National Park Service own extensive public lands, the Bureau of Reclamation manages Western water, and the Environmental Protection Agency has a hand in everything from water quality to the chemicals used by farmers and ranchers. The Bureau of Reclamation's subdivisions seem so bizarre because they follow watersheds, the most logical approach for managing natural resources despite the other agencies' straightlined borders. The overlapping authority of municipal, county, state, and federal agencies places each piece of land, and its resources, under the jurisdiction of up to a dozen agencies, each with its own regulatory authority.

A Region Compared

A drive from Boston to Washington, just under 500 miles, would pass through cities and suburbs containing upwards to 45 million people. A drive from the northeast to the southwest corner of Wyoming—the same distance, but certainly accomplished at higher speeds—would pass through communities adding up to perhaps 50,000 souls.

The Region Compared

lined. Only a small part of the Montana-Idaho border follows the lay of the land, and only a handful of mountain counties in Colorado, Utah, and Montana are drawn along watershed boundaries.

Federal agencies, such as the U.S. Forest Service and Environmental Protection Agency, ignore natural boundaries too. EPA is organized for simple political reasons along state lines, and USFS regions follow natural features only along the few watershed lines that are also county or state lines; the agency's regional and district breakdown pays little heed to the West's different forest ecosystems. The Bureau of Reclamation, dedicated to bending nature to human will, comes closer to nature by clumping large river basins into administrative units; still it arbitrarily throws most of New Mexico into the Upper Colorado jurisdiction, and calls it quits at New Mexico's straight-arrow eastern border, which has nothing to do with watershed or ecosystem. Even this book's "New West" boundaries are arbitrary, an attempt to limit our scope in some geographic way.

Western city governments live within these jumbled jurisdictions, reaching out across boundaries to get water or find places to dump trash and build airports. Denver and Los Angeles each bought land far away across the mountains to obtain rights to water they would someday need. Los Angeles built an aqueduct that finally gave the Great Basin an outlet to the Pacific Ocean, draining water from Mono Lake on the west side of the Sierra Nevada. Later the city was forced by environmentalists to buy further water rights to support Mono's unique ecology. The Denver Water Board reached into the Colorado River Basin, and even bought out the whole town of Dillon, Colorado, in the 1960s so that it could build a reservoir west of the divide. Turf battles flared when Denver wanted to build another reservoir in the mountains during the 1980s. Permits for the dam were needed from almost a dozen state and federal agencies, and one agency—the EPA—balked at another big Western dam on grounds that it would violate federal clean water laws. Neighboring towns, counties, and states also complained and the Two Forks Dam was never built—the first time that the feds have said no to Western cities' apparently insatiable thirst for someone else's water. Without a doubt water, given its tendency to ignore political boundaries drawn straight across the land, has spurred more bureaucratic squabbling than any other issue in the West.

A Blank Space on the Map

In *The Nine Nations of North America*, Joel Garreau labeled most of the Interior West the "empty quarter,"[1] distinguishing this "nation" chiefly by its sparse population. From the central Great Plains to the crest of the Cascade and Sierra Nevada ranges, the West remains sparsely populated. This reflects the region's recent settlement and landlocked geography, but also stems from Westerners' tendency, until recently, to settle in cities rather than rural areas. The Interior Western states are more urbanized than even the mid-Atlantic region. Roughly 75 percent of people in eastern "metropolitan" states like New York and New Jersey are urban dwellers, but fully 86 percent of Westerners live in cities. Urban-rural tensions play out in every Western statehouse. Raw political power in state assemblies belongs, as in much of the country, to the cities, but rural representatives still carry clout and symbolic appeal when they fight urban-led movements to, say, restrict gun ownership, preserve wilderness, transfer water, protect gay rights, or support higher education.

But the empty quarter is filling. The Interior West grew faster than the U.S. as a whole in the 1970s and 1980s, and the pace quickened in the 1990s. Colorado boasted ten of the fifty fastest growing counties in the U.S. during 1990–95; the fastest growing county was a Denver suburb. Second place went to Summit County, Utah, a piece of the snowy Wasatch Range preparing to host the 2002 Winter Olympics. Idaho, Colorado, Montana, Arizona, and Utah grew

Town-limit sign, Gold Hill, Colorado

A Blank Space

With most Westerners jammed into a few cities and their suburbs, the vast majority of the intervening geography is thinly settled. Only a few counties away from the cities contain population densities of even 25 souls per square mile, and some of the emptiest counties in the nation are found here, especially in those blank spaces of Nevada, which has the lowest population densities in the country. Each of the 4,540 residents of Nevada's Eureka County, if evenly distributed, would be alone in 3.5 square miles of land.

A Blank Space

Population per square mile by county, 1995

☐ 0–25

☐ 25–75

▨ 75–200

■ 200+

Black Hole

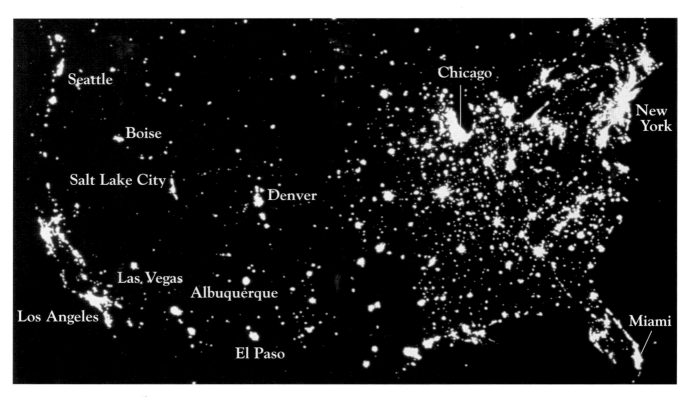

Black Hole

High-powered telescopes still dot the Interior West where the air is clear and city lights don't cloud supersensitive photographs of the galaxy. Viewed at night from orbit, the country's eastern metropoli, like Boston-New York-Washington, Miami, and Chicago stand out in a tapestry of cities and towns that thins noticeably midway across the continent. The larger Western cities show up, in an otherwise dark landscape, as a dispersed constellation of bright splotches: Phoenix, Tucson, El Paso, Albuquerque, Denver, Salt Lake, Boise, and, of course, Las Vegas, whose love affair with garish neon signs, spotlights, and now even lasers, has caught the eye of astronauts since orbital flight began.

faster than all the remaining states during 1995.

Westward movement is as American as cheeseburgers and interstate highways, and the West has always drawn at least a trickle, and often floods, of immigrants. The West's current boom, not tied to a particular commodity like silver or oil, seems different than past migrations and is difficult to characterize. Newspapers and magazines covering the new population shift offer anecdotes about high-tech telecommuters, retirees, and trust-funders seeking a western lifestyle.[2] The newcomers have been called lifestyle refugees, modem cowboys, lone eagle entrepreneurs, and amenity migrants. New Western homesteaders are also vilified for their precious lifestyles, inconsistent preservationist attitudes, and for carving up the West's open spaces. They are loathed by residents who stuck out previous boom-and-bust cycles, even though they are driving the boom that repaired economic damage from the 1980s mining and energy bust.

The richest immigrants, critics say, ride on the backs of an underclass of low-paid service workers, who migrate like camp followers to clean the condos and cut the lawns of western resort-town residents. Tension builds between the new immigrants and the dwindling corps of natural resource laborers and the service workers *they* supported—who all sneer at the new service workers catering to tourists and cleaning trophy homes sprouting up on the range.

Long-time residents are especially disturbed at New Westerners' enthusiasm to preserve, or "museumnize," the region's natural and working landscapes—they crave wilderness and like the look of cattle country, though they demand well-marked trails in the backcountry and call for animals rights when ranchers shoot coyotes or prairie dogs. Seasoned West-watcher Donald Snow claims that many of these "outback urbanistas" can't tell the difference between work and play, wilderness and Disneyland.[3]

The current settlement rush surpasses the energy boom of the late 1970s in parts of the Interior West, but shows a different complexion. Rather than the apartment buildings and trailer parks of the 1970s, the current boom features cookie-cutter subdivisions and mammoth houses spread across the landscape. Interior West immigrants, especially those from California's inflated real estate markets, arrive with more cash to invest in land and houses than the region has ever seen. The land consumed by this new homesteading is almost all former cattle country.

The pace of population growth in the West may slow in the future, but the region is probably losing its thinly settled geography forever. Of course, this latest land boom could bust, like other booms before it. Could the region be left with new types of ghost towns: ghost second-home subdivisions and ghost ski resorts? *High Country News* publisher Ed Marston argues that the neohomesteading boom is just like the mining booms, the energy booms, or the timber booms of the past.[4] Perhaps. But, maybe the new homesteaders have potential to stick. Such a thought chills no-growth'ers like former Colorado governor Richard Lamm, but it also engenders some hope for a mature and more stable Western social landscape. A more immediate question is how tensions between the old and new economy, and Old and New Westerners, can be resolved.

Filling the Void

This map of population growth rates is more telling for those very few Interior West counties not growing fast. Most of the rest of the country, outside of Florida, southern Texas, and a few other hot-spots, barely matches the national average annual growth rate of about 1percent, but only a handful of western places—mostly busted mining areas and declining timber communities—are growing less than 2.5 percent annually, growth rates that would double their population every 28 years. Several Western places, like Douglas County, Colorado, and Summit County, Utah, grew at 10 percent per year in the 1990s, a rate that would double their population every 7 years.

Filling the Void

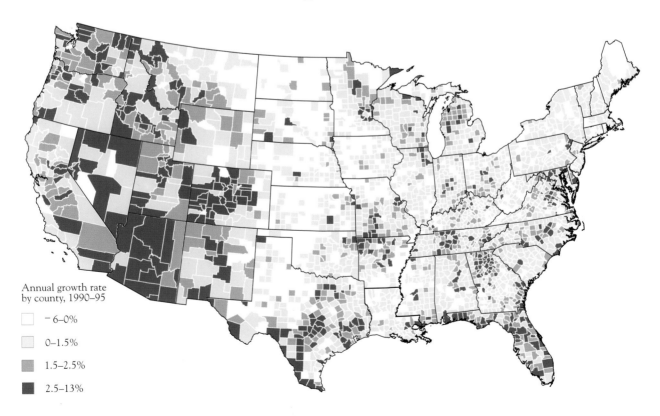

Annual growth rate
by county, 1990–95

- − 6–0%
- 0–1.5%
- 1.5–2.5%
- 2.5–13%

Public West, Private East

Though a few national parks and forests dot the eastern two-thirds of the country, 88 percent of the nation's federal public lands outside Alaska lie in the 11 Western states. Some counties in these states consist of 80–90 percent federal lands, leaving little room for private development, but providing millions of acres of open space, natural resources, recreation, and wildlife habitat.

A Wealth of Public Lands

Almost half of the eleven western states is federally owned land, while no state east of the Rockies is more than 13 percent federal. National forests, national parks, great swaths of Bureau of Land Management holdings, National Wildlife Refuges, military bases, and bomb (dumb, smart, conventional, and nuclear) testing grounds comprise up to 83 percent of Nevada, 62 percent of Idaho, and between roughly a third to a half of the other Western states. No wonder antifederal feelings, especially over land and water resources, run deep in the West, particularly in the most federalized states like Nevada.

The notion that the federal government should retain title to large swaths of the West—rather than hand it all over to homesteaders—first appeared with Congress's creation in 1872 of Yellowstone National Park. According to legend, the idea was born around a campfire in the summer of 1870. A group of "gentleman explorers," attracted by accounts of geysers and petrified trees, were exploring the Yellowstone country under the leadership of former Civil War general and congressman Henry Washburn. Camped near the confluence of the Firehole and Gibbon Rivers at the end of their expedition, they debated. Should each claim a homestead in Yellowstone and start tourist businesses, or should the group call for Yellowstone's preservation as a public reserve? Their public-mindedness won out. For a while, Yellowstone limped along under Army management as other Western parks were created: Yosemite in 1890, Mesa Verde in 1906, the

Public West, Private East

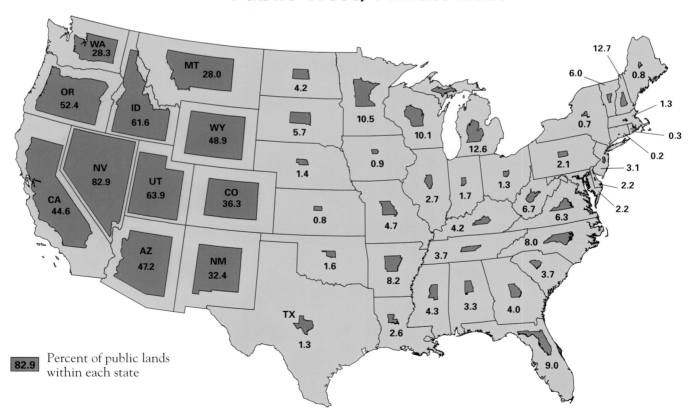

82.9 Percent of public lands within each state

Grand Canyon in 1908. Finally, in 1916, Congress founded the National Park Service to protect these landscape treasures. The rest of America was filling up fast. Only in the West was it practical to preserve large swaths of land in a natural state.

The parks were special cases full of natural wonders, and federal retention of more mundane lands, the forests and open range, started in earnest during the 1890s when Congress gave the president authority to set aside federal reserves to protect natural resources from unwise exploitation. Some 40 million acres of national forests were created by Presidents Harrison and Cleveland. President Theodore Roosevelt topped this off one March night in 1907 as he huddled over maps with Gifford Pinchot, first head of the Forest Service, to designate, in 33 separate presidential proclamations, additional national forests covering over 16 million acres of land. Why the rush? Pinchot and Roosevelt were trying to beat a congressional act retracting the president's authority to withdraw such lands from homesteading. Among these "midnight forests" were many of the West's greatest, like Cascade National Forest in Washington and Oregon and the Grand Mesa in Colorado.

The Big Federal Landlords in the Western States

Bureau of Land Management: **161.2 million acres**
The BLM is responsible for a land mass equivalent to California and Oregon combined, mostly drier rangelands used for grazing, mineral and energy exploration, and recreation.

U.S. Forest Service: **140.9 million acres**
The Forest Service manages an area of the West equivalent to the size of Maine, New Hampshire, Vermont, Massachusetts, Rhode Island, Connecticut, and New York combined. Their responsibilities range from protecting wilderness areas to encouraging developments like ski areas and regulating oil and gas drilling.

The West's remaining public domain, outside of the parks and forests, was mostly open range and desert—spurned by homesteaders but freely used by cattle ranchers. Congress and the administration neglected these "left over" lands until 1934 when unregulated use threatened to destroy their resource values. The Grazing Service, later to become the Bureau of Land Management (BLM), was handed almost 150 million acres—more land than any other federal land agency—of mostly dry and scrubby rangeland to care for. The agency spent much of its first few decades mollifying ranchers who resented the government telling them what to do with their sheep and cattle. Later, put in charge of federal minerals leasing, the agency made the public spotlight with James Watt's industry-boosting coal leasing and offshore oil drilling policies in the 1970s. New Westerners are now flocking onto BLM land to mountain bike, hike, and even hold New Age gatherings, and the BLM has adopted the split personality of the other federal land agencies, awkwardly balancing the demands of old and new interests.

Economists and sociologists say that these public lands drive the West's

A Wealth of Public Lands

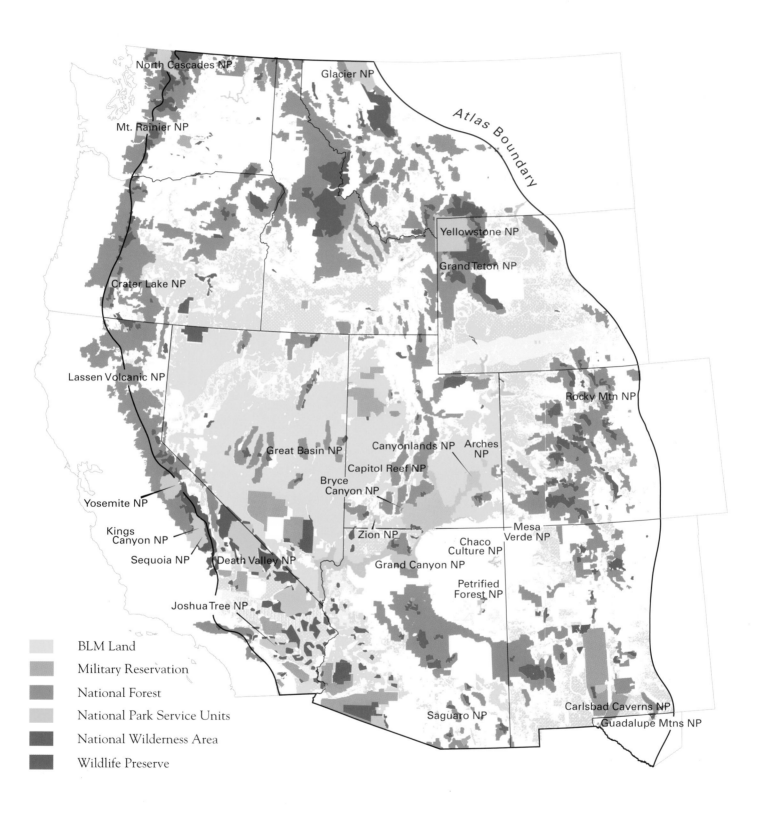

North Cascades NP

Glacier NP

Atlas Boundary

Mt. Rainier NP

Crater Lake NP

Yellowstone NP

Grand Teton NP

Lassen Volcanic NP

Rocky Mtn NP

Great Basin NP

Canyonlands NP

Arches NP

Capitol Reef NP

Yosemite NP

Bryce Canyon NP

Kings Canyon NP

Zion NP

Mesa Verde NP

Sequoia NP

Death Valley NP

Chaco Culture NP

Grand Canyon NP

Joshua Tree NP

Petrified Forest NP

BLM Land

Military Reservation

National Forest

National Park Service Units

National Wilderness Area

Wildlife Preserve

Carlsbad Caverns NP

Saguaro NP

Guadalupe Mtns NP

population growth—people are attracted by the natural vistas, wildlife, and recreation. The region's vaunted parks and wilderness playgrounds, besides luring outdoor types, also host the remaining grizzlies, wolves, bald eagles, and other endangered species. Much of the public lands has been mined, logged, roaded, and grazed, but the vast majority is not as developed as private lands and remains in something approaching a natural state—a rare commodity in the contiguous United States at the end of the twentieth century.

Westerners are ambivalent about Uncle Sam as landlord. They simultaneously take pride in the region's grand national parks and forests while complaining bitterly about the heavy hand of Washington land managers. Westerners aspire to rugged individualism, but crave federal subsidies for everything from water to skiing. Many believe that federal land ownership thwarts the region's economic development; they shout this at forest rangers in small-town public meetings throughout the West, ignoring the fact that they just spent the day on public land teaching their sons and daughters to fish. They feel controlled by the East, especially bureaucrats in Washington, D.C., yet many federal land policies are designed to curry local favor: below-cost timber sales keep local sawmills open, and ranchers graze public lands with little oversight from underfunded BLM field offices. Ski areas and other public lands concessioners energize local economies while paying below-market rates for exclusive franchises. Some Westerners look longingly at the private East and covet its property taxes, despite the federal government's longstanding practice of paying fees to counties in lieu of taxes.

Every decade or so a group of ranchers, or state and county officials, lobby for a transfer of federal lands to state or local government, or their sale to the highest bidder to improve the region's tax base and free it of land use restrictions. President Ronald Reagan and Interior Secretary James Watt, abetting the "Sagebrush Rebellion," a wave of antifederal insurgency in the late 1970s, proposed such transfers. Agency heads like Bob Burford at the BLM, whacked away at the agency's land protection powers, but in the end they achieved very little substantive change. Environmentalists and recreationists fought any land giveaway, and even a few Sagebrush Rebels, after the initial excitement, realized they had a better deal with the federal government than they would get from private landlords or even local government.

The Republicans tried again after the 1994 elections, seeking to sell some public lands, close national parks, and weaken federal land use authority. Their efforts resonated with the so-called "county supremacy" activists, pictured on the

A Wealth of Public Lands

Westerners recognize the fine distinctions among lands managed by, say, The National Park Service, Forest Service, and Bureau of Land Management (BLM) because each is used and managed in different ways. Parks are easy: Grand Canyon, Zion, Yellowstone, and Death Valley come readily to mind, but few Americans know the difference between national parks and forests, nor have most Americans outside the region even heard of the BLM, whose 160 million acres in the West (shown in yellow)—dwarfing both national parks and national forests—are open to public use. Complicating BLM management is the checkerboard of alternating private and public blocks in a swath right across the map. The public lands are a battlefield between Old and New West interests, the federal agencies bravely, or stupidly, trying to accommodate all users, from mountain bikers to coal miners. The 104th Congress even tried to close some national parks, but President Clinton responded by creating the Grand Staircase-Escalante National Monument, a brand new preserve of 1.7 million acres just east of Bryce Canyon in southern Utah, the first national monument to be managed by the BLM.

Entrance sign,   Riebsame

Entrance sign,   Riebsame

Sovereign Lands

A fifth of the Interior West is owned by Indian tribes. Just over a million Native Americans live in the eleven Western states, roughly half on reservations. The largest are the size of a small eastern state, and the smallest are like small towns. As sovereign governments the tribes make their own laws and land use decisions, sometimes in conflict with the states and federal government; tribes also wrestle internally over how much development or resource extraction to allow. Of the 135 reservations mapped here, 40 maintain fish and wildlife management operations, and 25, as members of the Council of Energy Resource Tribes, have joined together to improve energy resource management and to get better deals from coal, gas, and oil companies. Some 30 Interior West reservations offer casino gambling, an issue that strains tribal-state relationships.

cover of *Time* magazine in October 1995,[5] people like Nye County Commissioner Dick Carver, who believe the constitution gives at least land use control, if not outright ownership, of all public lands to county government. So far, though, a deep public care for public lands is beating back this rebellion too. The concern is national: New Yorkers fight to preserve southern Utah wilderness, and anyone who remembers seeing bears during a family vacations to Yellowstone is stirred to protect the Park and maybe support wolf reintroduction—even if it means a few ranchers' calves will be killed. *Time* quotes Western ecologist and author Karl Hess: "The public wants access [to the public lands]. They want to see wild country that looks wild; they want to see wildlife—and a lot of it; they want to see clear water, not muddy; they don't want to see cow turds everywhere."[6] They trust the federal government to meet these desires more than they trust private land owners or local government. Though contested and debated, a wealth of public lands looks to be an abiding geographic feature of the New West.

Indian Country

Indian tribes own roughly a fifth of the Interior West and increasingly control those lands with reduced federal interference, managing their natural resources, steadily reacquiring lost tribal lands, and governing their reservations through tribal legislatures and courts. They also control resources off the reservations: salmon in the Columbia River, water in nearby streams. Most legal interpretations of treaties between the tribes and the U.S. government suggest that they can legitimately claim significantly more water and wildlife resources in the West. This resurgence of Indian political power and cultural identity has become a significant characteristic of the New West.

The 1960s marked a turning point for American Indians. After a hundred years of decline, starting with their nineteenth-century defeat by European invaders and continued through this century in countless treaty violations, Indian fortunes are rising.

The quiet assumption among most Americans in the prospering 1950s and 1960s was that the Indians had already assimilated. Remade as "Americans" they could participate in the economic miracle just like everyone else. The civil rights movement among Blacks may have offered the Indians a model for civic

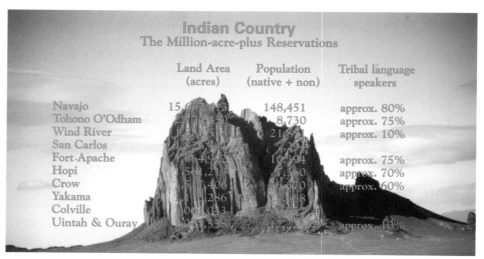

Indian Country
The Million-acre-plus Reservations

	Land Area (acres)	Population (native + non)	Tribal language speakers
Navajo	15,	148,451	approx. 80%
Tohono O'Odham		8,730	approx. 75%
Wind River		21,	approx. 10%
San Carlos			
Fort-Apache		10,	approx. 75%
Hopi			approx. 70%
Crow			approx. 60%
Yakama	286		
Colville			
Uintah & Ouray			approx. 10%

Sovereign Lands

Blackfeet

Colville
Kalispel   Kootenai
Spokane ♠
WA
Flathead
Coeur d'Alene ♠
Yakama Nation
Nez Perce
MT
Umatilla ♠
Crow   Northern
Cheyenne
Warm Springs ♠

OR   ID
Wind River

Burns Paiute
WY

Fort Hall ♠

Fort McDermitt
XL Ranch   Fort Bidwell
Cedarville   Duck Valley
Alturas Rancheria
Lookout Rancheria
Likely   Summit Lake
Rancheria
Pyramid Lake
Winnemucca   Shoshone
Susanville Rancheria   Battle Mtn.   Te-moak ♠   Skull Valley
Lovelock Colony
Reno-Sparks Community
Yerington   Fallon   Goshute   Uintah
Carson Colony   Walker River   and
Dresslerville Colony   Yomba   Ely Colony   Ouray   CO
Washoe   Duckwater   UT
Bridgeport Colony

Benton   NV   Ute
Bishop   Ute Mountain
Big Pine   Shivwits   Southern Ute ♠   Jicarilla Apache ♠
Fort Independence   Moapa River   Kaibab   Taos Pueblo ♠
Lone Pine   Havasupai   Navajo Nation   San Juan   Picuris Pueblo
Timbi-Sha Shoshone   Pueblo   Santa Clara Pueblo ♠
Las Vegas Colony   Hualapai   Jemez   Pojoaque Pueblo ♠
Hopi   Pueblo   Nambe Pueblo
Zia Pueblo   Tesuque Pueblo
CA   AZ   San Ildefonso Pueblo ♠
Canoncito   Cochiti Pueblo
Yavapai   Navajo   Santo Domingo Pueblo
Fort Mojave ♠   Zuni   San Felipe Pueblo
San Manuel ♠   Chemehuevi   Camp Verde   Pueblo   Laguna   Sandia Pueblo
Payson Comm. ♠   Ramah   Pueblo   Santa Ana Pueblo ♠
Morongo ♠   Twentynine Palms   Navajo   Alamo Navajo
Agua Caliente   Colorado   Fort   Isleta Pueblo ♠
Augustine   Cabazon ♠   River   Salt River   Apache   Acoma Pueblo ♠
Torres Martinez   Ft. McDowell ♠
Ft. Yuma ♠   Gila River   San Carlos   Mescalero Apache ♠
Gila Bend
Cocopah ♠   Maricopa   NM
Akchin   Pascua Yaqui
Tohono   San Xavier ♠
O'Odham   Ysleta Del Sur
Pueblo ♠
TX

▌   Indian Reservation
Nez Perce Member, Council of Energy Resource Tribes
Ft. Yuma Member, Native American Fish & Wildlife Society
♠   Gaming Legal on Reservation
🎓   Tribal College

and legal activism based on group identity. Much stronger, though, was simply the tribes' own sense that their unique cultures and sacred lands had been battered too much.

Add a tincture of higher education, law degrees, and an increasingly sympathetic white America, and the modern Indian resurgence gained strength. Treaty violations were challenged; access to natural resources like water and salmon were renewed; and, closest of all to Indian heart and culture, use of sacred sites, many on public lands, was reestablished. The practice of displaying Indian bones and artefacts as national history and prehistory was questioned, and museums began, some grudgingly, to repatriate Indian property.

White America probably hardly noticed this Indian advent in the West until Dee Brown published *Bury My Heart at Wounded Knee* in 1970; this subtitled "Indian History of the American West" described the treachery, butchery, and heartbreak of white conquest of Indians. Vine Deloria Jr.'s *Custer Died for Your Sins*, and even the film *Little Big Man*, started a demythologizing of Custer and his defeat ("Custer Had it Coming" bumper stickers appeared on Indian and Anglo cars), and the National Park Service formally renamed Custer Battlefield National Monument the Little-Bighorn Battlefield. By the time Paul Stekler and James Welch's film, *Last Stand at Little Bighorn*, aired on PBS's *American Experience* series in 1990, many Americans craved and appreciated a more searching, Indian account of the battle.

The Indians had barely survived. Despite much treachery, Euro-American policy in the 1800s officially treated Native Americans as sovereigns—signing treaties and ceding reservations rather than totally annihilating them. Once subdued, the logic of the times suggested, they could be absorbed, treaties broken, and white destiny on the continent completed. But the treaties and reservations were the tap root for future political power, and provided the legal firepower for claims to land and water. Indian culture remains a powerful part of Western geography, both on and off the reservations.

Writing the New West

A region is more than the sum of its parts; although the New West is built of expanded airports, sprawling cities, resurgent ethnicity, ski resorts, fiber optic lines, and even city slicker cattle drives, the words that speak regional coherence flow from the pens and computers of Western writers. No sharp break exists between Old and New Western literature, but certainly we can relegate the cowboy westerns of Zane Grey and Louis L'Amour to the Old West. A modern Western literature emerged, as did a modern literature of the South, during the

Offering flags, Medicine Wheel, Wyoming   Leiberman

Shiprock, New Mexico   Riebsame

NARF staff   Ramirez

1920s and 1930s, in the work of Willa Cather, John Steinbeck, and others. Western writing further matured in the 1940s, with historical fiction like A.B. Guthrie's *The Big Sky* and *The Way West*, and Wallace Stegner's *The Big Rock Candy Mountain* (1943), and regional perspectives like Stegner's biography of John Wesley Powell (*Beyond the Hundredth Meridian*, 1954), works that linked traditional Western themes with modernist notions of people, place, and land—while eschewing hackneyed cowboy and Indian imagery. Stegner fostered this new Western regionalism and bridged, with novels like *Angle of Repose*, to the modernist and postmodernist works, such as Rudolfo Anaya's *Bless Me Ultima* (1972) and Leslie Silko's *Ceremony* (1977). Even gonzo works like Tom Robbins's *Even Cowgirls Get the Blues* and Rob Swigart's *Little America*, though avant-garde, refract Old and New West themes: people's relationship to the land; identity quandaries among Hispanics, Indians, and Asians; urban-rural tensions; and, of course, the continuing presence, in Western consciousness, of cowboys, cowgirls, Indians, gunmen and bank robbers, loggers, miners, sheepherders, and ranchers.

Much New West writing seeks to exorcise Old West demons. The cowboy, according to Sharman Apt Russell in *Kill the Cowboy: A Battle of Mythology*, has

> much to do with our cultural dreams of freedom and solitude, of riding a horse across golden fields as thunderclouds roil across the sky, of sleeping peacefully under the arc of the Milky Way, of walking alone to the bitter light of dawn. In these dreams we test ourselves on the anvil of self-sufficiency. In these dreams, we know the grandeur of an untrammeled continent.[7]

But she warns that "dreams, as we discover again and again, are half seduction. And the cowboy, the seductive cowboy, has a dark side." That darkness includes an urge to kill as many coyotes, mountain lions, and wolves as humanly possible, to keep every inch of Western space open to grazing cattle, "to transform the West into something that resembles, prosaically, a feedlot." Judy Blunt, in her essay, "The Good and Bad of Ranching," skewers the cowboys succinctly by pointing out that their much reported hard work and care at calving time is necessary because their greed and interference with genetics makes cows have bigger calves than they can naturally or easily birth; cowboys nurture with hooks, chains and pulleys.[8]

Sense of place, a strong part of Western life, is actively nourished in the new Western literature. Women ranchers in particular seem able to articulate place in new ways linked to old landscapes. Teresa Jordan (*Riding the White Horse*

Writing the New West

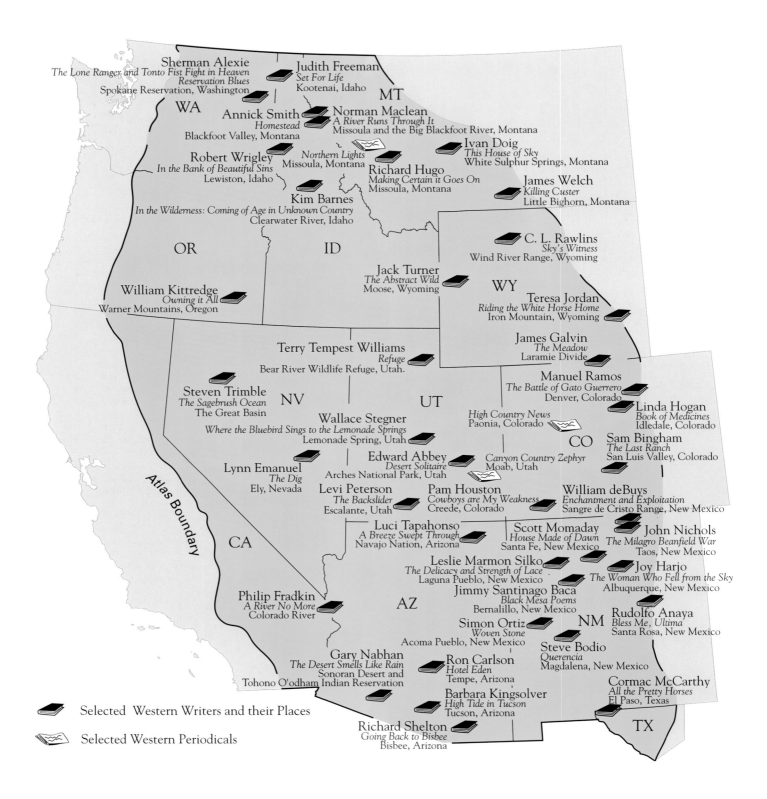

Sherman Alexie
The Lone Ranger and Tonto Fist Fight in Heaven
Reservation Blues
Spokane Reservation, Washington

Judith Freeman
Set For Life
Kootenai, Idaho

MT

WA

Annick Smith
Homestead
Blackfoot Valley, Montana

Norman Maclean
A River Runs Through It
Missoula and the Big Blackfoot River, Montana

Ivan Doig
This House of Sky
White Sulphur Springs, Montana

Robert Wrigley
In the Bank of Beautiful Sins
Lewiston, Idaho

Northern Lights
Missoula, Montana

Richard Hugo
Making Certain it Goes On
Missoula, Montana

James Welch
Killing Custer
Little Bighorn, Montana

Kim Barnes
In the Wilderness: Coming of Age in Unknown Country
Clearwater River, Idaho

OR

ID

C. L. Rawlins
Sky's Witness
Wind River Range, Wyoming

Jack Turner
The Abstract Wild
Moose, Wyoming

WY

William Kittredge
Owning it All
Warner Mountains, Oregon

Teresa Jordan
Riding the White Horse Home
Iron Mountain, Wyoming

James Galvin
The Meadow
Laramie Divide

Terry Tempest Williams
Refuge
Bear River Wildlife Refuge, Utah.

Manuel Ramos
The Battle of Gato Guerrero
Denver, Colorado

Steven Trimble
The Sagebrush Ocean
The Great Basin

NV

UT

High Country News
Paonia, Colorado

Linda Hogan
Book of Medicines
Idledale, Colorado

Wallace Stegner
Where the Bluebird Sings to the Lemonade Springs
Lemonade Spring, Utah

CO

Sam Bingham
The Last Ranch
San Luis Valley, Colorado

Lynn Emanuel
The Dig
Ely, Nevada

Edward Abbey
Desert Solitaire
Arches National Park, Utah

Canyon Country Zephyr
Moab, Utah

Levi Peterson
The Backslider
Escalante, Utah

Pam Houston
Cowboys are My Weakness
Creede, Colorado

William deBuys
Enchantment and Exploitation
Sangre de Cristo Range, New Mexico

CA

Luci Tapahonso
A Breeze Swept Through
Navajo Nation, Arizona

Scott Momaday
House Made of Dawn
Santa Fe, New Mexico

John Nichols
The Milagro Beanfield War
Taos, New Mexico

Leslie Marmon Silko
The Delicacy and Strength of Lace
Laguna Pueblo, New Mexico

Joy Harjo
The Woman Who Fell from the Sky
Albuquerque, New Mexico

Jimmy Santiago Baca
Black Mesa Poems
Bernalillo, New Mexico

Philip Fradkin
A River No More
Colorado River

AZ

Simon Ortiz
Woven Stone
Acoma Pueblo, New Mexico

NM

Rudolfo Anaya
Bless Me, Ultima
Santa Rosa, New Mexico

Steve Bodio
Querencia
Magdalena, New Mexico

Gary Nabhan
The Desert Smells Like Rain
Sonoran Desert and
Tohono O'odham Indian Reservation

Ron Carlson
Hotel Eden
Tempe, Arizona

Cormac McCarthy
All the Pretty Horses
El Paso, Texas

Barbara Kingsolver
High Tide in Tucson
Tucson, Arizona

TX

Richard Shelton
Going Back to Bisbee
Bisbee, Arizona

Atlas Boundary

Selected Western Writers and their Places

Selected Western Periodicals

Home) bound ranching to place and community—no ranch is an island—in ways most cowboys would disdain. Edward Abbey, in *Desert Solitaire*, linked place (Arches National Park) and persona in what became a standard of Western nature writing. And loss of place or, worse, destruction of place figures prominently in New West writing—William deBuys's account of cultural and ecological change in New Mexico's Sangre de Cristo Range, and William Kittredge's account of his family building and destroying a good place in *Owning It All*:

> The majority of agricultural people, if you pressed them hard enough, even though most of them despise sentimental abstractions, will admit they are trying to create a good place, and to live as part of goodness, in a kind of connection which with fine reason we call rootedness. . . . These are the thoughts which come back when I visit eastern Oregon. I park and stand looking down into the lava-rock and juniper-tree canyon where Deep Creek cuts it way out of the Warner Mountains, and the great turkey buzzard soars high in the yellow-orange light above the evening. . . .
>
> So, I ask myself, if it was such a pretty life, why didn't I stay? We were doing God's labor and creating a good place on earth, living the pastoral yeoman dream—that's how our mythology defined it, although nobody would ever have thought to talk about work in that way.
>
> And then it all went dead, over years, but swiftly. . . . For so many years, through endless efforts, we had proceeded in good faith, and it turned out we had wrecked all we had not left untouched.
>
> We baited the coyotes with 1080, and rodents destroyed our alfalfa; we sprayed weeds and insects with 2-4-D Ethyl and Malathion, and Parathion for clover mite, and we shortened our lives.
>
> We had reinvented our valley according to the most pervasive ideal given us by our culture, and we ended with a landscape organized like a machine . . . a dreamland gone wrong.[9]

A rich crop of writers who can articulate the West at the end of the twentieth century—a West rapidly filling with a new, landed gentry, high-tech businesses, and a desperate working class—has come out of Albuquerque, Missoula, Elko, Boulder, and other Western venues, to tell the region's stories and speak truth to its myths. They take strong stands: Edward Abbey rants against Western development and industrial tourism, and preaches a nearmisanthropic environmentalism; William Kittredge somberly laments the New West in *Who Owns the West* (1995); and Alston Chase argues, in *Playing God in Yellowstone*, that we destroy nature by our awkward attempts to preserve it.

New West writers may not get the attention they deserve; big publishing contracts are still rare, but a host of regional publishing houses, university presses, and periodicals like *Northern Lights* from Missoula, Montana, and Ed and Betsy Marston's *High Country News* out of Paonia, Colorado, and the *Canyon Country Zephyr* from Moab, Utah, have brought greater readership. At least they now have each other's work to build on.

Writing the New West

Western sense of Western place is actively nourished by the New Western writers. We map here a selection of authors whose writing especially links people and place in the Western landscape. Their "places" might be whole mountain ranges, as in C.L. Rawlins's book about his years collecting data on "acid snow" in Wyoming's Wind River Mountains, or William DeBuys' examination of land and community in New Mexico's Sangre de Cristo Range. Some authors use a small place to explore the bigger human predicament, as in Teresa Jordan's story of her wedding at Iron Mountain, Wyoming, while others range across the region and beyond: Wallace Stegner wrote about many Western places and about the West as a whole; Leslie Marmon Silko reflects the whole Indian experience from her home on the Laguna Pueblo.

Chapter 2: Infrastructure for the New West

Flying In and Out of the West

Airline service puts a town on the modern economic map, especially in an era of capital and labor mobility. The map shows zones within 60 highway miles of scheduled air service—less than an hour's drive at Western speed limits if it's not snowing. Small towns and rural hinterlands inside these perimeters are roosts for tele-commuting professionals and second-home owners. The Rocky Mountains, from Colorado to Montana, are especially well-served, partly because airlines find profit in catering to skiers. The thriving towns of eastern Washington have also created an air service zone based on the high-tech development attracted to the Hanford Nuclear labs, and the Interior West's sunbelt— from Albuquerque to Palm Springs—is also well-peppered with scheduled service.

Before they even got to the Sierra Nevada range that was their undoing, the Donner Party had lots to complain about in the fall of 1846. Their 2,000 mile trek from St. Louis, across the Rocky Mountains and through the Great Salt Lake desert ran afoul of bad advice, delays and wrong turns, poor equipment, and illness; now early snows had trapped them in the High Sierra. Only 47 of the 89 immigrants made it through to the lush valleys of California that winter, having survived on true grit and cannibalism. Three years later the California trail was better marked and lined by merchants offering supplies and fresh oxen to parties in need, selling maps and guide service, operating ferries and even hotels and restaurants along the way. By 1850 the California Trail was a reliable and safe thoroughfare.

First impressions endure, though. Hollywood belabors the obstacle course run by pioneering immigrants: swollen rivers, bad water, attacking Indians, and brutal, snow-clogged mountain passes. The West was hard, hard on travelers and the few who managed to settle. Western development was retarded by another kind of friction: lack of money. The West was built on Eastern capital; and investors outside the region still provided the capital and took the profits.

What have these images got to do with the New West?

The Too-Accessible West

According to legend, the deserts were littered with the bones of those who didn't make it across the wastes. But while Western mythology of impassable terrain is overblown, it is rooted in real events, especially immobilized travelers like the Donner group. Even the most experienced and hearty could get in trouble: celebrated explorer John C. Fremont's fourth Western expedition, mounted in 1848 to find a rail route through the central Rockies, bogged down in the snows of Colorado's San Juan Mountains—ten men in the party froze or starved. Inaccessibility seems to dominate Western geography, and basic geography teaches that poor access is not only hard on those passing through, but also retards economic development.

The merchants along the California trail started a trend, and the West is now laced with highways, airline service, and a telecommunications network growing with the surging demands of high-tech businesses and home-based information mongers. Getting into, out of, and around in the New West is easy and routine: fast, air-conditioned cars whiz across the deserts and mountains on good highways. Air service dispels any sense of isolation by bringing in daily loads of people; packages that were in Washington or Chicago one day arrive in Boise or Tucumcari the next; live lobsters and big city newspapers, the same day. A

Jackson Hole, Wyoming   Riebsame

Central Wyoming   Robb

Passenger Train, Colorado   Riebsame

Flying In and Out of the West

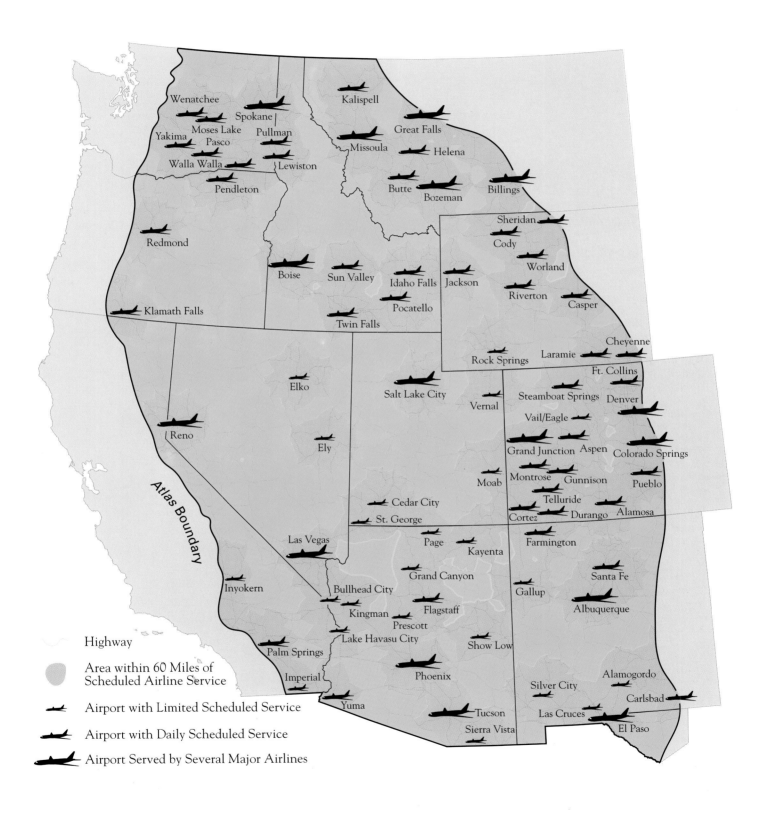

Highway

Area within 60 Miles of Scheduled Airline Service

Airport with Limited Scheduled Service

Airport with Daily Scheduled Service

Airport Served by Several Major Airlines

Jet-Setting the West

The high-end Western air traveler flies private jets, headed for landing fields near world-class trout streams or ritzy resorts. The Saratoga, Wyoming, jetport—on the North Platte River—is chock-full of corporate jets during the fly-fishing season, and tarmacs from Sun Valley to Tahoe to Driggs, Idaho (the latter hard by the west foot of the Grand Teton), are busy during the ski season. Corporate executives can visit the company's ranch near Pinedale, Wyoming, or Lone Pine, California, or get to the distant office quickly from their homes on the range.

wildlife documentary pans from a close-up of antelope to a vast desert background; another scene zooms to white dots on a castellated mountain peak, resolving them into mountain goats. But we don't see the highway overlook where the camera crew set up. The narrator doesn't mention that the crew flew into Kalispell, Jackson, or Telluride that morning from Los Angeles or New York City, rented a van, drove to a nearby national park or forest, and, having wrapped the wildland scenes, will fly out that evening. Tourists routinely land near Yellowstone, Glacier, or Grand Canyon National Parks; having breakfasted at home, they are, by dinner time, happily sipping wine in Old Faithful Lodge, Many Glacier Hotel, or the El Tovah dining room hard by the Grand Canyon's south rim.

Locals seem to have forgotten the region's vaunted inaccessibility as well; ski resort workers commute daily over 10,000-foot mountain passes, businessfolk attend lunch meetings at mountain resorts and return to their Denver, Salt Lake, Boise, or Tucson offices for an afternoon's work. Some even live in the West and work elsewhere. For its 1993 cover story about the New West, *Time* magazine interviewed several "commuting cowboys," with homes at the foot of the Tetons, or in Utah's canyonlands, and offices on either coast.[1]

The airfields used by these jet-setters emerged piecemeal, a lengthened runway here, an instrument landing system added there, funded with ticket tariffs, landing fees, and government subsidies. City councils and chambers of commerce crave better air service enough to subsidize it, and airports appeared to be the perfect development tool—taxing the rich so they could fly. That is, until air transport boosters decided to build Denver International Airport (DIA), the biggest one in the world. They poured great gobs of public money, sweetheart land and construction deals, and civic reputation into a tent-roofed facility on the Plains (its white, multipeaked tent roof emulating the snowy peaks of the Front Range west of the city), overstepping themselves. DIA's problems became the stuff of daily national news and even late–night TV comedy: multiyear opening delays, a Rube Goldberg automated baggage system still malfunctioning two years after the airport finally opened in 1994, and less than promised winter weather performance. The airport may turn out as the best public development investment of the twenty-first century, but, *High Country News* publisher Ed Marston believes that "DIA was an attempt by Denver's civic and business heads, the city's major media, and by all of Colorado's senators and representatives to

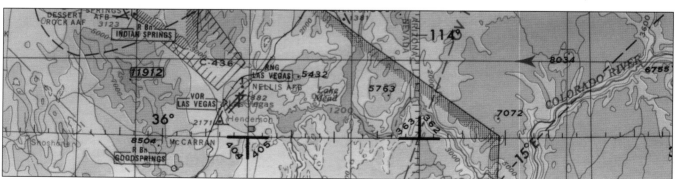

Sectional Aeronautical Chart, 1:50,000 - Las Vegas area

Jet–Setting the West

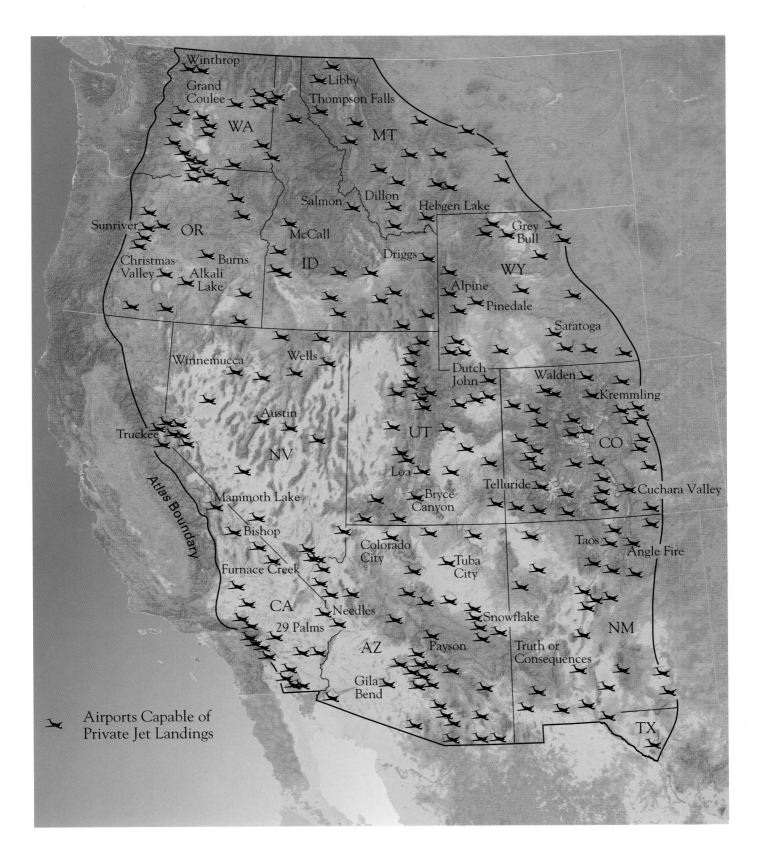

Winthrop
Grand Coulee
Libby
Thompson Falls
WA
MT
Salmon
Dillon
Hebgen Lake
Sunriver
OR
McCall
Grey Bull
Christmas Valley
Burns
Driggs
WY
Alkali Lake
ID
Alpine
Pinedale
Saratoga
Winnemucca
Wells
Dutch John
Walden
Kremmling
Austin
UT
CO
Truckee
NV
Loa
Telluride
Cuchara Valley
Atlas Boundary
Mammoth Lake
Bryce Canyon
Bishop
Colorado City
Taos
Angle Fire
Furnace Creek
Tuba City
CA
Needles
Snowflake
NM
29 Palms
AZ
Payson
Truth or Consequences
Gila Bend
TX

Airports Capable of
Private Jet Landings

blow Denver up into major-city status at the expense of the surrounding region."[2] Instead of improving roads and schools, the city, state, and feds sunk billions into a showy airport to replace one that served the region well enough, and, while aggrandizing itself, Denver drew resources off of the Rocky Mountain region it claims to be capital of—sucking up federal dollars and charging high landing fees that forced a cutback in commuter service to small towns.

Back on the ground, creating the Western road system was a Jekyll and Hyde proposition; construction crews faced a mixture of wide, intermontane basins with few barriers (not even trees), and the daunting terrain of mountains (those snowy passes that bogged down wagoneering immigrants in the mid-1800s), canyons, and searing deserts. But, Westerners quickly accepted the mass-produced automobile in the 1910s and 1920s and improved roads followed in a now well-established pattern of American development. To the Western mind, cars seemed the logical way to cross the region's large spaces; they also helped Western cities spread across that space. Southern California pioneered and exported an automobile-based urban society, and the interior cities, like Phoenix and Denver, though well-served by rail, quickly adopted automotive sprawl. As in so many aspects of American life, the middle-class automobile transformed the West, not just its city form, but also its twentieth-century economy. The railroads had made visiting the West "just to see it" popular with wealthy Easterners, but the automobile democratized tourism, which, in some years (say, when cattle prices slump) is the West's leading economic sector. Soon, national parks like Glacier and Grand Canyon, previously reached only by train, were opened to autos; the Park Service even encouraged car access. Enos Mills, founder of Rocky Mountain National Park, argued for the Western parks:

> There must be speedy ways of reaching these places and swift means of covering their long distances, or but a few people will have either the time or strength to see the wonders of these parks. The traveler wants the automobile with which to see America.[3]

Mills and many Park Service leaders argued, simply, that to protect the Parks they had to get as many people into them as possible, and roads did just that.

A Road Runs Through It

Westerners think nothing of 500-mile weekend outings on the region's network of good highways. The roads shown here allow a family sedan access to virtually all of the region's wide space. This places a premium on solitude, on the New West's "unpaved outbacks," mapped here as purple zones, at least 10 miles from a highway. The largest of these is central Idaho's River of No Return Wilderness. Other large unpaved outbacks show up in Nevada, Arizona, and New Mexico. Much of the roadless zone straddling the Utah-Arizona border was declared a national monument by President Clinton in 1996. Yet, many of the outbacks mapped here are crisscrossed by dirt roads used by four-wheeler's seeking "wilderness" adventure. Further inside them survive the last truly wild places, completely road-less wildlands whittled to ever smaller patches.

High Roads

Some Paved Mountain Passes in the West

Year-round	Elevation (ft)
Loveland Pass, Colo.	11,992
Hoosier Pass, Colo.	11,541
Monarch Pass, Colo.	11,312
Berthoud Pass, Colo.	11,307
Red Mountain Pass, Colo.	11,018
Wolf Creek Pass, Colo.	10,850
Vail Pass, Colo.	10,662
Cumbres Pass, N.Mex.	10,002
Bobcat Pass, N.Mex.	9,820
Powder River Pass, Wyo.	9,666
Togwotee Pass, Wyo.	9,658
Sonora Pass, Calif.	9,628
Palo Felchado Pass, N.Mex.	9,107
Galena Summit, Idaho	8,701
Teton Pass, Wyo.	8,429
Echo Summit, Calif.	7,382
Donner Pass, Calif.	7,209
Connors Pass, Nev.	7,723
Montgomery Pass, Nev.	7,132
Lost Trail Pass, Idaho	7,014
Chinook Pass, Wash.	5,440
MacKenzie Pass, Oreg.	5,325

Summer Only	
Trail Ridge, Colo.	12,183
Independence Pass, Colo.	12,095
Bear Tooth Pass, Mont.	10,947
Snowy Range Pass, Wyo.	10,800
Tioga Pass, Calif.	9,945
Logan Pass, Mont.	6,646

A Road Runs Through It

Paved Highway

"Outback" Area

Within Ten Miles of Paved Highway

Road touring took off after World War II—Americans had money, cars, time, children, and roads improved to move soldiers and war material around. And the parks accommodated them with lodges, campgrounds (some later became RV havens), and parking lots. Even Wallace Stegner, in his essay "The Rediscovery of America: 1946," savors the freedom of the road without gas rationing and travel restrictions in his first postwar camping trip:

> I have forgotten for too long how the tangled, twisted, warped and bent and bone-dry desert ranges lift out of their alluvial slopes, and how the road droops like a sagging rope from one dry pass to another. It is good to play the old game of guessing how far it is to that point, always fore-shortened and looking deceptively close, where the road curves and disappears into the rock.[4]

Park managers, well into the 1950s, hardly imagined smog obscuring the Grand Canyon, or mile-long "bear jams" in Yellowstone. Yet, by the 1980s most Park

No Roads Allowed

Federal wilderness designation protects some of the largest
unroaded Western landscapes. Some examples:

Frank Church River of No-Return Wilderness Idaho	2,364,500 acres
Bob Marshall/Scapegoat/Great Bear Wilderness Montana	1,536,100 acres
Selway-Bitteroot Wilderness Idaho/Montana	1,338,000 acres
Teton/Washakie Wilderness Wyoming	1,280,000 acres
Pasayten/Stephen Mather Wilderness Washington	1,230,000 acres
Absaroka/Beartooth Wilderness Montana	920,300 acres
Bridger/Fitzpatrick/Popo Agie Wyoming	728,500 acres
John Muir Wilderness California	580,000 acres
Glacier Peak Wilderness Washington	572,300 acres
Trinity Alps Wilderness California	498,000 acres
Wenminuche Wilderness Colorado	459,600 acres
High Uintas Wilderness Utah	456,000 acres

Not all of the West's remaining large roadless areas are protected as wilderness: the largest tract, over 1.3 million roadless acres, is inside southern Utah's new Grand Staircase-Escalante National Monument; the Utah Wilderness Coalition wants Congress to designate it formal wilderness to squash future road-building.
Source: U.S. Forest Service

Service planners were desperately trying to limit cars and get tourists on foot or mass transit (ironically, coming full circle). Not everyone, of course, wants fewer cars in national parks: the Wyoming congressional delegation recently fought the idea of a monorail system for Yellowstone as an infringement of tourists' ability to enjoy the park through their own windshields.

Starting in the late 1950s, the West, like the rest of the country, was laced with interstate highways. Westerners, used to driving fast on two-lane roads, could now travel 80+ mph to their favorite camping or fishing spot. Interstates served rural development, pork barrel politics, and even nuclear policy. The last stretches of Interstate 70 were forced through the Colorado high country in part to ease the anticipated shipment of high level nuclear waste to Nevada's Yucca Mountain. Off the main drags, backroads were paved and designated "scenic byways" by the U.S. Forest Service, county commissions, and local boosters, steamrolling residents who preferred their quiet back lanes quiet (their protests echo earlier dissent over highways that split neighborhoods in Boston and New York City).

Riebsame

Many Westerners think the region is altogether too accessible. Access has a cost. Snowplow drivers (and the occasional motorist) are caught in avalanches, and the mountains still swat small aircraft from the sky at an alarming rate. Salt and gravel do make mountain roads passable in snowstorms; but they also wash into streams, along with crankcase oil and toxic chemicals spilled by the occasional truck wreck, strangling the fish. Crime rates, house prices, and pollution increase in formerly isolated communities with each improvement in the passage of people, goods, and services. The West is as accessible as any other American region.

The Information Landscape

When the National Park Service announced that Yellowstone would get complete cellular telephone coverage by 1997, many Westerners found themselves conflicted: sure, the region has pushed hard on the government and

Calls from the Wild

Park and forest rangers in the West report increased cell phone calls for help from the wilderness; other wilderness calls are less critical:

A women called from near the top of El Capitan, in Yosemite National Park, demanding a rescue because she was too tired to descend.

Two climbers—on a rock wall near Tucson, Arizona—called a local outdoor shop to ask the owner about the climbing route ahead of them.

Calling friends from the top of Mt. Whitney, to say "Guess where I am!" and "What a great view," is routine; one climber overheard four cellular calls from the summit in one hour.

Sources: High Country News, Adventure West

Connecting the West

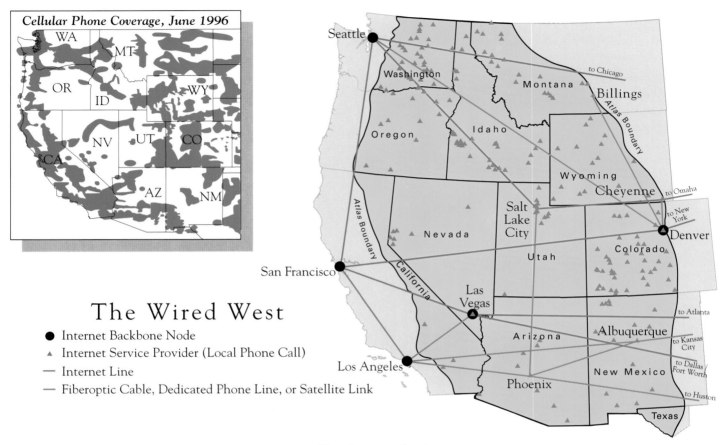

Cellular Phone Coverage, June 1996

WA
MT
OR
ID
WY
NV
UT
CO
CA
AZ
NM

Seattle
Washington
Montana
Billings
to Chicago
Atlas Boundary
Oregon
Idaho
Wyoming
Cheyenne
to Omaha
to New York
Atlas Boundary
Salt Lake City
Denver
Nevada
Utah
Colorado
California
Las Vegas
San Francisco
to Atlanta
Arizona
Albuquerque
to Kansas City
Los Angeles
New Mexico
to Dallas/Fort Worth
Phoenix
to Huston
Texas

The Wired West

- ● Internet Backbone Node
- ▲ Internet Service Provider (Local Phone Call)
- — Internet Line
- — Fiberoptic Cable, Dedicated Phone Line, or Satellite Link

Colorado's Digital Pipelines

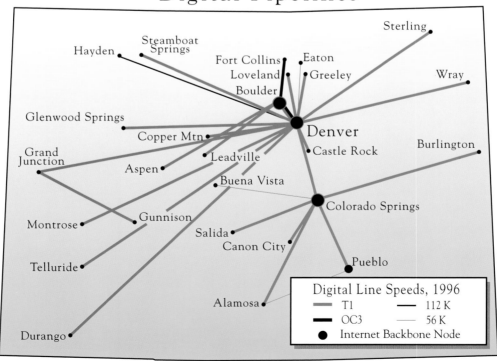

Sterling
Steamboat Springs
Hayden
Fort Collins
Eaton
Loveland
Greeley
Wray
Boulder
Glenwood Springs
Copper Mtn
Denver
Burlington
Grand Junction
Leadville
Castle Rock
Aspen
Buena Vista
Montrose
Gunnison
Colorado Springs
Salida
Telluride
Canon City
Pueblo
Alamosa
Durango

Digital Line Speeds, 1996
- — T1
- — 112 K
- — OC3
- — 56 K
- ● Internet Backbone Node

telecommunications companies to get it into the information age, but did the tendrils of info-space have to reach even into the heart of the wilderness? Yes, cell phones add a measure of safety in grizzly country, but do we really need to contact our brokers from camp?

Ready transportation of people and goods enabled Western development, but, like the rest of the postindustrial, global economy, the New West world turns on the generation and transfer of ideas and information. *Time* magazine's cover article hyping the region's newest boom briefly describes families escaping urban blight to watch sunsets behind snowcapped mountains, and then moves quickly on to the West's new economic raison d'etre:

> The Rockies' new ethos manages to combine the yearning for a simpler, rooted, front-porch way of life with the urban-bred, high-tech worldliness of computers and modems.[5]

Only in the cyberspace age could the imagery of laid-back rurality mesh so attractively with the standard urban frenzy. One interviewee writes daily stories for a computer magazine published out of Manhasset, New York, zapping them from a home office in Park City, Utah. Another modem refugee in that trendy Utah ski town designs training systems for a computer manufacturer. He tells *Time*: "With data communication and computers and faxes, distance is not an issue. We have easy access to our markets, most of which are on the West Coast. The airport's 45 minutes away."

Of course, not every Western ski resort town is just 45 minutes from a major airport, and the modem cowboys battle virtual and concrete obstacles in the West's information landscape. Telecommunications companies in the region simply did not anticipate the 1990s' boom in demand for multiple lines — one each for the home business, modem, parents, and kids; they also underestimated demand for the "high bandwidth" lines that accommodate large slugs of data (officially called ISDN lines, for Integrated Services Digital Network). The copper and fiberoptic cables needed to network all those computers and fax machines still concentrate in the big cities. Businesses and telecommuters removed from these sites either do without bandwidth or wait months for new lines. By the mid-1990s, Western public service commissions were fining the largest telecommunications providers for failing to meet demand for new lines. Businesses trying to establish sites on the Internet are frustrated, and lone eagles in small towns either pay large installation fees, or wait until more telecommuters join their rural retreat.

A few out-of-the-way places have succeeded in getting wired. Lincoln County, Montana, created public Internet access points in every town, becoming the envy of World Wide Web surfers in the rest of the state. A group of telecommuters in Telluride, Colorado, formed the INFOZONE, and bagged a node on the high-bandwidth network developed by the state. Still, information access problems get little mention in the hype about the West's emergence into info-space. *Money* magazine's list of 50 booming small towns cited several as computer age hot spots, but did not caution the fax and modem crowd to call ahead for reservations on the information superhighway.

Connecting the West

The telecommuter and cyberspace explorer needs connections: high bandwidth telecommunication conduits and "points of presence" where commercial and public providers offer local access to the Internet and World Wide Web. Despite the travails of telecommunications providers trying to meet rocketing demand, the wiring of the West proceeds apace and this map will be outdated quickly. Cellular telephone coverage (mapped here as of mid-1996) is also expanding—Yellowstone National Park in northwestern Wyoming should be covered by 1997. Some purists want cellular phones banned from wilderness areas or ski lifts. Unlikely, but perhaps a New West etiquette will emerge to proscribe all but emergency calls from backcountry campsites, ski runs, or mountain peaks.

A Corporate Void

Corporate America is head-quartered everywhere but in the Interior West. California tops the country according on the 1996 Forbes list of the 500 largest U.S. companies, but Montana, Wyoming, and New Mexico share with North Dakota and Vermont the distinction of hosting no companies on the list. Virtually all of the 119 listed firms in California, Oregon, and Washington are based in Pacific Coast cities, not in the interior.

Capital for the New West

Plundered province? The West still tends to run on Eastern or Pacific Coast investment; most companies extracting resources or manufacturing widgets in the Interior West answer to corporate headquarters outside the region. But indigenous firms are sprouting—a few making the lists of the country's biggest. Bernard DeVoto coined the term "plundered province" in a *Harper's* column in 1934,[6] and almost every Western essayist since has pondered the region's colonial relationship with the East. The East urbanized first and demanded resources, so it seems natural that an extractive economy would evolve in the resource–rich, but thinly settled, West to meet this demand. But the region's reliance on a monetary umbilical to the East is only half the story. California, by the second half of the nineteenth century, was a huge economy in its own right. And, like the East, it acted as a source of capital, innovation, and corporate control to the Interior. Western aircraft companies, missile builders, software firms, and tourist businesses are rooted not in New York or Chicago, but in Orange County, Silicon Valley, and on the San Francisco Bay.

Still, it makes little difference whether the Interior West was "plundered" by the East or by the Pacific Rim; like most extractive economies, the "value added" to and profit taken from Western production occurred somewhere else. If railroads were to stretch across the West, the capital would be raised in the East (or even Europe). With it would come strings of corporate control. Only a few

A Corporate Void

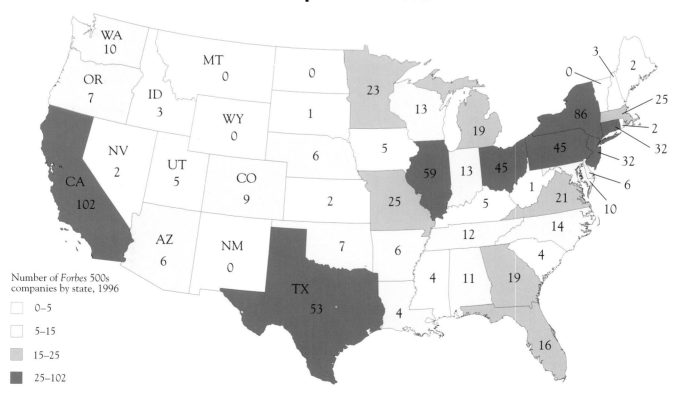

Number of *Forbes* 500s companies by state, 1996

- 0–5
- 5–15
- 15–25
- 25–102

well–known corporations have emerged in the Interior West (like Boise Cascade and Alberston's in Idaho; Novell in Utah; and TCI in Colorado), and though the region's political power increased dramatically in the 1980s with the Reagan Revolution, its capitalistic might hardly increased.

Corporate location even drives Western anger over the environment and public lands. Antilogging protestors in Colorado's Rio Grande National Forest like to point out that the main company cutting the area's remaining old growth forest is based in Chicago.

Capital for the New West

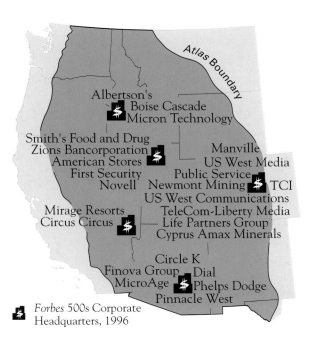

Forbes 500s Corporate Headquarters, 1996

Though few large corporations are based in the Interior West, the region's corporate ecology is more diverse than one might think. The extractive industries make a showing in the Forbes 500s list, of course: Boise Cascade (lumber) in Idaho, Cyprus Amax in Colorado (molybdenum), and Phelps Dodge in Phoenix (copper), but a larger number deal in the services economy, like American Stores in Salt Lake City (retail), Albertson's in Boise (groceries), Novell in Provo (software) and TCI in Denver (telecommunications and media).

Much of the wood, and most of the profits, leave the region. In southern Utah, Western senators cursed President Clinton for setting aside land that was slated for coal mining by a Dutch multinational firm. The coal would have gone straight to Pacific Asia (and the profits to Holland), leaving Utahns with, yes, a few hundred new jobs but also years of environmental clean-up. Many New Westerners living away from the coast would agree with DeVoto: they are a colony, and though better airports, highways, and telecommunications allow capitalists and their power to flow through the region less impeded, even the new economy of ideas and recreation seems colonial and extractive.

Arid, Extra Dry

Scholars refer to the 20-inch annual precipitation line, roughly paralleling the 100th meridian, as the edge of arid America. Unirrigated agriculture is nearly impossible west of this line, making lawn watering a way of life. Pockets of moisture exist in the West: the Colorado Rockies and Northern Idaho mountains stand out. But so too does the desiccated zone sprawling out from the junction of Nevada, Arizona, and California, a sprawl of true deserts like Death Valley, which can go years without significant rainfall.

Every school kid knows the West as the country's arid zone, a place of deserts crossed by a few precious rivers—rather like the Nile in Egypt. Aridity figures large in our understanding and expectations of the region, but in truth, the modern West is quite well-watered in spite of its sparse precipitation. Thanks to the utilitarian mindset of our century and a nexus of ingenuity, capital, and subsidies, the billions of gallons of snowmelt splashing from the region's high peaks—water that would normally go to "waste"—are ably captured and moved to "higher uses" by the most complex water collection and transfer systems on the planet. One result of this engineering miracle is that lawns in the suburbs of Denver, Phoenix, or Boise are just as green as those in Boston, Miami, or New Orleans.

Yes, the West offers a pleasantly dry climate—over 300 clear days a year in most places. But it is not stretched for water. In fact, it enjoys amenities native to more humid climes: impeccable lawns, lush gardens, long showers, swimming pools, and miles of green golf courses. John Wesley Powell, the 19th century explorer/scientist who saw water development as critical to the West's future, warned that the climate would not support large-scale irrigation or extensive human inhabitation.[1] Powell was wrong. Not only does the region support a multibillion dollar agricultural economy based mostly on irrigation, but people moving West have no trouble obtaining water for their lawns, pools, and hot tubs—just turn on the tap!

Aridity did not limit urban growth, thanks to the perseverance and ingenuity of engineers and developers and water laws and institutions designed to push development. Subdivisions on Colorado's Front Range with names like "Sandpiper" and "Water's Edge" project images of liquid abundance with artifi-

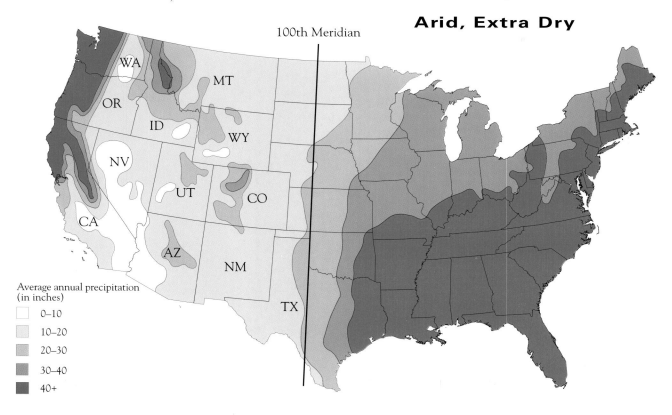

Arid, Extra Dry

100th Meridian

Average annual precipitation
(in inches)

- 0–10
- 10–20
- 20–30
- 30–40
- 40+

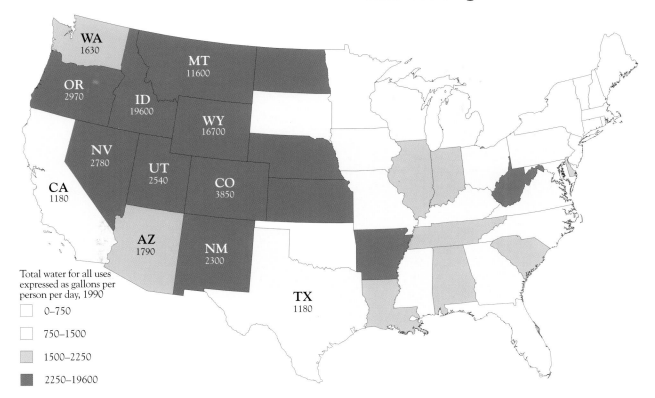

Total water for all uses expressed as gallons per person per day, 1990

- ☐ 0–750
- ☐ 750–1500
- ☐ 1500–2250
- ■ 2250–19600

cial streams at their entrances and vast expanses of verdant green lawns tended by automatic sprinkler systems doing duty even during the infrequent (though soaking) rainstorm. Sunbathers in Phoenix and Las Vegas loll on simulated beaches complete with make-believe oceans (of fresh water), waves, sand, cliffs, and waterfalls. On the Las Vegas Strip pirates reenact battles on the high seas, and water-based amusement parks thrill kids in this gambling-town-turned-family-theme-park. "Misters" spraying a fine drizzle on restaurant goers in Palm Springs keep outdoor patios cool in sizzling weather, and in Fountain Hills, a subdivision northeast of Phoenix, residents enjoy a 450-foot-high geyser, which shoots up from the middle of an artificial lake for 12 minutes every hour.[2]

Quenching the Thirst

Compared to other desert civilizations, the American West scoffs at aquatic moderation. Americans use three times as much water as Europeans and infinitely more than people in developing countries.[3] And Westerners lead the country. As a whole, Americans consume about 40 gallons per person per day, while in the Southwest, per capita daily consumption averages 120 gallons. In cities like Phoenix and Las Vegas, residents consume over 300 gallons per day, in large part because of their penchant for green lawns.[4] In Denver, for example, over half the water consumed is attributable to outdoor landscaping.

This watery lifestyle is not without its costs to urbanites, however: in parts of the Las Vegas Valley the earth has subsided five feet due to groundwater pumping, pulling houses into large holes; and excessive outdoor watering has made the microclimate of Phoenix humid and pollen-rich—the "eastern" climate

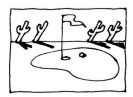

Quenching the Thirst

Water consumption is greater per person in the West than in other parts of the country, mostly due to the irrigation needed to grow anything in the region's dry climate. Though crops consume most Western water, more of the liquid that refreshes is shifting from farms and ranches to cities and suburbs every year. Western cities are fairly efficient water users, especially in parts of Arizona, where residents were coerced into a strict water conservation program in exchange for approval of the federally funded Central Arizona Project. CAP enables Arizonans to appropriate their share of the Colorado River, but with new conservation programs in place, residents are finding they don't need the new water!

Colorado River Uses

The Colorado River flows through seven states and Mexico, serving nearly 25 million people. Most of the beneficiaries of this water reside outside the basin and rely on transbasin diversions to slake their thirst. In Colorado, for example, 85% of the population served by the river lives on the other side of the Continental Divide! Eleven federal hydropower plants on the Colorado River system—Glen Canyon Dam, Hoover Dam, and others—generate enough power to meet all the electrical needs of 3 million people and partial electrical needs of 9 to 12 million. In the Upper Colorado River Basin alone, reservoirs provide 230,000 acres of water surface and 1500 miles of shoreline for recreation. The Bureau of Reclamation estimates over 9 million recreation visits to these Upper Basin reservoirs each year!

	Population Served	Irrigated Acres Served	Major Crops Under Irrigation
Arizona	3,080,000	560,000	cotton, alfalfa, lettuce, wheat, citrus, cauliflower, barley
California	16,000,000	650,000	cantaloupes, dates, grapes, lettuce, tomatoes, onions, carrots, alfalfa, wheat grass
Colorado	2,100,000	1,900,000	hay and alfalfa, grains, vegetables, fruit
Nevada	800,000	*	*
New Mexico	92,000+	60,000	alfalfa, wheat, potatos, corn, pinto beans, onions, grains
Utah	1,180,000	340,000	pasture, alfalfa, grains

Source: U.S. Bureau of Reclamation

Drenching the Fields

Eighty-seven percent of western water is used by farmers, but industrial and household uses—the latter mostly to keep lawns alive and green—consume an increasing share as farmers sell their water to cities. California consumes more water for both agriculture and domestic uses than any other state in the nation, but not far behind is the mostly agricultural state of Idaho, where potato fields can soak up 60 or more inches of water each summer, equivalent to the average rainfall of the country's wettest places, like New Orleans.

that many desert rats fled. To many, however, these minor inconveniences are a small price to pay for the pleasure of having it all.

As ridiculous as fountains, pools, and golf courses in the midst of desert country may seem to conservationists and some aesthetic sensibilities, in reality domestic and municipal water consumption accounts for only a small fraction of water used in the West—in many places less than 10 percent.[5] Most water conservation campaigns turn to urban spaces—turn off the water while brushing your teeth; flush only when necessary; use low flow showerheads and live with flat hair. But the real culprits in excessive water use ride out of the Old West: farmers, ranchers, and their hay balers and cows.

Drenching the Fields

Agriculture is declining in the New West, giving way to a service-based economy; but even so, the remaining irrigators still use most of the water. In some states, including urbanized Colorado, over 90 percent of water taken out of streams and aquifers is put on crops.[6]

Why do ranchers and farmers use so much water? One reason has to do with inefficient techniques like flood irrigation. In Idaho, for example, porous volcanic soils require constant watering—up to twelve feet of water an acre per season—to support the famous potatoes, Idaho's most lucrative industry. Another reason for agriculture's excessive water consumption has to do with the type of crops grown. When water is cheap and you can move it pretty much anywhere, water-intensive but lucrative fruit and vegetable crops pop up in unlikely places: lettuce and melons in the Imperial Valley, smack in the middle of the Mojave

Drenching the Fields

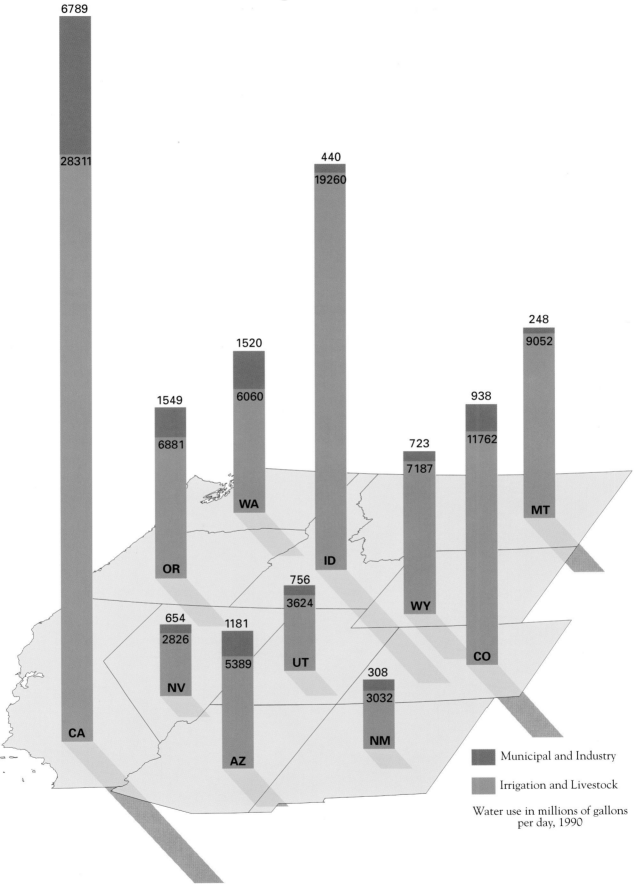

6789
28311
CA

1549
6881
OR

1520
6060
WA

440
19260
ID

248
9052
MT

938
11762
CO

723
7187
WY

756
3624
UT

654
2826
NV

1181
5389
AZ

308
3032
NM

Municipal and Industry

Irrigation and Livestock

Water use in millions of gallons
per day, 1990

Desert, oranges in southern Arizona, and sugar beets on Colorado's Front Range. In California's Central Valley, a southeast Asian climate is recreated each fall when rice fields are flooded with up to seven feet of water.[7]

But it is the alfalfa crops, which dot the Interior West and feed the nation's cows and horses, that absorb more water per acre than any other crop in the region. As author Philip Fradkin observes, "no other activity uses so much land area in the West, or for that matter in the entire nation, as cows eating grass . . . Nor does any other activity consume more water . . . Cows, not people, are the chief beneficiaries of western water."[8]

How did we get to this? When ranchers, farmers, and other settlers first came to the region over 100 years ago, they sought to put Western water to use with small, inefficient irrigation systems. Federal legislation like the Homestead Act and the Desert Lands Act lured rugged individuals west with grandiose promises of agricultural abundance, in spite of John Wesley Powell's warnings that only government assistance in water development would allow any kind of permanent Western settlement. When it became clear that limits on capital and labor would make the going much tougher than prophesied, Uncle Sam stepped in and began a long tradition of subsidizing original uses of Western water, such as farming and grazing cattle.[9]

Damming the West

The era of government-financed, large-scale water delivery and irrigation began around the turn of the century. In December of 1901, Teddy Roosevelt, a great admirer of Powell, proclaimed that "the western half of the United States would sustain a population greater than that of our whole country today if the waters that now run to waste were saved and used for irrigation."[10] Unburdened by doubt, and armed with a mission to populate and enrich the West by "reclaiming" the desert, Roosevelt fought for passage of the 1902 Reclamation Act, sponsored by Nevada Senator Francis Newlands. The federal reclamation program would make it possible for farmers to benefit from the harnessing of large rivers without having to supply capital up front.

The first government project under the act was indicative of what was to come: it realized Newlands' earlier goal of damming the lower Truckee River in Nevada and diverting most of its water into the neighboring Carson basin to help farmers grow alfalfa. Since that time, thousands of dams have been built by the Bureau of Reclamation and the Army Corps of Engineers, institutions full of people who long believed no river should run free. The skills of government engineers worked symbiotically with Western political agendas to accommodate water-poor but eager-to-farm constituents. Originally, Congress intended that farmers would pay back the federal government. But when it became apparent that farmers could not afford to repay much of their debts, the repayment laws were relaxed, resulting in a culture of large subsidized water projects in the West.[11]

What historians now call the "Big Dam Era" gained momentum in the 1930s, when New Deal policy encouraged public works to employ as many men as possible. In 1936, the four biggest dams in the world were under construction

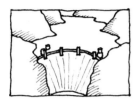

Damming the West

All the major Western rivers sport dams, built mostly between 1930 and 1980, to irrigate crops and produce hydropower. The biggest dams create enormous reservoirs: Hoover Dam flooded 115 miles of the Colorado River to create Lake Mead, and not far upstream lies the houseboat mecca of Lake Powell. In between the two bathtubs lies the greatest stretch of whitewater in the country, the Grand Canyon, which narrowly escaped damming and flooding in the 1960s when Western politicians proposed two "cash register" dams. The dams would have generated hydropower revenues to pay for pumping up to 1.5 million acre-feet of Central Arizona Project from the Colorado River up 2000 feet to Phoenix and Tucson each year. When David Brower of the Sierra Club and other environmentalists took out a full page ad in the New York Times decrying the proposal, the plan was nixed. In its stead today is a coal-fired power plant on the Navajo Reservation, which still manages to compromise the Grand Canyon experience by polluting the air and diminishing visibility.

Damming the West

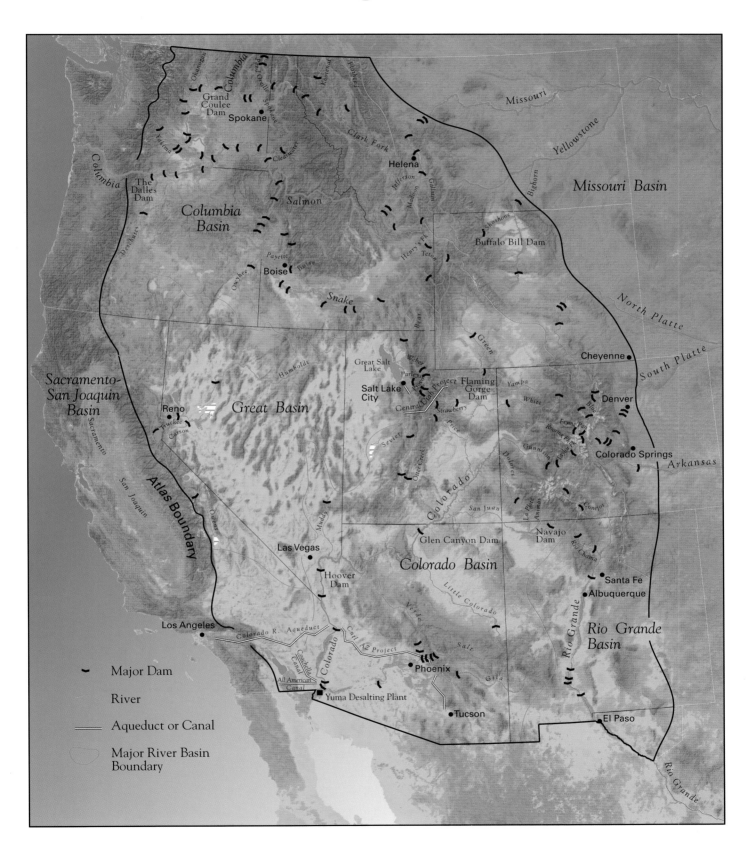

Columbia

Okanogan

Columbia

Pend Oreille

Spokane

Kootenai

Flathead

Missouri

Grand Coulee Dam

Spokane

Clark Fork

Yellowstone

Yakima

Clearwater

Helena

Bighorn

Missouri Basin

The Dalles Dam

Salmon

Jefferson

Madison

Gallatin

Shoshone

Buffalo Bill Dam

Columbia Basin

Deschutes

Payette

Boise

Boise

Henry's Fork

Teton

North Platte

Owyhee

Snake

Bear

Green

Cheyenne

South Platte

Sacramento-San Joaquin Basin

Humboldt

Great Salt Lake

Weber

Parley's

Yampa

White

Denver

Reno

Truckee

Carson

Great Basin

Salt Lake City

Central Utah Project

Flaming Gorge Dam

Strawberry

Roaring Fork

Fryingpan

Blue

Eagle

Sacramento

Sevier

Price

Gunnison

Taylor

Colorado Springs

Arkansas

San Joaquin

Otter Creek

Colorado

Dolores

La Plata

Animas

Conejos

Atlas Boundary

Mojave

San Juan

Navajo Dam

Las Vegas

Glen Canyon Dam

Colorado Basin

Little Colorado

Rio Chama

Rio Grande

Hoover Dam

Verde

Santa Fe

Albuquerque

Rio Grande Basin

Los Angeles

Colorado R. Aqueduct

Central AZ Project

Salt

Colorado

Coachella Canal

Phoenix

Gila

Rio Grande

All American Canal

Yuma Desalting Plant

Tucson

El Paso

⌒ Major Dam

River

Aqueduct or Canal

Major River Basin Boundary

Rio Grande

The Tallest Dams

	Height (feet)	Reservoir Capacity (acre-feet)	Drainage Area (sq mi)
Hoover Dam, Colorado River	726	28,537,000	167,800
Glen Canyon Dam, Colorado River	710	27,000,000	108,335
Hungry Horse Dam, Flathead River	564	3,467,179	1,640
Grand Coulee Dam, Columbia River	550	9,652,000	74,100

Source: U.S. Bureau of Reclamation and U.S. Army Corps of Engineers

The big dams work just as they were designed to, some of the reservoirs storing several years' worth of a river's total runoff. Lake Mead, behind Hoover Dam, is the nation's biggest reservoir, but Lake Powell is the longest, extending 186 miles up the Colorado River—the distance from New York City to Boston. Houseboaters on Lake Powell have 1900 miles of shoreline to explore! The Bureau of Reclamation's safety record is quite good, with the only major disaster occurring at Teton Dam in Idaho. The dam collapsed in 1976, sending a wall of water through the Mormon settlements of Ashton and St. Anthony, killing 14 people.

in the American West: Hoover, Shasta, Bonneville, and Grand Coulee. Between 1930 and 1980, the federal government built over 1000 large dams in the United States, 36 of them in the Columbia River Basin alone. These dams, many generating seemingly limitless electricity, helped the nation's war effort during the 1940s. More than half of America's planes in World War II contained aluminum processed with Grand Coulee hydroelectricity, and the region today still produces 43 percent of the aluminum made in the country, though the industry appears to be on the decline due to competition from the Russians, and to the credit of conscientious Americans and their aluminum can recycling.[12]

More than 80 percent of the Northwest's energy supply still comes from these highly subsidized hydroelectric dams, giving residents of the region the lowest electric rates in the nation.[13] Other beneficiaries of the dammed Columbia River system include farmers in Idaho, who draw water off of the many reservoirs for irrigation, and the barging industry. A series of locks and canals built by the Army Corps of Engineers at the taxpayers' expense makes it possible for Montanans to transport wheat to the coast via the little known ocean port of Lewiston, Idaho, 500 miles upstream from the mouth of the Columbia.[14]

Cheap electricity and free barge transportation comes at a high price though: the once wild Columbia and Snake Rivers have been reduced to a series of tepid reservoirs with little or no downstream current, a problematic situation for the once abundant wild salmon population. Standing in the fish observatory room at Bonneville Dam, one can watch salmon leap up the manmade fish lad-

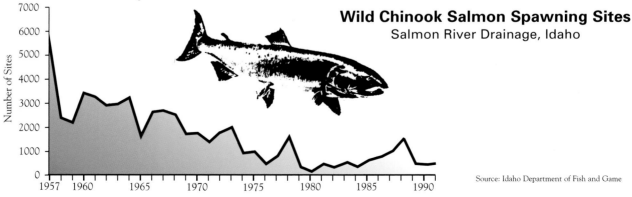

Wild Chinook Salmon Spawning Sites
Salmon River Drainage, Idaho

Source: Idaho Department of Fish and Game

der to the reservoir above, and marvel at how well the species has adapted to its new riverine environment. Unfortunately, it is the trip downstream that most often costs salmon their lives.

Born in the high country, as far inland as the west side of the Tetons in Idaho, juvenile salmon—called fry, fingerlings, or smolts depending on their life-stage—are normally swept downstream to the ocean within a year or two after birth, where they adapt to the saltwater environment and grow to maturity. On their way down—a process that can take as little as a week with natural flows but which now takes up to four months because of the slackwater—smolts are disoriented, consumed by predators, diseased, or simply chopped into salmon puree by turbines inside the hydroelectric dams. If they manage to make it through the reservoirs and turbines and out to the Pacific—only a small percentage do—the salmon then mature in the ocean until instinct calls them back home to spawn. Then these anadromous species must navigate commercial fisheries off the coast of Washington, Oregon, and Alaska, and climb past some of the tallest dams in the world, which have blocked off more than half of their spawning habitat.[15]

In short, the Columbia Basin's eight main-stem dams—all federally subsidized—account for over 95 percent of the Northwest's annual salmon mortality. In less than a century, salmon and steelhead populations have been reduced from an estimated 10 to 16 million to approximately 500,000 wild fish. The Snake River runs have been hit the hardest. In the 1950s, up to 5000 Snake River sockeye returned to Redfish Lake, in the Sawtooth Mountains of Idaho. Only one returned in 1992, and none in 1996. Over the years, two Snake River chinook stocks and the Snake River sockeye have been listed under the Endangered Species Act, while the Snake River coho has already disappeared.[16]

In a new spin on the concept of "reclamation," water institutions in the Pacific Northwest and their accompanying infrastructures have been modified in recent years in a slow tilt toward "reclaiming" aquatic ecosystems: the Northwest Power Planning Council has supervised the spending of more than $1.3 billion

Small Dams, Big Impact

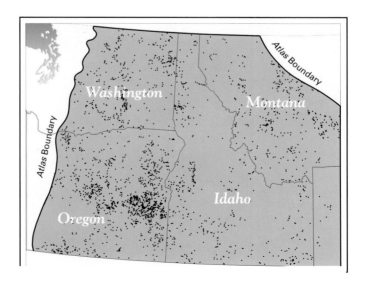

Small dams, ponds, and ditches proliferate in the West because catching, storing, and moving water is essential to Western development. In some ways, these small dams alter ecosystems more than their monstrous counterparts because they are nearly ubiquitous. The Interior Columbia Basin is blanketed with small and large dams that are wiping out the region's salmon populations by preventing their migration back and forth between the Pacific Ocean and the thousands of small streams in which they spawn.

Source: Interior Columbia Basin Management Project

in taxpayer and ratepayer money on three salmon recovery plans; turbine screens have been installed in many of the dams in an attempt to protect the smolts; salmon hatcheries have been established throughout the basin; and two of the main culprits in the salmon saga—the Bonneville Power Administration and the Bureau of Reclamation—have begun to lease senior water rights from Idaho farmers in order to increase springtime flows and aid smolts in their downstream journey.[17] The most desperate attempt to save salmon without rattling the status quo has been the "smolt transportation program," initiated in the early 1980s to literally carry juveniles down to the ocean. Using barges and trucks—called "iron coffins" by their critics—fish are collected in the Interior Columbia Basin, high on the Snake River in Idaho, and transported hundreds of miles to a point below the last dam before the ocean. Many of the fish die in the process, however, and some fisheries experts question the value of such bandaids in a watershed made ecologically sick from too much human impact.[18]

If none of these approaches is working, what needs to happen? Suggestions range from annual "reservoir drawdowns" which would transform the slackwater lakes back into flowing rivers during peak migration periods, to removal of several dams and even eradication of the aluminum industry. "Smolts over volts!" has become the battle cry for those critical of the subsidized and power-hungry smelting plants, which consume more electricity than any other entity in the basin. According to Andy Kerr of the Oregon Natural Resources Council—who has been labeled "an environmental Dr. Kevorkian" for wanting to put the ailing aluminum industry out of its misery—what's killing the salmon are economic activities that are being done inefficiently. "We can still produce a hell of a lot of power and still save the fish." [19]

If modern water resource managers and policymakers could muster the same kind of "can do" attitude that built the world's largest coordinated hydroelectric system, and apply that gumption to the salmon problem, perhaps the current downward spiral could be stopped.

Hardest hit by the transformation of the riverine ecosystem have been the Columbia River tribes that depended on salmon for spiritual, economic,

Selling Water to Nature

One way to protect the West's environment while heeding western water laws is simply to buy senior water rights—usually from farmers—in nature's name and, instead of diverting it onto alfalfa fields, leave it in the streams. In the Pacific Northwest, the Bureau of Reclamation—biggest of the big dam builders—now leases water from Idaho farmers it once supplied and lets the salmon use it as they have for eons. Colorado leads the pack in water transfers to nature because of the Colorado-Big Thompson Project, a federal project which has unusually flexible laws facilitating transfers to more economic uses. The Nature Conservancy has been particularly active in this arena, buying up water rights for instream flow purposes. Source: The Water Strategist.

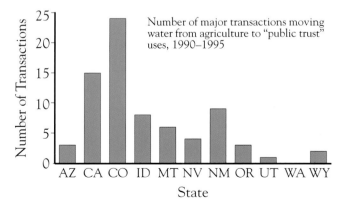

Number of major transactions moving water from agriculture to "public trust" uses, 1990–1995

6,516,208

Keeping the Promise

Currently irrigated Indian land vs.
potentially irrigable Indian land

- Current
- Potential

Acreage

600,000
500,000
400,000
300,000
200,000
100,000
0

AZ CA CO ID MT NM NV OR UT WA WY

Source: Western Governor's Association

and physical survival for over 11,000 years. Treaties signed in the mid-nineteenth century with white settlers promised the tribes fishing rights and "a fair and equitable share" of the salmon and steelhead runs, but with today's depleted state of affairs, even half of the catch is insufficient to maintain traditional life-styles. Four tribes in particular—the Umatilla, Warm Springs, Nez Perce, and Yakama—have been actively involved in the restoration agenda on the Columbia, working with the Northwest Power Planning Council, the Bureau of Reclamation, and the Bonneville Power Ad ministration to ensure the survival of the salmon as well as some semblance of their way of life.[20]

The plight of tribes in the Northwest illustrates a pattern seen throughout western history: not only have Indians and other original inhabitants been almost universally excluded from the benefits of federally subsidized western water projects, they have also been overtly injured by them again and again. On the Missouri River, three tribes were forced to relocate when the Bureau of Reclamation built Garrison Dam and flooded Fort Berthold Reservation in the 1940s. In 1962, several traditional Hispanic

Keeping the Promise

The Supreme Court decided in the 1908 Winters v. United States case that Indians had rights to sufficient water to make their reservations liveable. Since most tribes were encouraged and expected to farm, case law has defined these rights by measuring the "potentially irrigable acreage" on the reservations. For a tribe like the Navajo, with the biggest reservation in the nation, this translates to a potential entitlement to 50 million acre-feet of water, more than three times the entire annual flow of the Colorado River! Growing Indian political power and elevation of these "Winters rights" from historical curiosity to firm legal foundation make the Western water buffaloes—developers, cities, and federal agencies—increasingly nervous.

"Jurassic Pork"

The Animas-La Plata (A-LP) water project, if built, would divert up to half the flow of Southwest Colorado's Animas River, one of the last free-flowing streams in the West. The proposed project includes three dams, three pumping plants, a three-mile tunnel, 30 miles of canals, and 125 miles of pipeline. Water from the Animas River would be pumped 525 feet uphill to a reservoir two miles away. From there, some of the water would be pumped an additional 330 feet uphill to supply sprawling subdivisions and industries near Durango, and some would be pumped yet another 209 feet uphill to irrigate local fields. The energy needed to pump all this water annually would power a town of 63,000 people. Since the A-LP dams will provide no hydroelectric power—unlike most other large water projects in the West—a coal-fired power plant is needed to energize the pumps. The plant itself would evaporate approximately 26,500 acre-feet of cooling water each year to cool its coal generators. At an estimated cost of $710 million, A-LP would return, by one estimate, perhaps 36 cents to the dollar, the costliest and least beneficial Bureau of Reclamation project in history.

farming and ranching communities in northern New Mexico—Rosa, Arboles, Rio de los Pinos, and Los Martinez— were flooded by Navajo Dam and Reservoir, forcing residents to relocate. And with the creation of Glen Canyon Dam and Lake Powell, an estimated 10,000 Anasazi archaeological sites were lost forever. These are but a few of the many injustices borne by the original inhabitants of the West in the name of reclaiming the desert for newcomers.[21]

The federal government's reclamation activities

"Jurassic Pork"

Proposed Animas-La Plata River Project

often violated its trustee responsibility to Native American tribes. Federally protected Indian water rights have been well-established by the courts since the turn of the century, but the government failed to help Indians realize these rights. In *A River No More: The Colorado River and the West*, author Phillip Fradkin sheds light on this phenomenon, observing that "when it comes to distributing water in the West, it has been the politically strong and aggressive who get it. To be tenacious and knowledgeable helps. Moral rights, historical priority, and legal merit count for less."[22]

Fortunately for tribes, the legal might of their water rights is increasingly recognized in the West, and existing institutions are feeling pressure to conform to tribal demands. Armed with a growing legal savvy (and well-trained lawyers) tribes are getting their water rights adjudicated in courts or negotiated in Alternative Dispute Resolution (ADR) arenas. This is good for the Indians, but casts a pall of uncertainty over the West's Byzantine water institutions, unsettling water users whose rights have been recognized by state water agencies for generations. Accommodating these rights without rocking the boat too much has characterized recent negotiations; cost effectiveness, environmental sustainability, or maximum equity for the Indians take a backseat.

The best example of this questionable approach to satisfying Indian water rights is the proposed Animas-La Plata Project (A-LP) near Durango, Colorado, which would in theory benefit both Indians and non-Indians in the Four Corners region. The sprawling Bureau of Reclamation project was initially approved during the 1960s, but had been put on a back burner like many others with the close of the big dam era. It gained renewed momentum in 1988, however, when its proponents (alfalfa farmers in the La Plata Valley) joined forces with two southern Colorado tribes—the Southern Utes and the Ute Mountain Utes—looking to realize their reserved water rights. Because a project of this size would never be approved in today's political climate without its ties to Indian water rights, critics have dubbed the project "Jurassic Pork" because of its outlandish economic and environmental costs and questionable returns.[23]

According to Phil Doe, a disgruntled Bureau of Reclamation retiree, A-LP represents the old reclamation mind-set that "doesn't make any sense" in the New West. Huge sums of public money would be spent to help a few private individuals on private land, with questionable benefits for the Indians. In a surprisingly frank full page ad in the *Durango Herald*, a local group of proponents explained "Why we should support the Animas-La Plata Project: Because someone else is paying most of the tab! We get the water. We get the reservoir. They pay the bill."[24]

Politicians—including Colorado Senator Ben Nighthorse Campbell and President Clinton—downplay the $710 million construction cost to taxpayers saying that it is justified by the nation's duty to the tribes; it would, in theory, enable them to develop a thriving irrigated economy. But, like all modern water projects, the Animas-La Plata is highly controversial. On closer examination, it would benefit non-Indian farmers more than the Indians (2/3 of the Project water would go to non-Indians). Some critics have labeled A-LP an example of the "Indian Blanket Syndrome," where seemingly well-meaning politicians lobby for the rights of Indians, while simultaneously (and more surreptitiously) promoting non-Indian causes as well. Yet, the moral obligation to the tribes is compelling to most observers, even if it means an extension of the big dam era. Opponents and proponents of the A-LP are currently discussing less costly, more efficient alternatives, but negotiations are full of acrimony and are moving slowly.[25]

Animas-La Plata is often referred to as "the West's last major water project." By most accounts, the big dam era ended in the late 1970s, when President Jimmy Carter developed his infamous "hit list" and killed a number of Bureau of Reclamation Projects because of cost ineffectiveness and environmental impacts. Not surprisingly, these actions outraged Western politicians and may have cost him the 1980 election. Fiscal constraints and a new concern for nature spawned in the years following World War II had finally caught up with the Western water

Just the A-LP Facts Please

- Main justification for building the project: satisfy Indian water rights
- Amount of project water slated for Indians: less than 1/3
- Distance between project water and nearest Ute land: 10 miles
- Tribal delivery system: none yet
- Number of non-Indian farmers who would benefit: 20,000
- Federal investment per irrigated acre: $5000
- Current value of irrigated land per acre: $150–$350
- Acres of wetlands and vital winter elk habitat destroyed: 1000
- Number of endangered fish species further jeopardized by the project: 2
- Cost of increased salinity in the Colorado River: $800 million

Source: Colorado Rivers Alliance, Durango, Colorado

development machine. Since 1980, no major federal dams have been approved, and some have even been taken down.[26] Many observers see the federal refusal to fund Denver's proposed Two Forks Project on the Platte River in the late 1980s as the final nail in the coffin of the big dam era. As Jim Ogilvie, a retired water engineer for the Bureau of Reclamation, observed at a Two Forks hearing, there

Plumbing the Divide

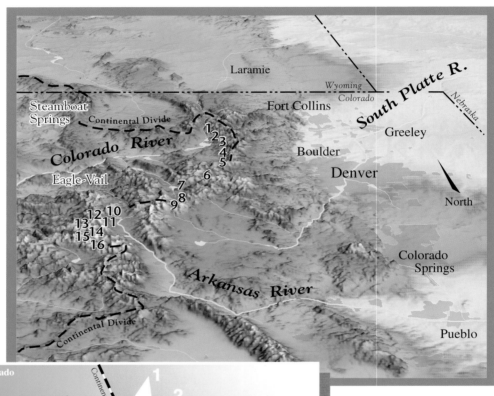

Water transfer from Colorado to Platte River Basin

1. Grand River Ditch
2. Vidler Tunnel
3. Eureka Ditch
4. Alva B. Adams Tunnel
5. Moffat Water Tunnel
6. Berthoud Pass Ditch
7. Harold D. Roberts Tunnel
8. Boreas Pass Ditch

Water transfer from Colorado to Arkansas Basin

9. Hoosier Pass Tunnel
10. Columbine Ditch
11. Ewing Ditch
12. Wurtz Ditch
13. Homstake Tunnel
14. Charles H. Boustead Tunnel
15. Bush-Ivanhoe Tunnel
16. Twin Lakes Tunnel

would have been no opposition to the dam if it had been proposed before the rise of the environmental movement in the late 1960s. "The biggest problem with the 1.1 million acre-foot Two Forks," he observed, "is that it wasn't built soon enough."[27]

The question remains: without more dams, how will we continue to meet the needs of newcomers to the West? According to most sources, water exists for much urban growth in the future—it just needs to be transferred from current uses, mainly agriculture. Often these transfers involve piping water under mountain ranges, from rural to urban contexts—water is moved from the Colorado River Basin to growing cities on the Wasatch Front, in the Los Angeles and Rio Grande Basins, and on Colorado's Front Range, for example. Such transfers are all the rage in the West right now, but many legal barriers still exist, which prevent water from moving easily to more efficient uses. Water law institutions designed to protect the status quo—using water for growing hay—are slowly evolving to accommodate changing needs and values. Cities are willing to pay big bucks for developed water, and as history has shown, water flows uphill to money.

For those hoping that aridity will limit Western population growth and development, who dream of settling into the idyllic New West lifestyle and shutting the door behind them (what geographer Gilbert White calls the "Last Settler Syndrome"), the news is not good: if farmers continue to sell their water rights to municipalities, as they are more and more eager to do, supplies could support a threefold or more population increase in the Interior West—and without significant new water development.

Plumbing the Divide

Engineers divert water under and over the continental divide all along Colorado's Front Range, the greatest concentration of trans-basin diversions in the West. In defiance of nature, more than 15 tunnels puncture the Continental Divide in Colorado, annually bringing 481,093 acre-feet of water naturally slated for the Pacific Ocean to the populated Front Range for use on hay, exotic fruit crops, and suburban lawns.

Selling Water to Cities

Water flows toward money in the West, and farmers have less of both as cities are willing to pay to get more water. To shift from one use to another, Western water must go through legal hoops that make the IRS tax code seem simple. But, if the planets are aligned properly, water will shift to industrial and residential users, and since the era of big dams and diversion projects has for the most part ended, new users want farmers' water. Legal reforms in many Western states will ease water transfers in the coming years. Colorado is leading the charge, reflected by the state's Colorado-Big Thompson irrigation project where almost half the water has shifted from farms to cities. If half the agricultural water throughout the West were shifted to municipal consumption at current urban use rates, the eleven western states— now with some 55 million people—could support, with water at least, 200 million more folks!

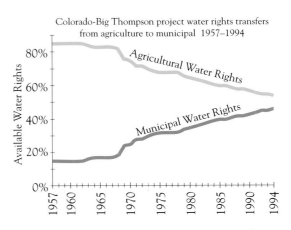

Colorado-Big Thompson project water rights transfers from agriculture to municipal 1957–1994

Source: Northern Colorado Water Conservancy District

Chapter 4: People in the New West

Americans created the New West by moving about, changing attitudes and jobs, and revising their relationships to each other and the land. In fact, the West has, more or less, been recreated every century or so. Indian home territories were in flux, owing to war or climate fluctuations or game movements, long before Europeans showed up. Once the Spanish got there in the fourteenth century, cultural change sped up in the Southwest. Each major shift—when the first humans hit the scene some 15,000 years ago or when white settlers unsettled the Indians—created a "New West." The Native West became a Euro-American West, and the cut-and-run economy of the Cowboy West was transformed, around the turn-of-the-century, into an economy based on scientific natural resources management. The emerging New West we describe here is the latest of these regional makeovers. Like the post–Civil War land rush, the current regional transformation is quite self-conscious: the latest New Westerners are embarked on a "national vision quest" to create a new American region, one that fits their lifestyles and desires for a new sense of place.[1]

Peopling the New West

The end of World War II marks the start of New West population growth. Military bases peppered the West and the atomic bomb was designed, built, and detonated at secret sites in the Interior. The West was even preferred for prisoner-of-war camps. Isolated from towns or railroads, Japanese, German, and Italian POWs cut timber in Wyoming's Medicine Bow Mountains and dug irrigation ditches in Arizona. American citizens with Japanese roots were banished to the interior, hauled from their Pacific Coast homes to internment camps at Heart Mountain, Wyoming, Minidoka, Idaho, Topaz, Utah, and Poston, Arizona. Airfields rolled out everywhere. Some still host top-gun military flight schools; some outback landing strips serve the drug trade and others transmuted into busy regional airports.

Many military veterans decided to stay on in the region, and the country's enduring westward migration quickened after the war, compelled by jobs, climate, and scenery, and eased by VA loans, GI tuition, and renewal of the great transfer of federal money to the West, money to resume the dam building, irrigation ditch digging, trail clearing, and subsidized grazing, mining, and logging. The natural resources rush that began with the first gold rushes climaxed in the 1970s' energy boom when, galvanized by the Arab oil embargo, American energy policy emphasized domestic sources, and, as Joel Garreau described in *The Nine Nations of North America*, coal miners, oil riggers, petroleum geologists, and refiners flooded into the West.[2] In the way of things Western, the energy boom busted by the late 1980s, the globe awash in oil and the roughnecks Garreau interviewed in Wyoming out of work and heading out of the region. Energy faltered as gold, silver, and cattle had before it. Still, the energy boom, and the quieter rise of services, tourism, and the high-tech economy that preceded and outlived it, set the stage for even more rapid population growth in the 1990s.

The great "sun belt" migration was on. Laid-off auto workers swept south and west from the Midwest, and retirees, weary of Florida real estate prices and crowding, created a second great geriatric heartland in the Southwest. The scientific, engineering, and business skills attracted by the energy boom were put to creating a new, more diversified economy. And the growing ease with which Americans move around, and even do their jobs, gives more folks the chance to live wherever they want, often where they can combine work and play.

Then something really unexpected happened: people started curling back east; that is, Californians began a reverse migration, from the coast into the Interior. By the early 1990s this reversal of the great American migration to California drew notice beyond statisticians at the Census Bureau. The Pacific Coasters weren't returning to Minnesota or Maryland; rather, they leaked (some called it a flood) east only as far as the Great Basin, Colorado Plateau, and Rocky Mountains. Idaho, Utah, Colorado, Montana drew Californians like a Royal Wulff attracts trout. The long western flow of Americans from New York, Illinois, Florida, and Texas continued, but the demographic headline of the early 1990s was the rush to the Interior by the Coasters. Even Washington and Oregon contributed to the flow, which surely contained some Californian migrants who had only stopped briefly in the Pacific Northwest before heading inland. In the spring of 1993, cashed-out Californians pursued homes in Boise, on Colorado's Front Range, and in resort towns throughout the region with a fervor that shot prices skyward. The mountains themselves all but levitated: Realtors—and sellers— were overjoyed. By 1995, one in five residents of Colorado's Roaring Fork Valley (topped by Aspen) was licensed to sell real estate.

The *New York Times* proclaimed, in a 1993 headline, "Eastward Ho! Disenchanted, Californians Turn to the Interior West":

Peopling the New West

In their endless to'ing and fro'ing, more Americans are ending up in the West. All of the country's other four census regions sent more people to the Interior West than they got back—a "positive net migration"—during 1990–94. The Pacific Region sent the most refugees inland, with California providing the lion's share—over 30,000 Californians moved into Colorado alone during 12 months starting in spring of 1993. The Northeast sent almost 119,000 more people to the West than it got back, most out of New York and Massachusetts. The Midwest comes next, with more Illinoisans than other Midwesterners joining the modern westward migration. This big immigration created knock-on effects within the region: Colorado absorbed the biggest slug of immigrants, and some 2,000 of that state's residents, disgusted with crowding and traffic, sold the newcomers land and houses and headed up to Montana in 1993, a place that reminded them of Colorado before the boom.

Peopling the New West

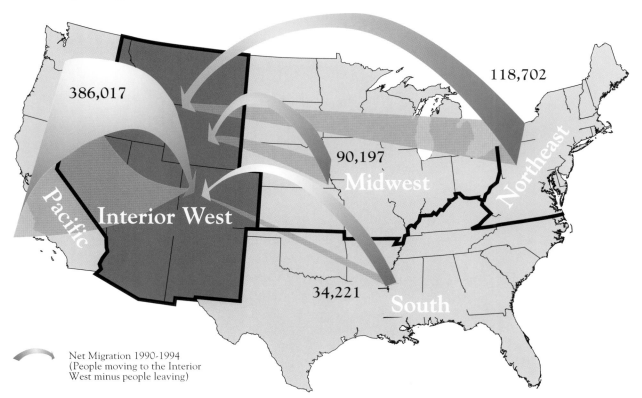

386,017

118,702

90,197

Midwest

Pacific

Interior West

Northeast

34,221

South

Net Migration 1990-1994
(People moving to the Interior
West minus people leaving)

The latest migrants are moving to Nevada, the fastest-growing state in the nation for the last two years; to central Oregon, where sports cars and sidewalks clogged with roller-bladers make the high desert country around the town of Bend look like Santa Monica North on weekends; to eastern Washington and the cities of Spokane and Richland, where home prices have doubled in three years; to Arizona, which grew by 35 percent over the last decade; to Utah, which boasts of "kidnapping" firms from California and bringing them to the cheap labor haven around the Great Salt Lake; and to southern Idaho, which led the nation in new job growth last year and is expected to do the same this year.[3]

But the empty quarter is filling. The Interior West grew faster than the U.S. as a whole in the 1970s and 1980s, and the pace further quickened in the 1990s. Colorado boasted ten of the fifty fastest growing counties in the U.S. during 1990–95; the fastest growing county was a Denver suburb. Second place went to Summit County, Utah, a piece of the snowy Wasatch Range preparing to host the 2002 Winter Olympics. Idaho, Colorado, Montana, Arizona, and Utah grew faster than all other states during 1995.

And Westerners sank into mourning—a favorite camping spot, fishing hole, or golf course fallen to the newcomers. Montana writer William Kittredge groused, in *Time* magazine, that:

> Seems like everybody is coming. We had our hundred years of solitude, and now the West is turning itself into a make-believe place where celebrities and tourists and retirees can roam and find homes. Beverly Hills in the highlands . . .
>
> Look down the two-lane highway, past the beauty of the Sawtooth Mountains . . . it's a bumper-to-bumper raceway—Jeeps and Winnebagos and Harleys, Californians and Canadians, illicit drug vendors on holiday, fly-fishing nuts who saw *A River Runs Through It*. Who knows? Some of them are tourists, but many are coming to stay.[4]

Interior West Growth Pole
Eight Interior West States are Among the Ten Fastest Growing in the U.S.

	1990–94 Pop. Growth	Doubling Time (yrs)
1. Nevada	21.2%	3.3
2. Idaho	12.5%	5.8
3. Arizona	11.2%	6.4
4. Colorado	11.0%	6.5
5. Utah	10.7%	6.7
6. Alaska	10.2%	7.0
7. Washington	9.8%	7.3
8. New Mexico	9.1%	7.9
9. Georgia	8.9%	8.1
10. Oregon	8.6%	8.4

One journalist captured the Montana mood: these were "new Okies" fleeing the cultural dust bowl they created on the Pacific:

> (Westerners) could probably deal with the Californians themselves if these interlopers didn't reflect a larger and more sweeping blight on the landscape that has come along with the economic shift away from a functional engagement with the land, namely, the loosing of postmodernism on a part of the world always considered so rugged, so permanent and so down-to-earth that residents have legitimately come to view it as reality itself.[5]

Right. The problem is not just people, but also imported ideas, and the desecration of old traditions: new residents upset the Old Westerners not with purple hair or Volvos, but by wearing cowboy hats, boots, and, by God, spurs! And driving pick-up trucks. Worse of all, the newcomers bought ranches! Two of them, Ted Turner and Jane Fonda, bought a ranch in Montana's Gallatin Valley and had the nerve to replace the cows with buffalo. Local ranchers took that as a reproach.

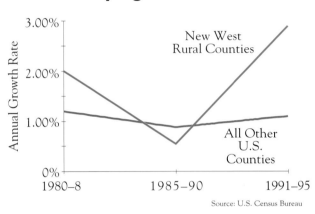

Gentrifying the Rural West

Source: U.S. Census Bureau

The current boom's ritzy extremes are fueled by a seemingly unlimited mass of capital in search of real estate: second, third, and fourth homes seldom used, large ranches not ranched, office parks enticing businesses with surprisingly low rents. Many New Westerners, attracted to wide-open spaces, are following their dreams of living and working away from the cities and suburbs that once held most white-collar jobs. Rural areas with the most open space and federal lands are developing faster than Western metropolitan areas. Counties with federally designated wilderness areas grew two to three times faster than all other counties in the country, rural or urban, from the 1970s to the 1990s; rural counties in the West grew twice as fast as other counties in the region and nation during 1990–95. Some rural refugees cite isolation and limited access as a desirable attribute—they value the rough dirt roads leading to their fancy, secluded homes on former ranches.

Origins

The U.S. Census Bureau recognizes only five ethnic classes in the U.S.: White, Black, Native, Asian (including Pacific Islanders), and what it calls "Hispanic origin," which includes all of Latin America, though the largest U.S. groups of Hispanics are from the Caribbean and Mexico. Like many Americans

Origins

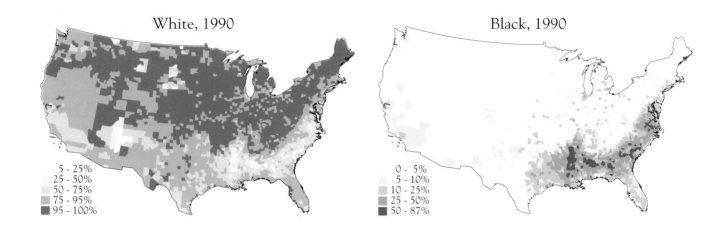

White, 1990

5 - 25%
25 - 50%
50 - 75%
75 - 95%
95 - 100%

Black, 1990

0 - 5%
5 - 10%
10 - 25%
25 - 50%
50 - 87%

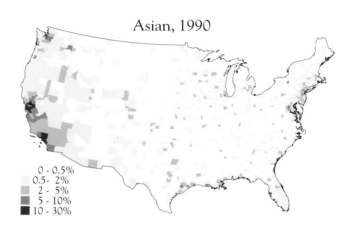

Asian, 1990

0 - 0.5%
0.5 - 2%
2 - 5%
5 - 10%
10 - 30%

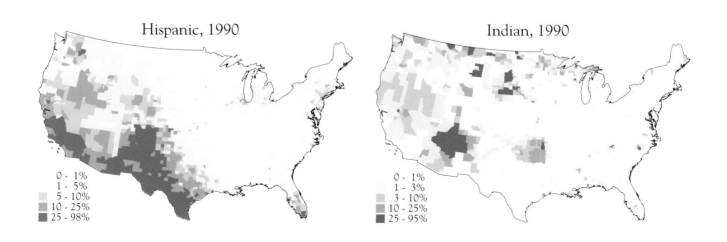

Hispanic, 1990

0 - 1%
1 - 5%
5 - 10%
10 - 25%
25 - 98%

Indian, 1990

0 - 1%
1 - 3%
3 - 10%
10 - 25%
25 - 95%

today, the census takers are not sure just what "race" means. And as social programs tied to old notions of race fade, census categories begin to lose their value. Yet, ethnic diversity, and, indeed, cleavage among groups, remains a sharp feature of the West's social landscape. Though Blacks make up substantial minorities in some Western cities, the strongest ethnic groups are Hispanics and Natives, and, on the West Coast, Asians. Much of the Southwest is authentically tricultural: Anglo, Native, and Hispanic.

Native American population declined steeply during White settlement, and they were largely restricted to reservations by 1890. There they languished under paternalistic federal policies that assumed, even demanded, their assimilation into "American culture." Indeed, many Indians were pushed to leave the reservations for cities, a policy that failed to "Americanize" them; most quickly returned to the reservation. The federal government ignored evidence, mounting through all of this century, that assimilation, which meant cultural annihilation to the Indians, would simply not occur. Revitalization of Native culture, at full speed by the 1960s, improved the lot of reservation residents and encouraged some Indians to live (voluntarily) off-reservation, where they got college degrees and better jobs. By the 1980s about as many Indians lived in Western cities as on reservations. Yet Indian Country still jumps out on our maps—in three major concentrations: central and northern Arizona and New Mexico, the Northern Rockies, and eastern Washington and Oregon.

The Spanish arrived in the Southwest in the 1520s, and soon outnumbered Natives in several areas. New Mexico is unusual among the states for having a non-White majority into the 1930s, when Anglos began to dominate. Hispanic concentrations, especially in cities like El Paso, Albuquerque, and Santa Fe, maintained a strong sense of identity. As with Indians, a resurgence of Hispanic culture occurred in the 1960s, with the florescence of Hispanic art, media, cuisine, and, often begrudged by Anglos, bilingual education.

The West's large-scale ethnic geography is curiously like the East's—both divide north from south along an ethnic line. The northern parts of the Interior West are predominantly White (no county north of Colorado holds a Hispanic majority), while the south remains strongly Hispanic. (Hispanics are a majority of 8 counties in New Mexico and their culture pervades the Southwest.) Indians provide a sort of north-south bridge across this ethnic divide.

Western Counties with an Ethnic Majority

% Hispanic

Santa Cruz, Ariz.	78
Imperial, Calif.	66
Conejos, Colo.	60
Cotsilla, Colo.	77
Dona Ana, N.Mex.	56
Guadalupe, N.Mex.	84
Hidalgo, N.Mex.	50
Mora, N.Mex.	85
Rio Arriba, N.Mex.	73
Santa Fe, N.Mex.	50
Taos, N.Mex.	65
Valenica, N.Mex.	50

% Native American

Apache, Ariz.	76
Navajo, Ariz.	50
Bighorn, Mont.	54
Roosevelt, Mont.	50
McKinley, N.Mex.	67
San Juan, Utah	54

Source: U.S. Census Bureau

Origins

Though Westerners might prefer other ways of labeling ethnicity, demographers are stuck with standard classes of White, Black, Indian, Asian, and Hispanic. We map them here for the whole country: A well-defined Hispanic zone emerges from Texas to California, with a splinter in northern Nevada and strength in southern Florida. Indian demographics cluster around the larger reservations, in the Great Plains (especially in Oklahoma and South Dakota), the Southwest, the Great Basin, and up along the Canadian border. Asians populate the Pacific Coast, but significant numbers have also settled in the Interior West and in pockets across to the East Coast. Except in a few West Coast cities, Black settlement is rather thin in the West.

Tuning into Diversity

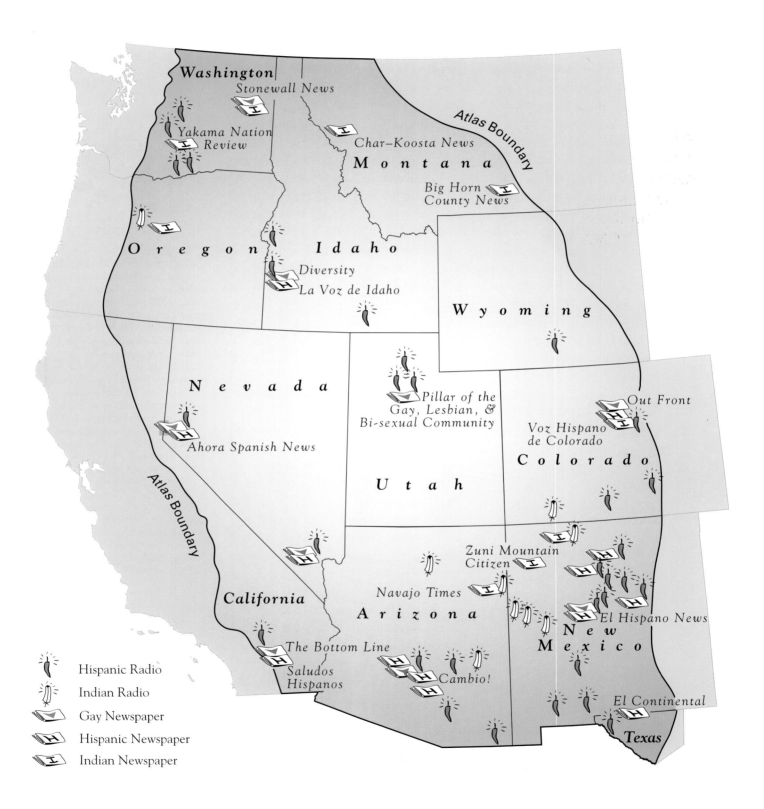

Washington

Stonewall News

Yakama Nation Review

Montana

Char–Koosta News

Big Horn County News

Oregon

Idaho

Diversity
La Voz de Idaho

Atlas Boundary

Wyoming

Nevada

Pillar of the Gay, Lesbian, & Bi-sexual Community

Out Front

Voz Hispano de Colorado

Colorado

Ahora Spanish News

Utah

Atlas Boundary

California

Zuni Mountain Citizen

Navajo Times

Arizona

El Hispano News

New Mexico

The Bottom Line

Saludos Hispanos

Cambio!

El Continental

Texas

Hispanic Radio

Indian Radio

Gay Newspaper

Hispanic Newspaper

Indian Newspaper

Blacks show up in significant numbers only in a few Interior West cities. After the turn of the century Blacks moved west from the South for the same reasons they moved to northeastern and midwestern cities: for jobs and less discrimination. They found both in California's early twentieth century boom, though the discrimination and tensions caught up with them in the 1960s, just as Blacks elsewhere were securing broader rights. The Watts district of Los Angeles erupted in protest, and resentment of white political power still festers and periodically wells up.

Asians, mostly Chinese, Japanese, and Korean, are concentrated along the West coast, making limited inroads to the Interior. But, if we map counties with even a small Asian population a more complex pattern emerges: interior California, Oregon, and Washington display Asian's slow inland migration; interior cities show up as landing spots for mobile coastal Asians; and counties along the railroads (as in southern Wyoming)—with more Chinese than other Asians—reflect the enduring legacy of railroad labor geography.

Asians, the newest large immigrant group to the region, fare better than Indians or Hispanics economically and politically. Perhaps because of the bigger hurdle crossed in migrating from Asia to America and the industrial wealth in Asia, Asian Americans in the West have more money than other minorities. Indeed, debates over affirmative action, especially on the Pacific Coast, pivot on the illogic of giving legal protection and public assistance to groups generally doing as well as the majority.

Indians, Hispanics, and Blacks in the West, though grasping for themselves stronger rights and respect during the civil rights movement, still suffer several vexing problems compared to whites: lower incomes, higher unemployment, lower education, and continued discrimination of all sorts. Yet the future prospect seems clear: the New American West will enter the twenty-first century with its ethnic groups displaying stronger identities and growing political and economic power.

Tuning into Diversity

A hint of Western cultural and social diversity comes from the map of Indian and Hispanic media. We add newspapers serving the gay community, evidence of strengthening gay identity in the New West.

Tuning into Diversity

Ethnic diversity in the West grows stronger: some political power wrested from Whites in municipal, state, and federal elections; more formal recognition in many Western cities and states; and Westerners—native and non-native—increasingly respecting Indian culture. Burgeoning Indian and Hispanic media illustrate one aspect of this ethnic florescence, though also hint at the debates over whether an "American" culture can emerge where ethnic groups hold on dearly to their identity, especially through language.

Social diversity is also illustrated by strengthening gay identity in the West. Conservative Western towns are not known for welcoming gays, and Colorado voters even passed an amendment denying gays any "special" treatment; it was later found unconstitutional. Yet, gay communities sufficient to support specialized newspapers have developed in several Interior West cities.

And the large role of women in Western politics lends weight to claims that women in the West were "liberated," at least in terms of political power, sooner than their eastern sisters. Wyoming was the first state to give women the

Electing Women

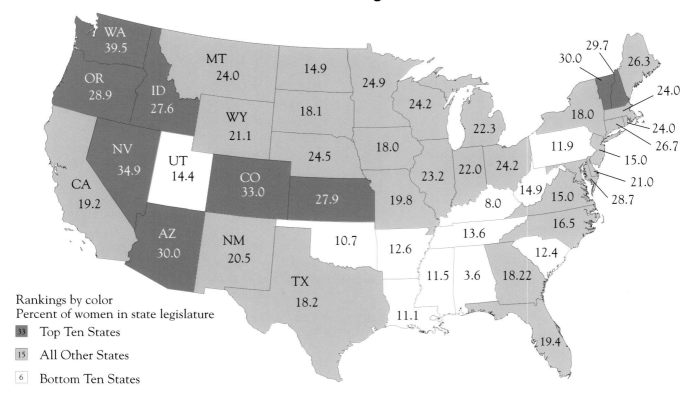

Rankings by color
Percent of women in state legislature

33	Top Ten States
15	All Other States
6	Bottom Ten States

Electing Women

With the obvious exception of Utah, where Mormonism holds to strong traditional roles for women, Western states have elected more women to their legislatures than eastern, especially southern, states.

vote, though some historians claim this was more about luring settlers than social equity. With the glaring exception of Utah, Western states have elected more women to state assemblies than their Eastern counterparts; fully a third of the state legislators in Washington, Nevada, and Colorado are women. Mormonism, which holds to strong traditional roles for women, has kept female political profiles low in Utah.

Owning a Home on the Range

Population growth turned the West's early 1980s housing glut to a shortage by the early 1990s. Busted energy towns, like Rifle, Colorado, rebounded. Moribund since the scheme to bake oil out of local shale deposits succumbed to a world awash in crude, Rifle dusted itself off, spruced itself up, and joined the region's booming service economy. Building began anew. West coasters rushed in, capital gains cash burning a hole in their pockets. And right behind, a rush of construction workers began taking the place of miners and oil riggers. The West's house prices rose smartly. A map of home values shows pockets of western real estate fetching prices near those in the Boston-Washington corridor, Chicago, and on the Pacific coast. With each pulse of coastal out-migration, the Pacific housing market cooled while Interior West prices soared. Resort towns like Aspen, Jackson, Santa Fe, Prescott, and Ketchum, offered not only extreme skiing or mountain biking, but also extreme house prices. Even middle-class towns like Bozeman, Montana; Ogden, Utah; and Boise, Idaho, saw sharp housing cost increases in the early 1990s. A common complaint echoes through the

New West: only newcomers can afford to live there.

Aspen's superstar reputation and fetching scenery attracts not merely the rich, but the superrich. Star watchers report that billionaires have replaced millionaire Aspenites, the latter pushed to lesser digs further down-valley or in Crested Butte, Colorado; Wilson, Wyoming; or Sun Valley, Idaho. In 1990, the median home value in Pitkin County (which includes Aspen) reached over $450,000, second in the country only to New York City. And Colorado mountain real estate is appreciating faster than New York's. A species rarely sighted before in the West, the monster home, sprouted up on sagebrush slopes, ridgetops, and along trout streams. Aspen's city council, stung by a Saudi prince's 55,000 square foot home, enacted (and enforced) a home size ordinance—no new construction may be larger than 15,000 square feet. It did not help that such big homes stand empty much of the year; according to Aspen Mayor John Bennett, they "sit like great, silent tombstones" amid neighborhoods of modest Victorian mining cottages.[6] Teton County, Wyoming, home to nouveau ritzy Jackson and Wilson, put the limit at 8,000 square feet. Nobody but public authorities are building for working people. Affordable housing crises hang like a pall above all of the Western resort towns. Some towns offer incentives for worker apartments attached to new construction, but even professionals cannot afford the freight: police and firefighters in Vail, Colorado, must commute from faraway, more affordable towns, raising public safety concerns.

The Santa Fe experience adds an ethnic facet to tensions between wealthy immigrant and long-term resident. Median home value in Santa Fe edged above $200,000 in 1993, not so high as other booming Western towns, but

Owning a Home on the Range

Western housing is no bargain, with much of the region showing house prices like those in the Northeast or South Florida. The hyperinflated real estate markets of resort towns like Aspen and Vail have pushed the median house price to over $500,000, not unlike Manhattan. While resort areas stand out on this map— like Colorado's ski counties and Jackson in northwestern Wyoming—house prices are climbing even in less swank areas like southern Utah or eastern Washington, with many rural counties attracting new, more affluent residents to their open spaces and rural lifestyles.

Owning a Home on the Range

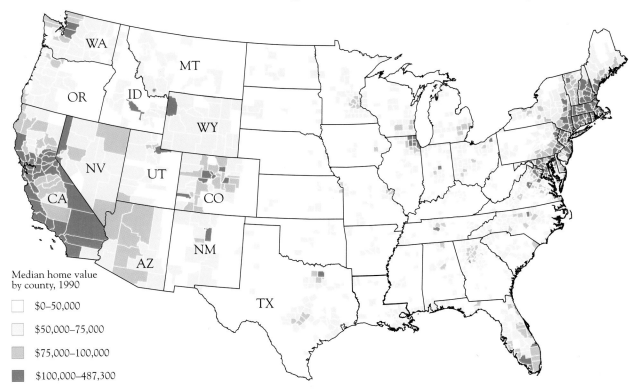

Median home value by county, 1990

- $0–50,000
- $50,000–75,000
- $75,000–100,000
- $100,000–487,300

Santa Fe's monster homes glare very bright in an area with average annual income of less than $16,000. Only incoming Anglos were building these big new homes in a town long cherished as a center of Hispanic culture. In 1994's nasty mayoral election, populist Debbie Jaramillo won on a platform of "Santa Fe for Santa Fe'ans" and of promising to brake the town's hyperdevelopment and cultural alienation. Locals were fed up with gated and walled subdivisions surrounding the town, and with the fancy galleries, Southwestern trinket shops, and espresso bars that had transformed the downtown plaza into a caricature of the New West.

But Jaramillo had a problem not unique to Santa Fe. Any attempt to limit development runs smack into the West's deeply rooted antipathy to regulation by any government. Ranchers might wince to see productive spreads turned into ranchette estates, but they will fight for every owner's right to do what they please with their land.

After residents spent years writing a comprehensive plan to guide rapid development that many felt was ruining Flathead County, Montana, the "Wise Use" movement blocked its implementation. This confederation of traditional industries like mining and ranching, and the property rights movement, sided with developers and won a court order against the plan. They claimed that the plan, by limiting development of some property, was an unfair taking of property by the government; to the Wise Use clan almost any form of land use planning, outside traditional zoning for health or safety, is unconstitutional. Readers who crave a piece of the New West should note the region's weak zoning and planning. The views, open space, and wildlife that attracted you may not last.

Trailer homes, Colorado   Theobald

Rural home, Wyoming   Riebsame

Adobe home, New Mexico   Barber

Ghost Houses

Mountain cabin with no running water, two-bedroom condo in Jackson Hole, or 10,000-square-foot rambler in Aspen: the West sports thousands of homes occupied only a few weeks a year. Owned by folks from the West's own cities, or New York, or Riyadh, or Tokyo, these thousands of second, third, and fourth homes have confounded planners, even as they filled local property tax coffers, and evoked resentment among locals of modest means. A swank two-thousand-house development near Vail in Eagle County, Colorado, yielded big property taxes but added only a couple of kids to local schools. Places like Vail, Park City, Tahoe, Sedona, and Steamboat Springs report that up to 70 percent of their housing is owned by non-residents, most of it not rental property but rather sitting empty until owners can get away to enjoy it. Entire "ghost" subdivisions may be empty during the off-season,

Vail, Colorado has the highest proportion of "second-homes" of any resort town in the West. A 1996 survey found that 66% of Vail's property owners list somewhere else as their principal residence. Two-thirds of those live outside Colorado, many outside the U.S. Vail planners say the survey also showed that a large number of Vail's temporary residents plan eventually to settle there permanently.

and use may be brief even in winter at ski resorts; and these houses are heated, cleaned, and the driveways cleared of snow by an army of house-watchers and maintenance workers.

Geographic concentrations of second homes in the U.S. show, simply, where rich Americans like to spend their free time: northern New England, the Caskills, along the spine of the Appalachians, Florida, the Upper Midwest lake country, coastal Washington, and the mountains and deserts of the Interior West. All the ski zones, up and down the Rockies and along the East Front of the Sierra Nevada, attract second homes, as do the deserts and canyonlands of southern Utah and northern Arizona. Right in the heart of the West, however, covering much of Nevada, southeastern Oregon, far southern Idaho, and northwestern Utah, lies a donut hole of geography with apparently little appeal. These areas may be yet undiscovered gems of Western real estate, or dull salt flats and sage brush wastes.

Working ranch, Colorado   Riebsame

Condo construction, Idaho   Pike

Ridgetop home, Colorado   Riebsame

The West's booming second-home landscape depends not just on American affluence and recreational tastes, but also on the tax break accorded holders of home mortgages. All of this could change. *High Country News* publisher Ed Marston, a savvy and forward-looking Western observer, worries about what to do with the monster second homes if the bust does come; Westerners surely will not have money to heat, much less buy, them.[7] And places that charmed wealthy itinerants in the past have not always maintained their cachet: Atlantic City, Saratoga, even Florida's Gold Coast, have lost much of their past attraction. Still, the vacation homes of places like Cape Cod and the Smoky Mountains have long been part of the residential landscape, and those of the West may endure. Westerners living near ghost subdivisions might wonder what happens to their towns if all those nonresident owners suddenly decide to telecommute from, or retire to, their dream homes on the range.

Ghost Houses

Percentage of second
homes by county, 1990

☐ 0–5

☐ 5–0

▨ 10–25

■ 25–76

Ghost Houses

Many Americans who haven't moved to the West own homes there nonetheless. Most of the second-home zones that stand out on this map are mountain or desert resort areas, anchored on ski areas, lakes, and reservoirs. Entire "ghost subdivisions" of second, third, or even fourth homes sprout next to ski runs, wilderness areas, or trout streams. Two-thirds of the homes in ski towns like Vail or Park City are owned by out-of-towners who drop in for occasional stays. The proliferation of second homes confounds Western planners, fills local property tax coffers, and evokes resentment among permanent residents. The non-resident homeowners in Telluride, Colorado—claiming taxation without representation—recently won the right to vote in municipal elections, a precedent that worries other resort town officials who face new limitations on how they spend nonresidents' property taxes.

Working and Earning in the New West

A diminishing few Westerners cut trees, dig minerals, or graze cattle for a living; most work in the region's booming service economy. The term "services sector" brings to mind low-paid workers flipping hamburgers and cleaning motel rooms, and this is a big chunk of Western job growth. But the West's growing nonfarm, nonmanufacturing economy is also fueled by growth in health, finance, construction, engineering, education, and small businesses of all sorts, from environmental consulting firms to software companies.

First, though, the underside of the new economy. An immutable economic logic tethers society's lowest paying jobs to the ritziest and most expensive western places. The resort towns' "servant economy"[8] is rich in jobs waiting tables, mowing lawns, and cleaning hotel rooms, jobs that offer full-time take-home pay of less than $1,000 a month. Even skilled lift operators and trail groomers at the ski resorts are lucky to make $12/hour. Two-bedroom apartments in Vail or Aspen or Jackson run to over $1500/month, and groceries, gas, and even hamburgers cost more in the ski resorts than they do in major cities. Workers don't even dream of owning homes in these hyperinflated real estate markets. So, the service workers of Vail commute 40 miles over a 10,400-foot pass from Leadville—a busted mining town now serving, like many other Western towns, as bedroom community to the resorts. Workers in Jackson do the same, coming in from Idaho over Teton Pass, at least when avalanches haven't closed it. Job rich and housing poor, ski area workers have resorted to working up to three jobs, living in cars (Telluride first banned the practice, then set aside a place for "camping" workers), and commuting longer distances. The counties and ski corporations provide some worker housing, but one ski company argued that the Forest Service should provide public land for worker dorms, and fewer than half of Aspen's workers live in the town.

The other, brighter side of the service economy makes for gleeful chambers of commerce. A great deal of Western employment is professional: educators, scientists, lawyers' and the whole high-tech crowd. In fact, economic studies of the West's booming service economy show that the bulk of new jobs are not in retail, restaurants, or lodging—the tourist economy—but rather in business, health, legal, and engineering services. One study found this even in ski resorts like Summit County (Park City), Utah, and Blaine County (Sun Valley), Idaho.[9] Thus, although service jobs are often derided as paying less than the disappearing resource extraction jobs, Western wages remain higher than in most other U.S. regions.

A study of the area around Yellowstone National Park, covering parts of Idaho, Wyoming, and Montana, found 2100 new business starts in the 1980s; self-employment accounted for over half of these 15,141 new jobs. During the same time, mining jobs dropped by half and oil and gas jobs dropped by a quarter.[10] Economists argue that the natural landscape is fueling this economic boom, attracting entrepreneurs and small businesses. Yet every tilt by the Park Service or Forest Service toward preserving nature evokes claims from lumber, minerals, oil, and cattle interests that the region's economy still runs on resource extraction. Less than 1 percent of employment in the West is supported by mining, and only .06 percent of jobs are associated with ranching.[11] Instead, retirement income alone brings more money into areas like Yellowstone than resource extraction. Slavish support of the old economy, often in the forms of subsidies and political protection, actually reduces the region's economic well-being by hurting the new economy.

Yellowstone's Service Economy

The area surrounding Yellowstone National Park epitomizes the Western economy's nature-tourism-based boom. Some Westerners disparage the services economy as providing only low-wage jobs, and bemoan the fading of logging, mining, ranching, and energy industries—which, despite claims to the contrary, provided few jobs even two decades ago. The postindustrial economy is not just jobs serving ice cream to tourists at Old Faithful; the Yellowstone area, and the West more broadly, is also growing high-paid jobs in financial, health, and legal services, in software development, telecommunications, and education. Investment and retirement income equals or exceeds wage incomes in many areas, especially near national parks and other amenity-rich landscapes.

Yellowstone's Service Economy

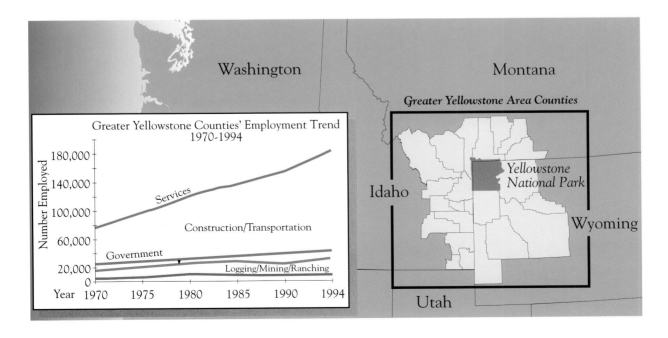

Strongholds of the Traditional Economy

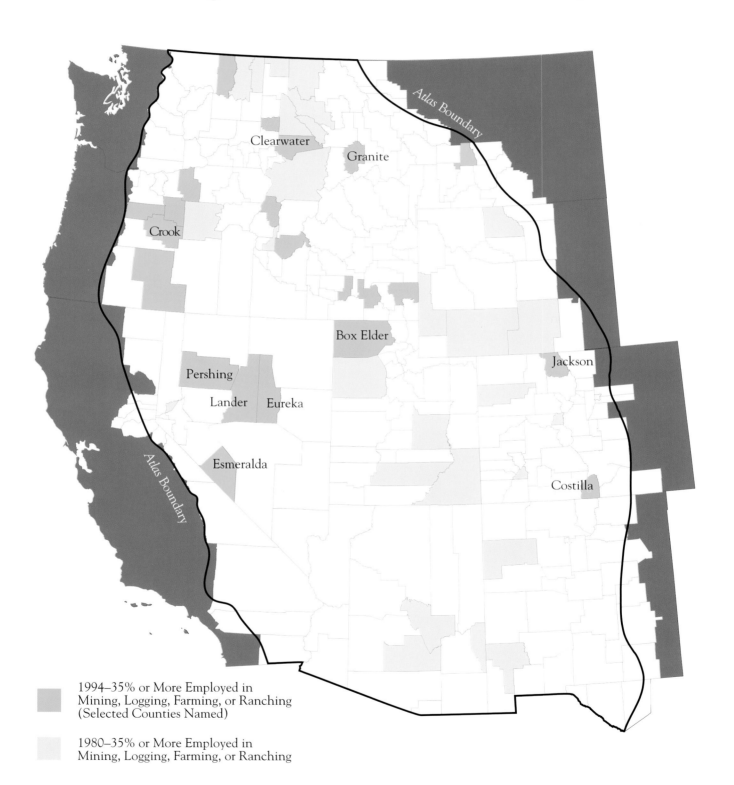

Clearwater

Granite

Atlas Boundary

Crook

Box Elder

Jackson

Pershing

Lander   Eureka

Atlas Boundary

Esmeralda

Costilla

1994–35% or More Employed in
Mining, Logging, Farming, or Ranching
(Selected Counties Named)

1980–35% or More Employed in
Mining, Logging, Farming, or Ranching

Some of the Old West economy survives. Pockets of ranching, logging, and even a few mining economies lend, in their own way, an economic diversity fast disappearing in the suburbanizing West. Ranch hands still herd cattle in Jackson County, Colorado; mining is still big business in Sweetwater County, Wyoming, and around the pits and mills of Jefferson County, Montana; and logging still means jobs in Custer County, Idaho. A few places remain one-industry towns, whose fortunes rise or fall with the price of copper, lumber, or molybdenum. Up to 70 percent of the jobs in the small timber towns of Clearwater County, Idaho, are in the local timber mills.[12]

Mostly, though, the West has moved beyond extracting natural resources to appreciating them in place: mountainsides not excavated for copper or molybdenum; rangeland homes for wolves instead of cattle; and old growth forests rather than clear-cuts. Economists point out that the West is moving beyond even a wage economy. Much of the money Westerners now earn comes from non-labor sources like investment and what economists call transfer payments: trust fund income, retirement, and welfare. So-called "current earnings" (wages for work) make up less than half of the region's income and are declining especially in the amenity areas around national parks, ski resorts, and retirement hot spots.

Those economists, impressed with new money in the West, are also reassessing the standard economic development model that starts with industries creating jobs, which then lure people. Now the West lures people first, who then create jobs, by starting their own businesses or attracting footloose industries from metropolitan areas.[13] The New West, then, is truly built by New Westerners, not by the commodities industry nor even the corporate logic of economies of scale.

Strongholds of the Traditional Economy

The traditional Western economy—logging, ranching, farming, and mining—holds on in a few places, highlighted here where it provided at least 35 percent of jobs in 1994; comparison with 1980s strongholds illustrates the boom and bust of commodities. The energy boom brought mining back to southern Wyoming and eastern Utah in 1980, but by 1994 energy had busted like gold and silver before it. Jobs extracting natural resources are rarer than ever, but ranchhands still find work in Jackson County, Colorado, or Eureka County, Nevada; and loggers still feed the sawmills of Clearwater County, Idaho.

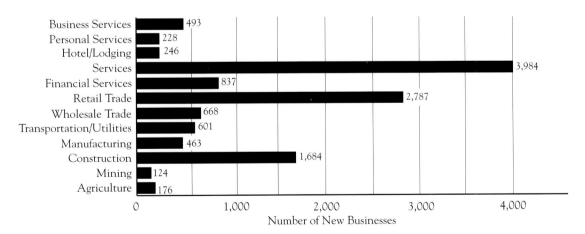

Making Business on the Colorado Plateau

Like the Yellowstone country, and other Western areas rich in natural beauty and open space, as well as national parks and resorts, the Colorado Plateau is booming, its economy shifting away from its two historical mainstays: agriculture and mining. Service companies like law and engineering firms have led the pack of new businesses over the last twenty years, followed by retail businesses and the construction trades that boom wherever new homes, shopping malls, and utilities go in.

Source: Walter E. Hecox and Bradley L. Ack, Charting the Colorado Plateau (Flagstaff, Arizona: Grand Canyon Trust, 1996)

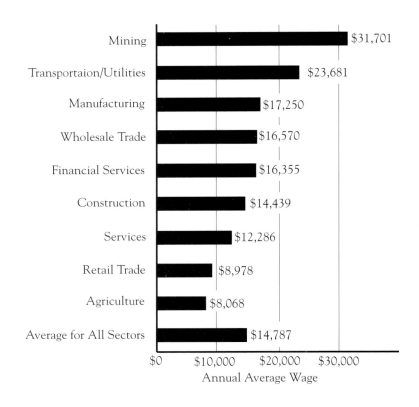

Mining	$31,701
Transportaion/Utilities	$23,681
Manufacturing	$17,250
Wholesale Trade	$16,570
Financial Services	$16,355
Construction	$14,439
Services	$12,286
Retail Trade	$8,978
Agriculture	$8,068
Average for All Sectors	$14,787

$0 $10,000 $20,000 $30,000

Annual Average Wage

**Earning a Living on the
Colorado Plateau**

*The expanding Western new services econo-
my is routinely disparaged as offering only
low-paid jobs. Although some economists
point out that services include high-paying
professionals like doctors and lawyers, many
service and retail jobs pay barely half what
mining did, though they do pay better than
most agricultural jobs.*

Source: Walter E. Hecox and Bradley L. Ack, Charting the Colorado
Plateau (Flagstaff, Ariz.: Grand Canyon Trust, 1996)

Retirement Hot Spots

Scottsdale, Palm Springs, Lake Havasu City are place names long syn-
onymous with retirement, and with desert climates, golf courses, and climate-
controlled shopping malls. Retirement far from the last career-based home is relatively new in America, though a few places, like Phoenix, Arizona, attracted
retirees since early this century. The trend accelerated after World War II; some
soldiers, sailors, and pilots had developed a taste for the Sunbelt during military
service and fled to the Southwest at retirement.

We are talking about deserts here, but retirees settling in Kalispell,
Montana; Ketchum, Idaho; and other snowy Rocky Mountain retreats? These are
not much like the great American Sunbelt. Las Vegas, sure, Phoenix, Tucson,
and even Colorado Springs, not surprising, but Kalispell? This puzzle partly yields
to a nuance of Western climate—even cold, snowy places enjoy dry, sunny
weather most of the time; shirtsleeve afternoons pepper the winter, and 45 inches of snow a winter in Colorado Springs, where each storm is followed by dry,
melting winds, has little in common with 45 inches in, say, Buffalo or Detroit.

Nor is climate retirement destiny. Younger, healthier retirees want more
action than can be found in Sun City, Arizona. Ski areas, trout streams, and
wilderness now vie with health care and housing cost in retirement planning. We
map top-rated Western retirement places from three rankings that take account
of everything from climate to crime. Several Western towns get high rankings,
but the important message is that Western retirement geography has been liberated from its hackneyed rut of desert golf communities. Dozens of towns like

Kalispell have the requisite qualities: Provo, Utah, has good skiing, low crime, and excellent health care; Grand Junction, Colorado, is dry and warm with snowy mountains a few miles east and the alluring canyonlands of the Colorado Plateau spread out to the west; Wenatchee, Washington, on the mercifully dry side of the Cascades is not too far from Seattle and the ocean. Babyboomers, who will start to retire en masse around 2010, will probably search out more obscure places that meet their recreational, travel, and housing desires, places that don't show up in today's rankings. More small Western towns will match those requirements by then—places like Moab, Utah; Elko, Nevada; Saint Anthony, Idaho; and Thermopolis, Wyoming.

Even young retirees eventually get older and less robust, and a new pattern of "multiplace retirement" is popping up. They start in, say, Kalispell or Pagosa Springs for the first retirement decade, then relocate (hopefully with some capital gained from their resort-town homes) to the retirement communities of Arizona.

A big bulge of babyboomer retirement is on the way. Nothing will stand in its way, certainly not the economy's inevitable ups and downs. Retirement may not be fully recession-proof (though it is countercyclical in that many firms use early retirement to cut workforces in tough times), but analysts see it as an enduring boon to the West: retirees bring permanent incomes with them, incomes independent of resource extraction, industrial production, or even the services economy of tourism and recreation. Economist Thomas Power, taking a close look at the Greater Yellowstone economy, points out that retirement brings more money to the region than commodity exports and a retirement dollar has the same multiplier effect as one made cutting trees or drilling for oil. Furthermore, he argues, retirees bring different cultural facets, new ideas, and community service to their chosen places. The West's great retirement boom has just begun.

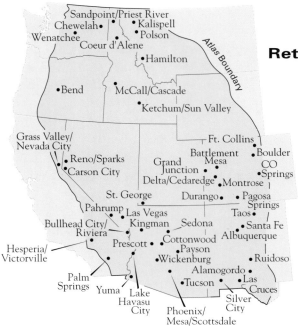

Retirement Hot Spots

The desert Southwest is famous as a retirement magnet, but with millions of babyboomers retiring during the next few decades experts expect more dispersed retirement patterns. Younger, healthier retirees from the baby boom will still play golf but they'll also ski, fly-fish, and mountain bike, and settle into places far from traditional retirement meccas. Here we map recommended retirement towns according to Retirement Places Rated and New Choices for Retirement Living. Northern locales like Polson, Montana, or Wenatchee, Washington, are a far cry from the desert golf communities in California and Arizona, but, like much of the West, they offer pleasant climate—including enough snow to play on—and a small-town atmosphere that increasingly includes services the retirees need, from investment brokers to good hospitals. The southern spots still beckon with endless summers, and some Western retirees will surely flit north and south as the seasons change.

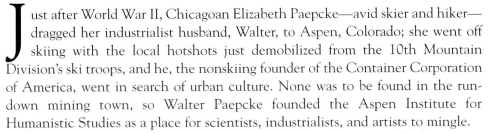

Chapter 5: New West Lifestyles

The Cultured West

Long associated with the region's rural, rugged image, and its Hispanic, Indian, and cowboy heritage, the "cultured West" now includes not only cowboy poetry, mariachi bands, and Native American art, but also symphonies, plays, and film festivals— trappings previously enjoyed mostly on the east and west coasts and a few cities in between. Many of these cultural amenities appeared in ski towns like Telluride and Sun Valley in the 1970s as the summer attraction that made them year-round tourist economies. Four-year colleges and even National Public Radio and Pacifica Radio member stations add a sophisticated, in-touch ambiance even to smallish Western towns like Laramie, Wyoming, or Gunnison, Colorado.

Just after World War II, Chicagoan Elizabeth Paepcke—avid skier and hiker— dragged her industrialist husband, Walter, to Aspen, Colorado; she went off skiing with the local hotshots just demobilized from the 10th Mountain Division's ski troops, and he, the nonskiing founder of the Container Corporation of America, went in search of urban culture. None was to be found in the run-down mining town, so Walter Paepcke founded the Aspen Institute for Humanistic Studies as a place for scientists, industrialists, and artists to mingle.

Aspen's mix of good skiing and high culture made it a world-class resort, a mix now replicated in several Western places. Cultural trappings previously concentrated on the east and west coasts have cropped up around the region. New Westerners demand the right edifices (galleries, bookstores, gourmet restaurants), entertainment (symphonies, plays), information sources (National Public Radio and the *New York Times*), addictions (espresso, boutique beer), pastimes (squash, golf, heli-skiing) and gear (the elegance and practicality of Range Rovers, Orvis flyrods, and Patagonia outdoor clothing). At the same time, they appropriate and remold what the West has always offered—rich Indian and Hispanic culture and spirituality, cowboy mythology, great fishing, and a host of mountain and desert sports.

The Cultured West

Outside of the few big cities, it was skiing's awkward seasonality that helped give the West high culture. Ski towns like Sun Valley and Telluride dragged during the off-season until the town boosters and ski corporations hit on an idea to liven up the summer and, not incidentally, bring in more tourist dollars: summer arts festivals. Aspen's music festival got going with the 1949 Goethe Bicentennial celebration, thanks to the Paepckes, and most of the resort towns now have significant summer music, art, film, and theater events. Robert Redford's Sundance ski resort in Utah hosts the region's best-known film festival, though Telluride's film fair draws directors and stars too.

The Aspen Music Festival also set a precedent that was both practical and evinced a kind of reverse chic: it was held in a big tent. Tents full of musicians now sprout like alpine wildflowers in most of the West's mountain resorts. Add the year-round cultural attractions of the few large cities to the arts action on any college campus, and the region is quite well-served. Symphonies, operas, film festivals, and Shakespeare troupes dot the West.

New Age in the New West

Dramatic scenery and room to do your own thing attract alternative lifestyles to the West, starting with Brigham Young leading the Mormons to the valley of the Great Salt Lake. Today the West lures New Age gurus, healing centers, and communes to such nodes of crystal power and psychic vortexes as Crestone, Colorado, and Sedona, Arizona. But, like city slickers who annoy real ranchers with their cowboy apparel, the New Age crowd irks Native Americans by appropriating and misusing their ceremonies and spiritual sites. Conflating old and new, the New Agers create their own versions of medicine wheels at places like Bell Rock, Arizona, known to New Age mystics as a convergence point for

The Cultured West

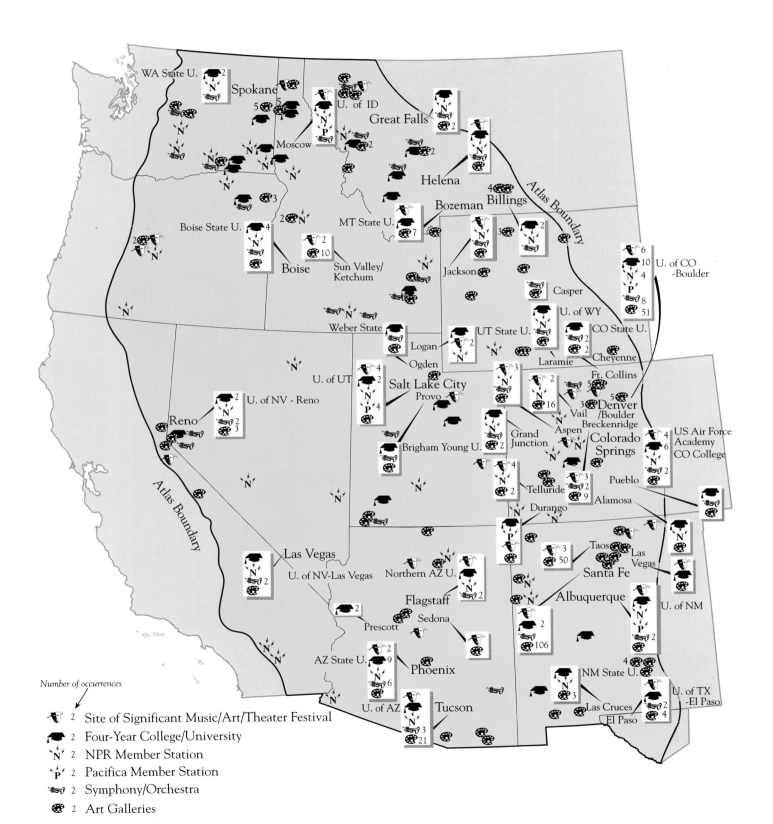

New Age in the New West

Dramatic scenery, rich Native American heritage, and isolation attract New Age practitioners to the West. Channelers, healing centers, and communes populate the region's nodes of crystal power and psychic vortexes, like Crestone, Colorado, or Sedona, Arizona.

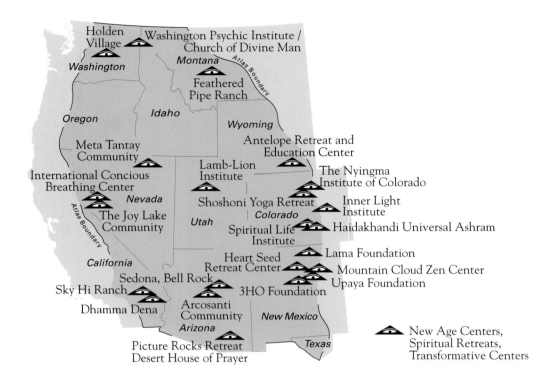

Opportunities to Join the New Age

Lama Foundation, Santa Fe, N.Mex.: religious practices, vision quests incorporating dreamwork, deep image journeys, ceremonial drumming, fasting.

Meta Tantay, Carlin, Nev.: community living following Native American lifestyle and culture.

International Conscious Breathing Center, Sierraville, Calif.: conscious breathing technique.

Stillpoint Center, Wetmore, Colo.: Taoist meditation to achieve inner tranquility and participate in the cosmic process.

Feathered Pipe Ranch, Helena, Mont.: natural medicine, yoga, drum building, women's wisdom.

Heart Seed Retreat Center, Santa Fe, N.Mex.: training in earth energies, dowsing and deep sensing, silent retreats.

Antelope Retreat and Education Center, Savory, Wyo.: vision quests.

New Age Fair, Santa Fe, N.Mex.: annual extravaganza of crystal power, channelers and healers.

Sources: The New Consciousness Sourcebook; Vacations that Can Change Your Life

what one journalist called "multiple-choice ethereal dimensions."[1] We chose not to map Indian spiritual sites because their representation, in maps or photographs, degrades their sacredness. But New Agers exhibit no such qualms about appropriating Indian spirituality and are probably largely unaware that several tribes declared war against New Agers and their use of Native traditions and places.

Those looking to transcend the daily grind and enter the New Age in the New West, find a bevy of opportunity. Retreats and spiritual centers offer Native American vision quests, Buddhist ritual, and training in shamanism.[2] What do oil industry executives, environmental activists, a public radio broadcaster, three American Indian elders, a literature professor, and a former member of a girls' street gang have in common? They all went through a recent three-day survival course in New Mexico's desert, learning aboriginal bush skills such as making fire with sticks, tracking wild pig, and charting their way by the stars. The director of the program studied with aborigines in Australia before starting his business. He points out that "you can get a Ph.D. in a few years, but it can take your whole life to become a good bushman."

The region also hosts alternative life-forms, if one can believe the UFO crowd, who haunt Nevada's "Extraterrestrial Highway" (State Highway 375 next to the Air Force's supersecret testing grounds) and Utah's "San Rafael Triangle," an empty swath of canyons and buttes, one of which, Luna Mesa, is apparently preferred by flying saucers. A visitor to the International UFO Museum and Research Center in Roswell, New Mexico, learns that the Air Force hides the

Declaration of War on the New Age

At their fifth international summit in June, 1993, the Lakota, Canadian Lakota, Dakota, and Nakota nations passed a "Declaration of War Against Exploiters of Lakota Spirituality." Some excepts:

Whereas for too long we have suffered the unspeakable indignity of having our most precious Lakota ceremonies and spiritual practices desecrated, mocked and abused by non-Indian "wannabes," hucksters, cultists, commercial profiteers and self-styled "New Age shamans" and their followers; and . . .

Whereas our Sacred Pipe is being desecrated through the sale of pipestone pipes at flea markets, powwows and "New Age" retail stores; . . .

Whereas the absurd public posturing of this scandalous assortment of pseudo-Indian charlatans, "wannabes," commercial profiteers, cultists and "New Age shamans" comprises a momentous obstacle in the struggle for an adequate public appraisal of the legitimate political, legal, and spiritual needs of real Lakota people; . . .

Therefore we resolve as follows:

We hereby and henceforth declare war against all persons who persist in exploiting, abusing and misrepresenting [our] sacred traditions and spiritual practices . . .

We call upon all [our people] to actively and vocally oppose this alarming takeover and systematic destruction of our sacred traditions [through] demonstrations, boycotts, press conferences, and acts of direct intervention.

We especially urge [action] to prevent our own people from contributing to . . . the abuse of our sacred ceremonies and spiritual practices by outsiders . . .

We urge all our Indian brothers and sisters to act decisively and boldly in our campaign to end the destruction of our sacred traditions, keeping in mind our highest duty as Indian people: to preserve the purity of our precious traditions for our future generations, so that our children and our children's children will survive and prosper in the sacred manner intended for each of our respective peoples by our Creator.

Consuming in the New West

○ *New York Times*

■ Gourmet Coffee (espresso, fancy brewed coffee)

■ Land Rover

▲ Full-Line Orvis Shops

● Patagonia Outfitter

wreck of an extraterrestrial spacecraft and its occupants—which purportedly crashed in 1947—inside a nearby hanger, repudiating both the government's noted inability to keep secrets and supposed alien engineering skills. Interstellar visitors to the West attract earth-bound tourists, and good money is to be made off of both cultures.

Consuming in the New West

High culture doesn't appeal to all New Westerners, but they do like their amenities. The New West lifestyle has a lot to do with the flood of well-off newcomers and their consumption patterns. Urban and suburban refugees come to the Interior West looking for salvation from the rat race; they appreciate the rugged landscape, the big sky, the mythical "Wild West," and opportunities to make money and spend it. But there can be a problem. Not all places in the Interior offer the requisite amenities. The neighbors may not all be nice, either. Much of the West is still a working landscape where oil is drilled, coal dug up, and poison set out for coyotes. And though little true wilderness remains, some of the region's long-term residents—like bison, mountain lions, and rattlers—make unwanted appearances in rural subdivisions, ranchette estates, and on the urban fringe.

Interior cities, though few and far between, offer most of what the New Westerners need, and towns blessed with, say, a four-year college or fancy resort, are one step ahead with bookstores, espresso bars, and cultural events. Firmly established New West places like Scottsdale, Boulder, Santa Fe, Aspen, Jackson, Sun Valley, and even Moab provide all the perceived necessities. For cool, understated Southwest style in Moab, formerly strictly trinkety and blue collar, go to the Slickrock Cafe for a fancy sandwich, and for the best selection of books about the West in the West, try Back of Beyond Books. Beyond these outposts, the New West pioneer might wish to wait until the frontier is better supplied with the essentials—like the daily *New York Times* and NPR or Pacifica Radio outlets—and people don't think you're Italian when you ask for an Americano.

It might not be long until most Western towns are gentrified. Driving through the Utah countryside, one sees vast expanses of space punctuated by small, dusty towns, formerly dependent on local farmers and ranchers to frequent their shops. Coming begrudgingly to the realization that tourists and recreationists are likely to be their economic

Consuming in the New West

New Western immigrants bring with them their information sources (the New York Times), addictions (good coffee, good beer), pastimes (fly-fishing and golf) and consumer values (the understated elegance and practicality of Range Rovers and Patagonia clothing). It's no surprise that well-established New West entrenchments like Scottsdale, Boulder, Santa Fe, Aspen, Jackson, Sun Valley, and even Moab provide most of the perceived necessities of the good life. But New West outposts, like Panguitch, Utah; Dubois, Wyoming; and Saratoga, Wyoming, also offer gourmet coffee, five-hundred-dollar Orvis fishing poles, and the latest in outdoor clothing.

Cowboys in Other Lines of Work

Cowboy Blues Diner, Escalante, Utah
Cowboy Aviation, Kanab, Utah
Reel Cowboys, Taos, N.Mex.
The Canine Cowboy, Santa Fe, N.Mex.
Cowboy Computer Corp., Frisco, Colo.
Psychic Cowboy-Tarot, Palm Springs, Calif.
Cowboy Logic, Victor, Idaho
Cowboy Coffee Co., Jackson, Wyo.
Cowboy Cooking and Supply, Jackson, Wyo.
Cowboy Snowmobiles, Dubois, Wyo.
Cowboy Computers, Tempe, Ariz.
Cowboy Pest Control, Apache Jct., Ariz.
Le Cowboy, Scottsdale, Ariz.
Cappucino Cowboy Coffee House, Ronan, Mont.
Cowboys and Lace Antiques, Haxtun, Colo.
Cowboy Heaven, Sedona, Ariz.

mainstay in the future, such places have decided to give them what they want. In Panguitch, Utah, Buffalo Java stands out like a sore thumb, imposing its chic on the rest of the rundown town. Inside you can find every thinkable variety of espresso drink and organic tea, which you sip while browsing the New-West-for-sale: denim backpacks with old (looking) Montana and Utah license plates sewn on; juniper flavored incense; barbed wire art (which, as the clerk pointed out, is pricey because of the expensive and time-consuming process involved in giving the barbed wire that old, rusted look; Charles Wilkinson, Edward Abbey, and Wallace Stegner on audiotape; and books on where to find authentic dude ranches.

Buffalo Java is emblematic of coffee's signature status in yuppiedom. Seattle has no monopoly on the newly emerged coffee culture west of the Mississippi. Phoenix boasts dozens of coffee spots and a coffee culture rag, *Java Monthly*, offering coffee and art reviews, plus an "I Saw You" page of personals: "I saw you at the Coffee Plantation wearing ripped jeans and a tank top and can't get you out of my mind . . ."

Santa Fe, of course, is *the* hot spot for New West lifestyle and consumption. Strolling along the main plaza one finds a pleasant mixture of old and new: on one side of the plaza Indians sell their jewelry from blankets on the ground, usually willing to bargain with tourists eager for Indian crafts; across the way, window after window displays the prolific howling coyote, complete with nifty red bandanna; pricey Southwest art; and more silver and turquoise than a body could support. These staples of Southwest style inspired the well-known cartoon seen around town on posters and postcards: "Another Victim of Santa Fe Style," on which a portly woman bedecked with a billowing, colorful skirt, peasant blouse, cockleshell belt, enough silver and turquoise to sink a battleship, and, of course, cowboy boots, has keeled over dead in her adobe home, which is complete with cow skull, hanging red chile peppers, Georgia O'Keeffe print, and other Santa Fe accoutrements.

Some sites of New West consumption are obvious: of course there's a Land Rover dealership in Aspen, and the fly-fishers flying into private ranches on the North Platte near Saratoga, Wyoming, couldn't live without a full-line Orvis shop. But when did they start drinking gourmet coffee in Douglas, Wyoming, Alamosa, Colorado, or Henderson, Nevada? Who wears Patagonia gear in Sand Point, Idaho, retirement hotspot for LA policemen?

What's Brewing?

Beer is a national pastime, so how can it also be an indicator of the New West? Twenty years ago, microbreweries wouldn't have thrived among old Western beer drinkers unwilling to pay six to eight dollars for a six-pack. The Old West was the land of Bud and, of course, Coors. But today Adolf Coors' brew is considered un-PC among the left-leaning. The beer of the New West differs from Coors in that much of it comes from small distributors in 22 ounce "bombers" (rather than six-packs) with exotic labeling and trendy names like Fat Tire, Avalanche, Hubcap Ale, and Red Lady. Many of the four to six new microbreweries that open every week in America are in the West, and their range of distribution is increasing. Some microbreweries choose to remain local and distribute

What's Brewing in the New West

What's Brewing in the New West? Lot's of beer, that's what, in microbreweries producing nectar named Fat Tire or Avalanche ale, and in basements throughout the region. Homebrew clubs started a tradition of colorful names, often reflecting local features, like the Atom Mashers near the Los Alamos nuclear labs, or political sensibilities, as in the Northern Utah Militia of Brewers.

What's Brewing in the New West

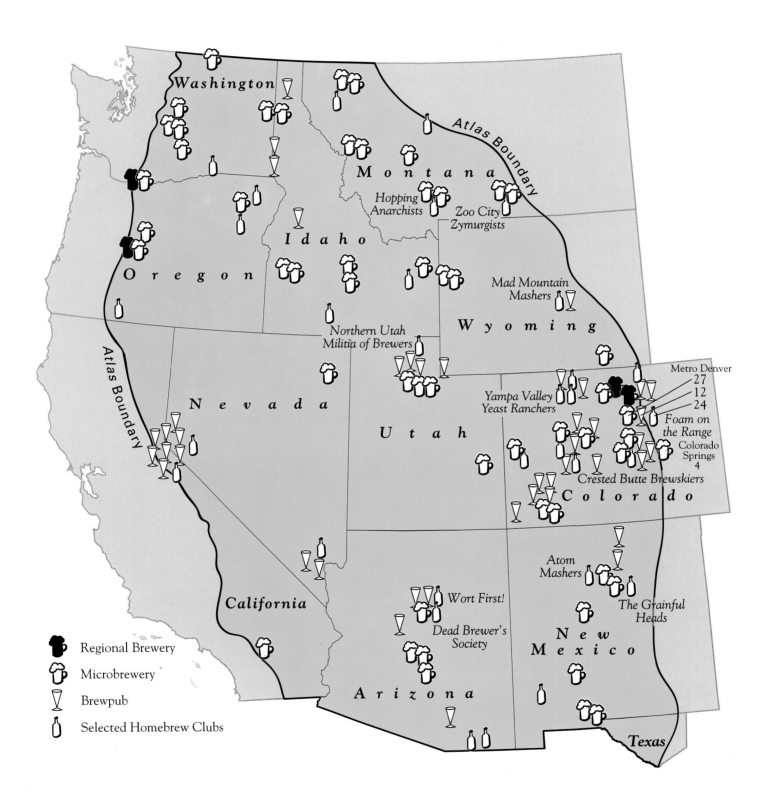

Washington

Montana

Hopping
Anarchists

Zoo City
Zymurgists

Idaho

Oregon

Mad Mountain
Mashers

Wyoming

Northern Utah
Militia of Brewers

Nevada

Yampa Valley
Yeast Ranchers

Metro Denver
27
12
24
Foam on
the Range
Colorado
Springs
4

Utah

Crested Butte Brewskiers

Colorado

California

Atom
Mashers

Wort First!

The Grainful
Heads

Dead Brewer's
Society

New
Mexico

Regional Brewery

Microbrewery

Brewpub

Selected Homebrew Clubs

Arizona

Texas

primarily to customers onsite. Many of these so-called "brewpubs" naturally pop up in cities, but more and more, the small-town West is getting its own beer label. Together with fancy coffee places like Starbucks, these pubs provide a much appreciated scene for congregation. Sampling the latest raspberry wheats, oatmeal stouts, hot chili beers, and java ales (perhaps the ultimate nexus of New West beverages), New Westerners can put on a buzz without ever feeling crude or uncouth. Coors' response to the yuppification of beer drinking? A new slogan: "Coors, the last *real* beer."

Inspired by the growth of microbreweries, brewing at home catches on in the West as well, and homebrew clubs with names like the Yampa Valley Yeast Ranchers and the Northern Utah Militia of Brewers call up images of old-time whiskey brewing and New West suburbanism. A certain ruggedness attaches to fermenting your own hops and barley and ale, and testing the prototypes along with the perfected batches.

Old West Lives On

The greatest amenity for New Westerners, the one that sets their urban and ex-urban lifestyles apart from the same scene in, say, Atlanta or Albany, is the Old West. Rodeos and cowboy poetry gatherings everywhere from Elko, Nevada, to Clovis, New Mexico; gambling in old mining towns like Central City, Colorado, and Wells, Nevada; mountain man rendezvous in Wyoming; and even city slicker cattle drives at fancy dude ranches—all these trade on Old West imagery and mythology. Authenticity, though, is in the eye of the beholder and Western booster: Moab's Apache Motel flaunts its coveted connection to a connection to the Old West: "Stay where John Wayne stayed!"

Gambling may be a national pastime, but its homeland lies in the heart of the New West—Nevada. Its traditional imagery of Doc Holliday and Old West saloons has been transfigured by the Las Vegas casinos into fantastic theme parks based on Camelot, ancient Eqypt, or even Manhattan. Originally quarantined by the Great Basin's trackless wastes, legal gambling spread from Nevada to Indian reservations and small towns throughout the Interior West—mostly towns that got their start in the gold or silver rushes. The new gambling boom emulates the Old West more than modern community leaders might wish to admit. Studies of

The Old West Lives On

Rodeos are held in just about every Western town, but the ones mapped here, sanctioned by the Professional Rodeo Cowboys Association, are the big-bucks events drawing 22 million spectators and doling out over $25 million in prize money during 1995. Dude ranches also dot the West, and run the gamut from fancy operations with pools and hot tubs to working ranches where guests check cattle and mend fences alongside the ranch family. When not hanging on to a bronc for dear life or catering to guests, modern cowboys also write and read poetry: the annual cowboy poetry gathering at Elko, Nevada, attracts some 10,000 people. Recreated mountain man rendezvous—concentrated in Wyoming where the real things were held—attract fewer participants because strict rules limit attire, food, and even sanitary facilities to mid-1800's custom. Finally, though they compete with indigenous species and deplete the range, wild horses and burros, introduced by Spanish conquistadors and prospectors, are managed by federal agencies as a national legacy in several areas.

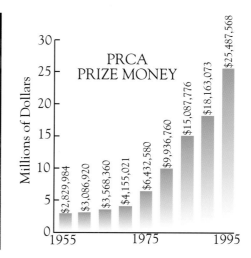

Rodeos are Hot

According to the Pro Rodeo Cowboys Association, rodeo is booming! Over 22 million people attended PRCA-sanctioned events in 1995, and a recent study says that those fans are predominantly urban, and 44% earn annual household incomes greater than $50,000, half expect to purchase Western apparel during the coming year, and fully a third of them expect to buy a truck or car in the next year. Rodeo advertising budgets are way up too, and sponsors' cash, along with entrance fees, make for bigger and bigger purses.

PRCA PRIZE MONEY

Millions of Dollars

- $2,829,984
- $3,086,920
- $3,568,360
- $4,155,021
- $6,432,580
- $9,936,760
- $15,087,776
- $18,163,073
- $25,487,568

1955　1975　1995

The Old West Lives On

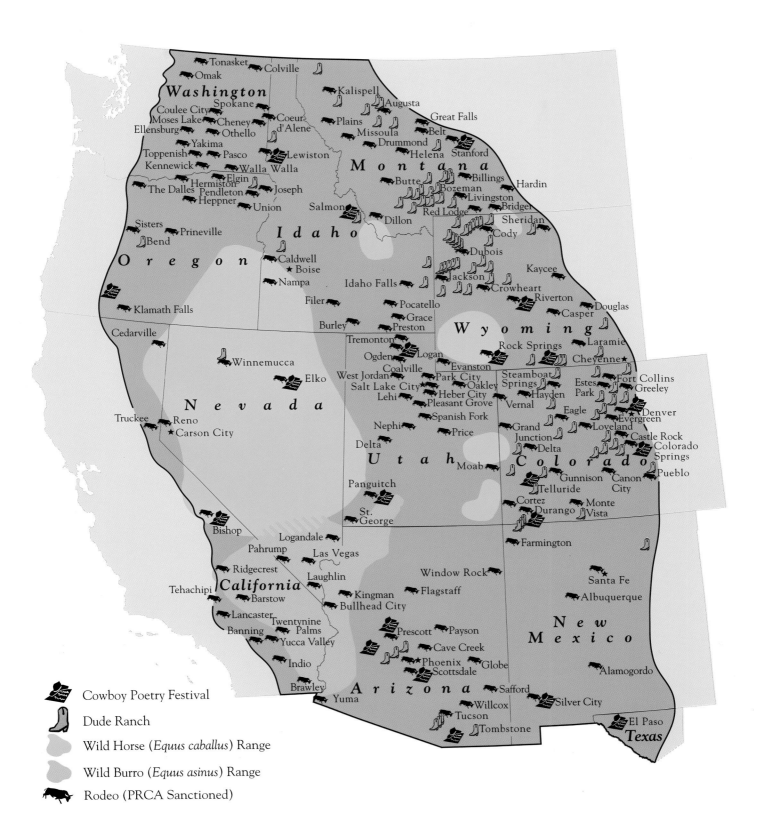

Tonasket
Omak
Colville
Washington
Coulee City
Spokane
Kalispell
Augusta
Great Falls
Moses Lake
Cheney
Coeur
Plains
d'Alene
Ellensburg
Othello
Missoula
Belt
Yakima
Drummond
Toppenish
Pasco
Lewiston
Helena
Stanford
Kennewick
Walla Walla
Montana
Elgin
Hermiston
The Dalles
Joseph
Butte
Billings
Hardin
Pendleton
Bozeman
Livingston
Heppner
Union
Salmon
Red Lodge
Bridger
Idaho
Dillon
Sheridan
Sisters
Prineville
Cody
Bend
Oregon
Caldwell
Dubois
Kaycee
★ Boise
Nampa
Jackson
Crowheart
Idaho Falls
Riverton
Filer
Pocatello
Casper
Douglas
Grace
Klamath Falls
Burley
Preston
Wyoming
Cedarville
Tremonton
Ogden
Logan
Rock Springs
Laramie
Winnemucca
Coalville
Evanston
Cheyenne ★
West Jordan
Park City
Steamboat
Fort Collins
Elko
Salt Lake City
Oakley
Springs
Estes
Greeley
Lehi
Heber City
Hayden
Park
Nevada
Pleasant Grove
Vernal
Eagle
Denver
Spanish Fork
Evergreen
Truckee
Reno
Nephi
Grand
Loveland
★ Carson City
Price
Junction
Castle Rock
Delta
Delta
Colorado
Utah
Moab
Colorado
Springs
Panguitch
Gunnison
Canon
Telluride
City
Pueblo
Cortez
Monte
St.
Durango
Vista
George
Farmington
Bishop
Logandale
Pahrump
Las Vegas
Santa Fe
Ridgecrest
Laughlin
Tehachipi
California
Window Rock
Albuquerque
Barstow
Kingman
Flagstaff
Lancaster
Bullhead City
New
Banning
Twentynine
Mexico
Palms
Prescott
Payson
Yucca Valley
Cave Creek
Indio
Globe
Alamogordo
Phoenix
Brawley
Scottsdale
Arizona
Safford
Yuma
Willcox
Silver City
Tucson
El Paso
Tombstone
Texas

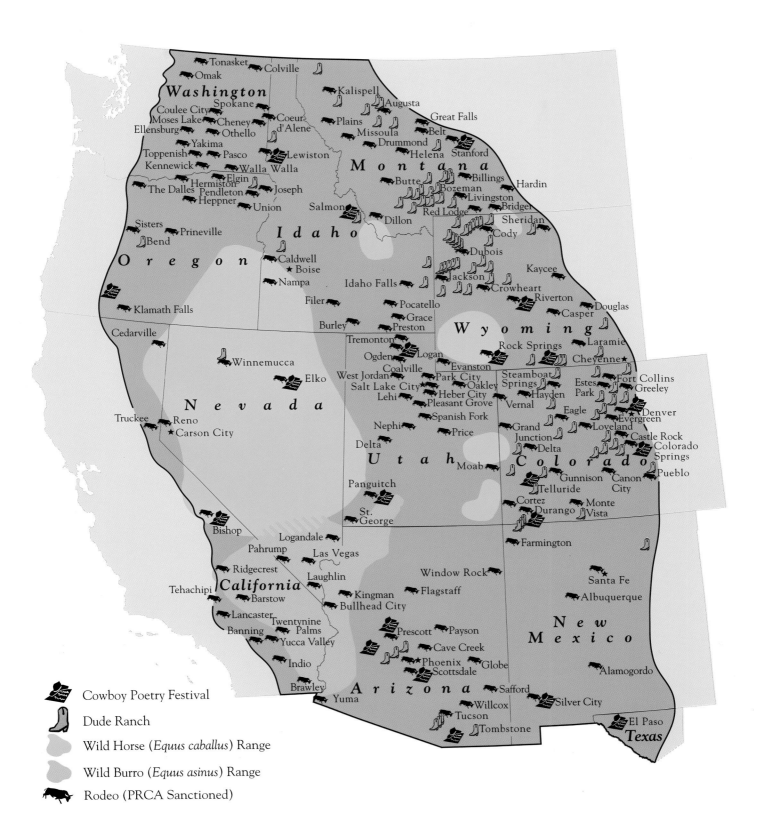 Cowboy Poetry Festival

Dude Ranch

Wild Horse (*Equus caballus*) Range

Wild Burro (*Equus asinus*) Range

Rodeo (PRCA Sanctioned)

new gambling towns find that the economic boost is not all it's cracked up to be: yes, locals get jobs and the town gets more sales tax, but the control comes from the outside, and most of the money leaves town. The towns and the reservations that invite in casinos lose the fabric of local community.[3]

Dude ranching is also booming in the 1990s, hitting another heyday like the boom of the 1920s. Back then the typical dude was an Easterner whose name appeared on the social register; today dude ranching appeals to a more eclectic, but still urbane, crowd, portrayed by Billy Crystal and his sidekicks in the movie *City Slickers*. Many dude ranches are pure tourist operations: meet the van at 8:00, saddle up and move some cattle around, and finish with an authentic chuck-wagon lunch. Some offer special week-long programs for gay and lesbian greenhorns. But others are working ranches that invite city slickers to try their hand at the real thing. At the Three Quarter Circle ranch near Lander, Wyoming, "guests get to participate and do things the ranch cowboys do in their everyday life"; the ranch "places emphasis on beef production instead of swimming pools and golf courses." Guests are also warned that "living on a ranch can be risky and dangerous . . . the weather can drastically change, trails may not be maintained, horses are unpredictable, and travel conditions are rough, dangerous, and tiring . . . many miles from . . . help and medical attention." Ranches naturally endowed with trout water now also make side-money by renting their private riversides to fly fishers tired of crowded public fishing—at the going rate of roughly $50 a day per fishing rod.

New Westerners leery of actually getting on a horse are happy to watch others not only get on, but also be unceremoniously thrown off. Rodeo, according to proponents, is the only major sport derived from skills of the workplace: bronc riding, steer wrestling, and calf roping. Bull riding, the sport's most popular and dangerous event, was invented to liven it up, and women's barrel racing is appended unofficially to degenderize this all-male sport. Rodeo is also a big, rapidly growing business in the West. Rodeos sanctioned by the Professional Rodeo Cowboys Association (PRCA)—the largest rodeo organization—increased from 509 in 1960 to 754 in 1990, with total attendance over 22 million.[4] Thirteen million viewers watched the 1995 Wrangler World of Rodeo series on ESPN, and corporate sponsors like Coca-Cola and Dodge add millions

They Eat Horses, Don't They

Some of the wild horses rounded up from the Western range and adopted for a $125 fee wind up on the menu of European restaurants. The Bureau of Land Management's 25-year-old adoption program has gathered over 160 thousand horses; according to a 1996 Associated Press investigation each costs the government an average of $1,100 to round up, vaccinate, and place with adopting owners. After a year the new owners are allowed to do as they please with the horses, and 90 percent of them are sold to slaughterhouses for around $700 each. According to one meat processor, a select few horses get special treatment: "killed on Friday, processed Monday, and Thursday we load the truck, and then it's flown to Europe. Monday it's sold in Belgium, Tuesday eaten."

to rodeo purses. Big money can be made by rodeo competitors, most of whom are not working cowboys and learned the sport in college or rodeo school. Total purses on the PRCA circuit range from $10,000 at the small-town events to $100,000 at semifinals in Pendleton, Oregon, and $150,000 at the Cheyenne, Wyoming, Frontier Days Rodeo (the "Grandaddy of them All"). Las Vegas's national finals outbids them all with a $3 million-plus purse. Smaller prizes but similar action mark the Black Cowboy Rodeo circuit and the International Gay Rodeo Association's events around the West.

Cowboys aren't the only Old West group to capture modish imaginations. An industry has grown up around American fascination with the mountain man, like Jedediah Smith, who scoured the Rocky Mountains in search of furs during the mid-nineteenth century. The original trappers spent long months trampling the backcountry, and then gathered in rendezvous for resupplying, companionship, and trading. The rendezvous system died out in 1840, the beaver trapped out. History buffs now reenact the gatherings in exacting detail. Twentieth century buckskinners wear clothing made of leather they tanned themselves. They practice shooting muzzle-loading rifles, knife throwing, wilderness survival, and other early American skills. Strict rules require period dress, and vehicles and other stuff of modernity are prohibited in the encampment.[5]

Modern day "mountain men" populate the New West, but they have shucked off the buckskin and moccasins for Lycra, GoreTex, and Vibram soles. They hike, climb, bike, fish, and kayak the nation's outdoor playground.

America's New West Playground

In 1858, Lieutenant Joseph C. Ives, topographical engineer, stood on the rim of Grand Canyon after the first scientific survey of the area and remarked:

Boaters in the Grand Canyon

Boaters in the Grand Canyon look to Major John Wesley Powell as the grandfather of all whitewater enthusiasts. In 1869 he set off with nine men in four river dories to explore the depths of the Grand Canyon of the Colorado River. Three months later, in the heart of the Grand Canyon and less one boat and low on supplies, three of the crew, dreading the next rapid, decided to leave the canyon—at a point now called Separation Rapids. Those three were killed by Indians, while the main party made it safely to a Mormon outpost a few days later. Today's river runners dream of being allowed in to the hallowed, now oft-travelled, canyon. The average wait for a private permit to run the Grand Canyon is now about ten years. If you want to go with a commercial guide, dozens of companies will eagerly take your money (a couple of thousand dollars per person), and convey you down the river in safe rafts, feeding you gourmet dinners and wine at each riverside camp. Over 23,400 folks floated in the "footsteps" of Powell during 1996.

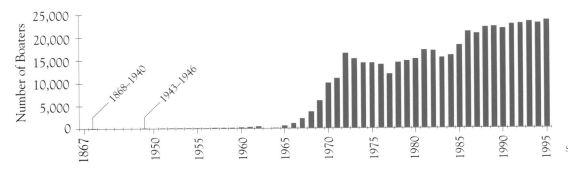

Source: National Park Service

America's Playground

Glacier Peak
Leavenworth
Kelly Creek
Blackfoot
Missouri
Atlas Boundary
Washington
Mt. Adams
Lochsa
Clark Fork
Big Hole
Madison
Gallitan
Yellowstone
Bighorn
Mt. Hood
Deschutes
Hells Canyon
Selway
Snake
Middle Fork
Granite Peak
Metolius
Smith Rock
Payette
Salmon
Borah Peak
Henry's Fork
Grand Teton
Shoshone National Forest
Oregon
South Fork Boise
Silver Creek
S. Fork
Snake
Dubois
Owyhee County
Idaho
Lander
LaBarge
Shoshone National Forest
City of Rocks
Green
Wyoming
McCloud
Flaming Gorge
North Platte
Vedauwoo
American ForkCanyon
Yampa
Lumpy Ridge
Longs Peak
Nevada
Gates of Lodore
Colorado
Eldorado Canyon
East Fork, Carson
Green
Fryingpan
Roaring Fork
South Platte
Torreys Peak
Grays Peak
Lover's Leap
Desolation and Gray Canyons
Utah
Westwater Canyon
Moab
Mt. Elbert
Wheeler Peak
Gunnison
Upper Arkansas
Mammoth Mtn.
Canyonlands
Colorado
Owens River Gorge
Cataract Canyon
Ouray
Crested Butte
Mt. Whitney
Durango
Death Valley
National Park
San Juan
Animas
San Juan
Wheeler Peak
Box Canyon
Red Rocks
Lee's Ferry
Grand Canyon
California
Humphreys Peak
New Mexico
Granite Mountain
Sedona
Joshua Tree
Salt
Mt. Lemmon
Arizona
Hueco Tanks
Texas

Peak Bagging
Four-Wheel Drive
Mountain Biking
Rock Climbing
Fly-Fishing
Whitewater
Whitewater and Fly-Fishing

The region last explored is, of course, altogether valueless. Ours has been the first and will undoubtedly be the last, party of whites to visit the locality. It seems intended by nature that the Colorado River, along the greater portion of its lonely and majestic way, shall be forever unvisited and undisturbed.[6]

If Ives were around today, he'd be surprised to find himself at the bottom of a ten-year waiting list for a permit to float the Grand Canyon. Fifteen thousand white-water adventure seekers set out each year from Lee's Ferry, Arizona, at the regulated rate of 150 commercial passengers and one private party a day. From there, they bob down the seemingly wild waves of the highly controlled Colorado River. Without the strict permitting system, river traffic would be jammed up raft-to-raft. Indeed, it was the crowds, the trash, the competition for beach camping, the looting of archaeological sites that led to a stringent river management plan in the 1970s.[7] Today one can float the Grand Canyon and still feel relatively alone and adventurous, even if your guide frets about getting to a good campsite ahead of other commercial companies and wonders how the latest water release from Glen Canyon Dam—producing electricity for air conditioners in Phoenix—might affect the size of an upcoming rapid.

Overcrowding, strict rules, and conflict among recreationists and between recreationists and other land users dog the New West playground. At Vedauwoo, a well-known climbing area near Laramie, Wyoming, rock jocks wait in line half an hour for popular routes. Brown's Canyon on Colorado's Arkansas River, the nation's most commercially boated stretch of whitewater, is a nonstop parade of rafts carrying their screaming cargos down the river every summer's day, at least until the Bureau of Reclamation turns the water off on August 15. No backcountry experience here. If you want to camp in Yellowstone during July and August, make your reservations months in advance. Even so, fantastic recreational experiences can still be had in the West—as long as you keep up with the latest *Outside* magazine list of the best, most secret, most remote places for solitude.

Over 200 people set out each summer day in the Sierra Nevada to trudge the 101 switchbacks to the top of 14,494-foot Mount Whitney—the highest peak in the lower 48. In Moab, over 120,000 mountain bikers ride the same, well-worn Slickrock Trail each year. These are pilgrimages, to the meccas of a civil religion sweeping America: experiencing the wonders of nature through hiking, boating, skiing, biking, or climbing. The pilgrims often report near mystical experiences: crossing over to the other world, finding themselves, reprioritizing their life.

America's Playground

Dotted with outdoor recreational meccas, from world-class trout streams like Idaho's Henry's Fork to top-ranked rock climbing areas like California's Joshua Tree National Monument, the New West lures sports enthusiasts of all sorts in large numbers. We highlight only a few outdoor meccas—the blank spaces, mostly public lands (shown earlier) attract millions of visitors: Yellowstone National Park alone sees over 3 million visitors annually and the Western national forests attract millions of campers, hikers, fishers, ORV'ers, and hunters every year. Tourists bring with them (or purchase locally) all kinds of equipment—from climbing ropes to jet skis, take home memories, photographs, aching muscles, and increased self-confidence, while leaving behind more than a little money. Most Interior West states now reckon recreation and tourism as the first or second largest part of their economies.

Yellowstone Visitors

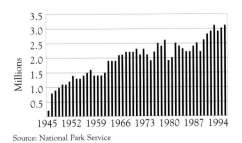

Source: National Park Service

Backpackers in Canyonlands

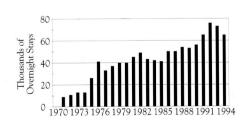

What is so cathartic about bushwhacking into seldom-seen places and not showering for days on end? Life for most Americans has become so mechanized, predictable, comfortable, and safe, that a person could go downright crazy. Exposure to danger, dirt, and larger-than-life scenery makes us feel more alive, and connects us to the simple things, like how to boil water, and where to pee far from a toilet. As the ever philosophical Doc Sarvis observes in Edward Abbey's *The Monkey Wrench Gang*,

> The reason there are so many people on the river these days is because there are too many people everywhere else. . . . The wilderness once offered men a plausible way of life. Now it functions as a psychiatric refuge. Soon there will be no wilderness. Soon there will be no place to go. Then the madness becomes universal.[8]

No doubt about it, though, recreational meccas are more plentiful in the West, with its wide open spaces, abundance of wild mountains and rivers, and plenitude of federal land. Those who can't afford land of their own take comfort in knowing that the Western parks and forests are just as much theirs as anyone's. As Wallace Stegner once wrote, "We simply need that wild country available to us, even if we never do more than drive to its edge and look in. For it can be a

Paying to Play

The recreational elite flock to the New West's costlier playgrounds: elite golf courses, backcountry ski huts, alpine ski resorts, and heli-skiing areas. A day with the family on the slopes at Vail can run $400–$500 all told for, say, four lift passes, rentals, lodging, food and, of course, parking. A heli-skiing day runs the same just for the air lift. The latest recreational craze is actually an indoor sport: climbing gyms, with walls made up to simulate famous routes across the West, now attract paying customers who prefer their sport out of the weather.

Big Western Drops

The West's exaggerated terrain makes for tall ski mountains and the greatest altitude drop from top to base in American skiing. In fact, the ski areas compete for "vertical footage." Big Sky added a tram up Lone Peak in 1996, giving it 41 feet over Jackson Hole. But, according to Powder magazine, Jackson Hole's 4,139-foot descent can be skied in one continuous swoop while skiing Big Sky's total vertical requires a lift ride part of the way down to access another run. We keep Jackson Hole on top; you choose.

Ski Area	Vertical Drop (feet)	Longest Run (miles)
1. Jackson Hole, Wyo.	4,139 (continuous)	7.0
2. Big Sky, Mont.	4,180 (with a lift ride)	3.0
3. Beaver Creek, Colo.	4,040	3.5
4. Steamboat, Colo.	3,668	3.0
5. Aspen Highlands, Colo.	3,635	3.5
6. Snowmass, Colo.	3,612	4.1
7. Heavenly Valley, Tahoe, Calif.	3,500	5.5
8. Sun Valley, Idaho	3,400	3.0
9. Breckenridge, Colo.	3,398	
10. Vail, Colo.	3,330	4.5
Also Ran's: The 3,000 foot plus club:		
Aspen Mountain, Colo.	3,267	3.0
Snowbird, Utah	3,240	
Telluride, Colo.	3,165	2.8
Killington, Vt.	3,100	10.2
Mt. Bachelor, Wash.	3,100	2.0
Park City, Utah	3,100	3.5
Crystal Mountain, Wash.	3,102	3.5
Winter Park, Colo.	3,060	4.5
Mammoth Mountain, Calif.	3,100	2.5

Sources: Ski area literature and World Wide Web pages; *Powder: The Skier's Magazine*

Paying to Play

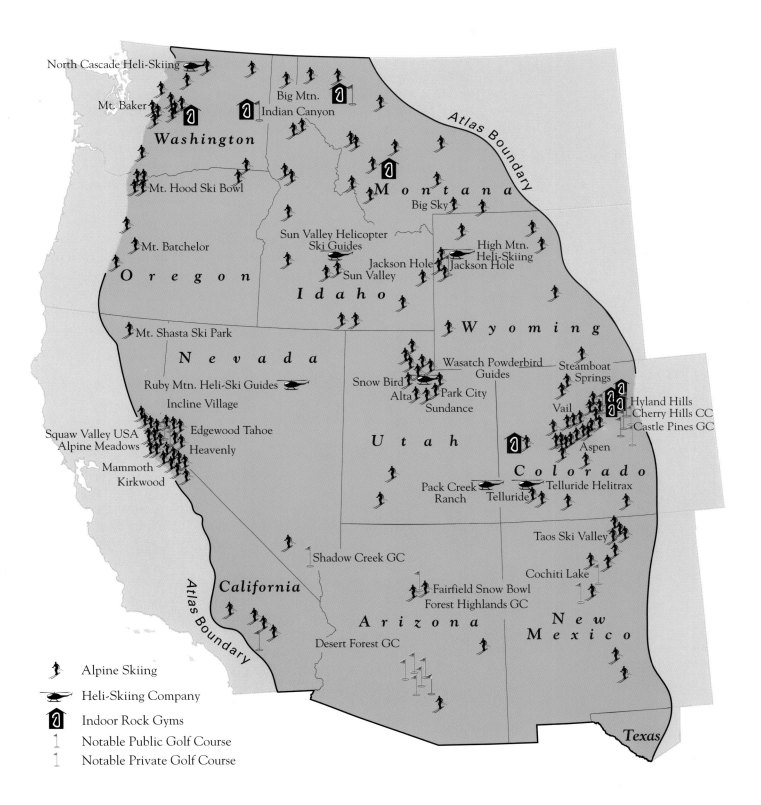

North Cascade Heli-Skiing

Mt. Baker

Washington

Indian Canyon

Big Mtn.

M o n t a n a

Big Sky

Mt. Hood Ski Bowl

Mt. Batchelor

O r e g o n

I d a h o

Sun Valley Helicopter Ski Guides

Jackson Hole

Sun Valley

High Mtn. Heli-Skiing
Jackson Hole

W y o m i n g

Mt. Shasta Ski Park

N e v a d a

Ruby Mtn. Heli-Ski Guides

Incline Village

Wasatch Powderbird Guides

Steamboat Springs

Snow Bird

Alta

Park City

Sundance

Vail

Hyland Hills
Cherry Hills CC
Castle Pines GC

Squaw Valley USA
Alpine Meadows

Edgewood Tahoe

Heavenly

U t a h

Aspen

Mammoth

Kirkwood

C o l o r a d o

Pack Creek Ranch

Telluride

Telluride Helitrax

Taos Ski Valley

Shadow Creek GC

California

Cochiti Lake

Fairfield Snow Bowl
Forest Highlands GC

A r i z o n a

N e w
M e x i c o

Desert Forest GC

Texas

Atlas Boundary

Atlas Boundary

Alpine Skiing

Heli-Skiing Company

Indoor Rock Gyms

Notable Public Golf Course

Notable Private Golf Course

means of reassuring ourselves of our sanity as creatures, a part of the geography of hope."[9]

The West's role as playground has its roots primarily in hunting, fishing, and mountaineering. Theodore Roosevelt hunted mountain lions in Colorado's North Park; John Muir, David Brower, and Royal Robbins bagged peaks in the Sierra; and Norman MacLean mythologized Montana fly-fishing in *A River Runs Through It*. Outdoor recreation is a full-blown industry now. The West's fastest growing counties lie next to wilderness areas and other public lands. Recreation and tourism comprise the second biggest share of western state economies (after agriculture), making up for lagging energy or beef income.

Is this new industry and economy really all it's cracked up to be? Strip-mining and clear-cutting leave sharper scars, but the recreation industry has brought with it a slew of social and ecological impacts. Alpine ski areas cut swaths through the national forests. Snowmaking—gotta keep those skiers happy—dewaters streams and threatens aquatic species, as do the irrigation and chemicals required for golf links. Snowmobiling, a noisy and air-polluting sport, is expanding rapidly, even in some national parks. In the Mojave Desert, off-road vehicle enthusiasts have reduced the desert tortoise population, putting it on the Endangered Species Act, and kangaroo rats, whose large ears are adapted to desert silence, are literally deafened by muffler-less vehicles.

Climbers trying to "bag" all of Colorado's "fourteeners"—the 54 mountains over 14,000 feet—have wrecked the peaks' delicate ecosystems. The Colorado Mountain Club has mounted a big new campaign to educate the tens of thousands of people who climb these fourteeners every year.[10] The message: go climb a less-used peak.

The playground West also sometimes pits old ways and new: ranchers and mountain bikers must share public lands; climbers and Native Americans have different ideas about proper behavior in some of the West's most spectacular "sacred" places. In many cases the parties work conflicts out among themselves: in Crested Butte, Colorado, self-proclaimed mountain biking capital, ranchers and bikers coauthored a brochure telling bicyclists how to behave around cows, and to leave every gate as they found it, open or closed.

Another peaceable truce was struck at Shiprock, a spectacular rock formation on the Navajo Reservation in New Mexico. Shiprock, long a climbing mecca, is listed in Steck and Roper's *Fifty Classic Climbs of North America* (often referred to as "Fifty Crowded Climbs"). But the climbers' ropes, calls of "OFF—BELAY!" and camping sites mar Shiprock's spiritual value to Navajos. The tribe asked that no one climb there without explicit permission to avoid conflict with tribal ceremonies, a request that the climbing community has largely respected.

Yampa River, Colorado   Robb

Flat Tops, Colorado   Abbott

Wind River Range, Wyoming   Robb

At Devil's Tower National Monument in Wyoming, however, it is war. The lava tower is sacred to the Lakota Sioux, and Indians and rock climbers have shared it uneasily for years, finally taking their issues to court in 1996. The National Park Service tried to accommodate the spiritual needs of the tribes by closing the Monument to commercial rock climbing during June, when the Tower is most used for rituals. A local climbing guide sued, and the Mountain States Legal Foundation, which often represents extractive industries and commercial interests against the government, joined the suit to protest what they called a First Amendment violation. Many in the climbing community abhor this aggressive stand; a voluntary closure of the Tower to climbing during June 1995 decreased use by 83 percent. Still, prayer bundles began to disappear from the park, and signs reminding visitors to respect Native American rituals were vandalized. The court ruled in favor of the climbers—sport won out over religion.[11]

The growing use of nature in the West makes for interesting social dynamics, not just between oldtimers and newcomers, but also amongst recreationists themselves. Kayakers and fly-fishermen compete for eddies, and argue over dam management policies. Mountain bikers and ORV'ers vie for control of public land, especially in the red rock country around Moab. When two different user groups consider the same town the epicenter of their sport, conflict is inevitable. In 1993, at Sand Flats east of Moab, an area of spectacular sandstone outcrops seemingly created just for mountain bikers and jeepers, too many of both showed up on the same weekend and the local police had to separate them.

Places Rated, Places Raided

The "places rated" industry got going in the 1970s, when some geographers and demographers figured out that people want to hear how cities rank against one another in jobs, climate, crime, house prices, and recreation. The first *Places Rated Almanac*[12] was a big hit. Now dozens of lists appear each year, rating the best places for outdoor sports, the best small towns for job prospects, the most liveable big and small cities, and the best retirement places.

No one knows if showing well in a places-rated list actually entices new residents; in all likelihood good ratings in *Money* magazine or *The Places Rated Almanac* little affect the cities. High ratings for small towns in terms of art, culture, or outdoor sports probably lag their "discovery" by people searching out refuges, rather than revealing undiscovered gems. Yet, each list evokes lament of locals who already know they live in a great place and don't want hordes of newcomers. Sometimes the ratings do wake up a "sleeper" town. *Money*'s list of the best small towns for job opportunities and lifestyle is probably the best at finding small-towns ready for growth. It recognizes the postindustrial economy, and hon-

Fraser, Colorado   Riebsame

Green River, Utah   Riebsame

Estes Park, Colorado   Robb

Places Rated, Places Raided

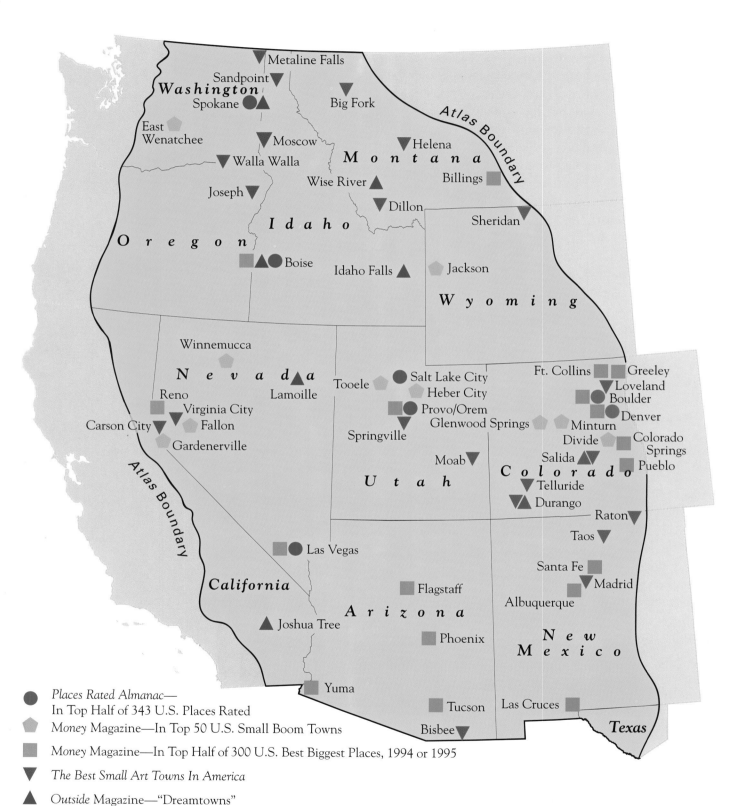

Metaline Falls

Sandpoint

Washington

Spokane

East
Wenatchee

Big Fork

Moscow

Helena

M o n t a n a

Walla Walla

Wise River

Billings

Joseph

Dillon

Sheridan

I d a h o

O r e g o n

Boise

Idaho Falls

Jackson

W y o m i n g

Winnemucca

N e v a d a

Reno

Lamoille

Tooele

Salt Lake City

Heber City

Ft. Collins

Greeley

Loveland
Boulder

Virginia City

Provo/Orem

Denver

Fallon

Glenwood Springs

Minturn

Carson City

Springville

Divide

Colorado
Springs

Gardenerville

Salida

Moab

C o l o r a d o

Pueblo

U t a h

Telluride

Las Vegas

Durango

Raton

California

Taos

Santa Fe

Flagstaff

Madrid

A r i z o n a

Albuquerque

Joshua Tree

N e w
M e x i c o

Phoenix

Yuma

Las Cruces

Tucson

Bisbee

Texas

● *Places Rated Almanac—*
In Top Half of 343 U.S. Places Rated

⬠ *Money Magazine—*In Top 50 U.S. Small Boom Towns

◼ *Money Magazine—*In Top Half of 300 U.S. Best Biggest Places, 1994 or 1995

▼ *The Best Small Art Towns In America*

▲ *Outside Magazine—*"Dreamtowns"

estly evaluates small-town problems, like lack of cultural diversity. In the West, it revealed great little places that only a few folks knew about: Divide, Colorado, near the new gambling halls of Cripple Creek; Grantsville, Utah, a bedroom town one mountain range west of Salt Lake City (perhaps a bit too close to Tooele's chemical weapons depot for some tastes, however); and Fallon, Nevada, a military town riding Reno's boom.

Some rankings might mislead trusting migrants. *Outside* magazine lists Lamoille, Nevada, as a hot new place to live, presumably because of its location amidst the recreation-rich and virtually deserted Great Basin. True, helicopter skiing is offered in the nearby Ruby Mountains, but what does an urban transplant do when the snow's no good? The nearest *New York Times* is in Salt Lake City, 250 miles away; bagels are rare in Nevada too, but you can get them in Reno, Las Vegas, Carson City, and Lake Tahoe. Not in Lamoille, though. Metaline Falls, Washington, is listed in *The 100 Best Small Art Towns in America*, but as the author points out, "the closest place to get a pastrami sandwich" is in Nelson, British Columbia, an hour north, or in Spokane, 90 minutes south.[13] A lot of people don't care about such amenity gaps, but those who do beware.

Places Rated, Places Raided

The top-ranked Western towns, according to the Places Rated Almanac, Outside magazine, Money magazine, and The 100 Best Small Art Towns in America, include obvious places like Sante Fe, New Mexico, and Jackson, Wyoming. Many less known spots show up, and Money warns readers to look before they leap into one of its top small boom towns, which include such out-of-the-way places as Winnemucca, Nevada, and Heber City, Utah, and The 100 Best Small Art Towns in America notes that some of its picks lack urban amenities. Outside magazine is less circumspect, touting recreational nirvanas like Lamoille, Nevada, Wise River, Montana, and Joshua Tree, California—after all, what more does one need than good skiing, a trout stream, and rocks to climb?

Rating Places

Rankings of Interior West towns in the *Places Rated Almanac*

Salt Lake City, Utah	8	
Denver, Colo.	32	
Spokane, Wash.	47	
Boise, Idaho	59	Top Half of 343 U.S. Places
Boulder, Colo.	142	
Las Vegas, Nev.	144	
Provo, Utah	172	
Reno, Nev.	180	
Fort Collins, Colo.	183	
Colorado Springs, Colo.	191	
Santa Fe, N.Mex.	204	
Richland, Wash.	205	
Billings, Mont.	220	Bottom half of 343 U.S. Places
Great Falls, Mont.	229	
Las Cruces, N. Mex.	241	
Cheyenne, Wyo.	274	
Yuma, Ariz.	297	
Casper, Wyo.	323	

Of the eighteen Interior West places rated, only seven are in the top half of the 343 U.S. places ranked. Western towns often received lower ranks due to high house prices and climate extremes.

Chapter 6: The Ugly West

In "The Clan of the One-Breasted Women," epilogue to her book *Refuge*, Utah writer Terry Tempest Williams recalls telling her Dad about a childhood dream, a recurrent image of a flash of bright light in the desert. Their conversation occurs about a year after her mother died of breast cancer, the ninth woman among Williams' parents, aunts, and grandparents to contract the disease. His reply:

> "You did see it," he said.
> "See what?"
> "The bomb. The cloud. We were driving home from Riverside, California. You were sitting on Diane's lap. She was pregnant. In fact, I remember the day, September 7, 1957. We had just gotten out of the Service. We were driving north, past Las Vegas. It was an hour or so before dawn, when this explosion went off. We not only heard it, but felt it. I thought the oil tanker in front of us had blown up. We pulled over and suddenly, rising from the desert floor, we saw it, clearly, this golden-stemmed cloud, the mushroom. The sky seemed to vibrate with an eerie pink glow. Within a few minutes, a light ash was raining on the car."[1]

The ugly West was built on mostly good intentions but also inconsistent policies: Invent and test nuclear weapons in the vast West to win the war and stave off the fascists and then the communists. Make "clean" electricity with the atom then bury nuclear waste in a Western hole in the ground far removed from most Americans. Exterminate wolves so that cows and sheep can graze safely. Protect forests from wildfire so that they can be clear-cut. Build tourist roads and parking lots so visitors can gaze into the Grand Canyon. Advertise trout fishing to lure tourists to your state, then give permits to gold mines likely to foul mountain streams. Americans get national security, jobs, affordable housing, good roads, and cheap water. They give up uncontaminated soil, clear views, some part of their health, and spotted owls, salmon, and a host of other species. Western development is a devil's bargain, and, by some accounts, the devil got the better deal.

The Nuclear West

The human affair with radioactive elements comes full circle in the West: uranium is dug out of the ground, milled into high-grade ore, exploded in cataclysmic atomic blasts, used in nuclear power plants, and eventually put back into the ground as waste—including the waste from plants all over the country. Fissile material has leaked out of this cycle, contaminating land and water. Above-ground nuclear bomb tests in Nevada rained radioactive plumes down on villages of southern Utah in the 1950s, and rivulets of contaminated groundwater still seep from bomb factories and mill tailings. Hot spots in the nuclear West include the Hanford Nuclear Reservation in eastern Washington, the Idaho National Engineering Laboratory, the nuclear bomb trigger factory at Rocky Flats just west of Denver, Frenchman Flat in Nevada, where most of the bombs were exploded, and planned dumps for nuclear waste near Carlsbad, New Mexico, and under Nevada's Yucca Mountain. The mining and milling of uranium in fact already gave the West a contaminated landscape as well as busted atomic cities. As information leaked out of a tight-lipped Atomic Energy Commission, and later the U.S. Department of Energy acknowledged the mess, citizens demanded nuclear clean-up. Radioactive material was used in the sidewalks of Grand Junction, Colorado. An open pile of uranium tailings sat uncovered in a Salt Lake City suburb for decades. The clean-up began slowly in the 1970s and gained momentum after the Cold War ended.

Other parts of the country got nuked too, and every nuclear power plant in the U.S. stores high-level waste on site, awaiting the Nevada dump. But many Westerners truly live in a radioactive landscape. More uranium, radium, and vanadium was mined from the spectacular geology of the Colorado Plateau around Moab, Utah, than anywhere else in the country. The boom started in 1952, as the federal government—the only buyer—geared up for the cold war. Raye Ringholz, in *Uranium Frenzy: Boom and Bust on the Colorado Plateau*, says that literally thousands of small mines popped up: "Real estate salesmen, school-teachers, hashslingers, and lawyers competed with trained mining engineers on a near-insane quest to discover uranium in the redrock deserts of the Colorado Plateau."[2] Some prospectors got rich and a lot more miners and uranium mill workers got radiation sickness. Only a few really big mines evolved, like diggings on the Navajo Indian Reservation in northern Arizona. Uranium mining there and elsewhere, originally valued for the jobs, eventually degenerated into claims of worker illness and environmental injustice.

Some residents of New Mexico, Nevada, and Utah are the only American civilian eyewitnesses to exploding atomic bombs. They watched the clouds of fallout streak toward them. Parts of western Colorado, northern New Mexico, and northern Nevada were chosen to demonstrate "peaceful" uses of A-bombs in the 1960s. Two underground explosions in Colorado were meant to extract natural gas (which would be radioactive); other A-bombs were exploded to test their efficacy as engineering tools for building harbors or moving mountains; near Fallon, Nevada, a bomb was exploded to see whether we could verify other countries' claims that they were *not* testing bombs. Efforts to prove that all this bombing—and the whole nuclear industry—hurt people's health have been unsuccessful. Former Secretary of the Interior Stewart Udall brought suit against mining companies and the government on behalf of sick miners. He also argued the landmark "downwinders" case for people exposed to fallout from above-

Rest in Nuclear Peace

The country's two permanent depositories for the most dangerous radioactive wastes are in New Mexico and Nevada.

New Mexico's Waste Isolation Pilot Plant is slated for tons of "transuranic" wastes, especially plutonium-contaminated clothes and tools used by nuclear bomb workers. Hundreds of storage rooms have been carved out of a salt deposit 2,100 feet below the surface near Carlsbad Caverns. Collection of waste from all over the country should start in 1998; the material must be securely stored for 10,000 years.

Nevada's Yucca Mountain is slated for the high-level waste repository. Years behind schedule, the underground facility should start receiving waste in 2010, mostly uranium fuel rods from commercial nuclear power plants, some 20,000 of which now sit in ponds at the plants scattered across the country. By one estimate, the facility's 70,000-ton capacity will be exceeded a decade after it opens. The material must be sequestered for at least 30,000 years.

A Nuked Landscape

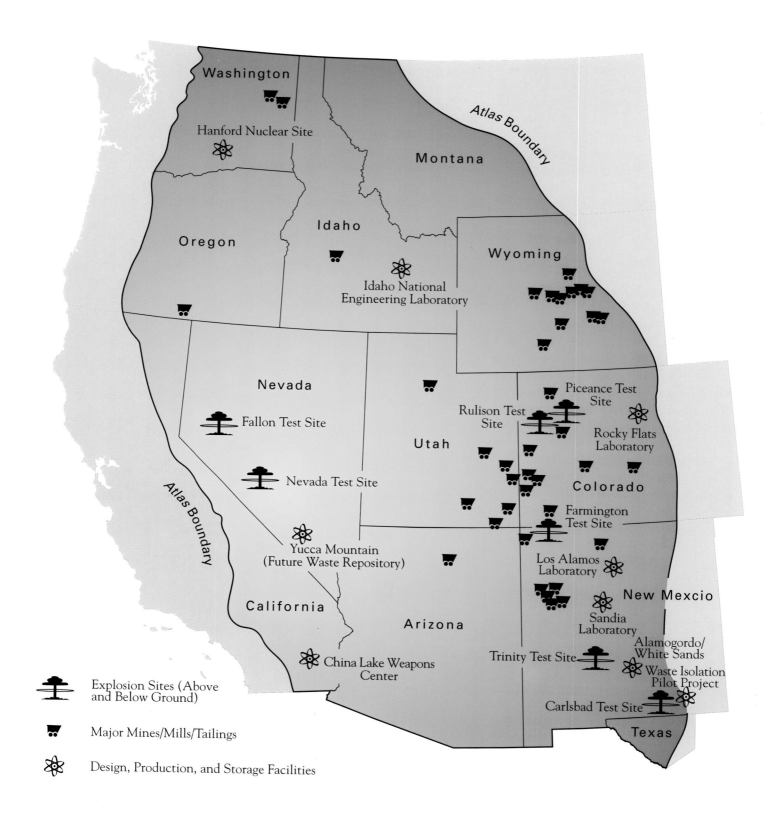

Washington

Hanford Nuclear Site

Montana

Atlas Boundary

Oregon

Idaho

Wyoming

Idaho National
Engineering Laboratory

Nevada

Piceance Test
Site

Fallon Test Site

Rulison Test
Site

Rocky Flats
Laboratory

Utah

Nevada Test Site

Colorado

Farmington
Test Site

Atlas Boundary

Yucca Mountain
(Future Waste Repository)

Los Alamos
Laboratory

California

Arizona

New Mexcio

Sandia
Laboratory

China Lake Weapons
Center

Trinity Test Site

Alamogordo/
White Sands

Waste Isolation
Pilot Project

Carlsbad Test Site

Texas

Explosion Sites (Above
and Below Ground)

Major Mines/Mills/Tailings

Design, Production, and Storage Facilities

ground tests in the 1950s. They all lost.

The West is littered with busted nuclear places: Jeffrey City, Wyoming; Uravan, Colorado; and Atomic City, Idaho. Towns near some nuke facilities are booming—Richland, Washington; Las Vegas, Nevada; and Denver, Colorado— and that's a new problem: more people near these once-isolated places means greater demand to have the stuff moved somewhere else. But engineers worry: carting radioactive material around might be worse than leaving it in place. Can the sites ever be made safe, and whose backyard should get the stuff if it is relocated?

Spectacles of the Ugly West

Compared to the nation's industrial heartland in the Northeast and Midwest, the West is less polluted with toxic material. Yet, it harbors more detritus of industrial civilization in its wide spaces than many visitors, and more than a few residents, might imagine. The county's largest superfund clean-up site is in Butte, Montana, home to big silver and copper digs spewing some of the pollution that hurt fish on the Big Blackfoot River, setting for Norman Maclean's *A River Runs Through It*. The 1996 list of EPA's superfund national priority sites (a small subset of all the seriously polluted places in the country) shows that both Old West (copper and gold mining, railroad tie treating) and New West (chemical manufacturing and missile building) enterprises leave a noxious legacy on the land. Spokane, Washington, touted as a top place to live and a preferred retirement community, has more current superfund sites than any other western town.

Toxic material inevitably results from many industrial processes; the biggest releases come from mining and smelting plants which extract small quantities of valuable mineral from huge amounts of ore. The latest big superfund clean-up in the West is a spanking new gold mine at Summitville, Colorado, on the Alamosa River. This heap-leach mine, where arsenic is seeped through piles of ore to extract minute quantities of gold, made money for a Canadian mining firm until the pollution became too big a liability and its American subsidiary company filed for bankruptcy. The federal government was left to clean up thousands of gallons of polluted

A Nuked Landscape

The atomic age started here in the 1940s and boomed during the Cold War, creating a landscape nuked by the atomic research labs (Alamogordo, Sandia, and Los Alamos, New Mexico; Hanford, Washington; and the Idaho National Engineering Lab), bomb factories (Rocky Flats, Colorado), A-bomb detonations (Nevada Test Site and Trinity Site in New Mexico), and "peaceful" underground bomb tests (Piceance and Rulison, Colorado; Fallon, Nevada; and Farmington, New Mexico). Add to this the dozens of mines and mills and busted uranium towns and the nation's nuclear waste dumps at Nevada's Yucca Mountain and New Mexico's Waste Isolation Pilot Plant near Carlsbad Caverns, proposed final resting spots of the country's hottest radioactive dregs. Unless nuclear power gains better public acceptance, the nuclear future of the West looks to be one of clean-up and long-term watchfulness; atomic leftovers remain potent contaminants for thousands of years.

The Biggest Toxic Releases in the West
(1994)

Corporation	Pounds of toxic material
Magnesium Corporation of America Rowley, Utah	55.8 million
ASARCO, Inc. East Helena, Mont.	43.6 million
Coastal Chemical, Inc. Cheyenne, Wyo.	21.5 million
ASARCO, Inc. Hayden, Ariz.	17.9 million
Kennecott Utah Copper Magna, Utah	9.7 million
Phelps Dodge Hildalgo, Inc. Playas, N.Mex.	9.6 million
Cyprus Miami Mining Corp. Claypool, Ariz.	7.8 million
Chino Mines Hurley, N.Mex.	7.4 million
Louisiana-Pacific Corporation Samoa, Calif.	4.1 million

Source: U.S. Environmental Protection Agency, Toxic Releases Inventory, 1994

water leaking into the Alamosa River, killing the trout and almost everything else for seven miles downriver. This modern story continues the long saga of mining waste and leaks that pollute thousands of streams in the West.

Mines around Leadville, Colorado, acidify the Upper Arkansas River. Few fish can live now in what should be trophy trout water. The fisher, working downstream, finally finds trout where the pollutants are well-diluted; stunted fish at first; then, further downstream, with the grace of a few more clean tributaries adding fresh water, some sizeable Browns.

Dead, dying, and recovering trout streams mark the West: the Upper Eagle above Vail, Colorado; the Yankee Fork of the Salmon and South Fork of the Coeur d' Alene in Idaho; and the Clark's Fork of the Yellowstone below Butte, Montana. Some rivers are recovering from too many years of a cocktail of acid mine drainage and heavy metals: Panther Creek near Salmon, Idaho, is coming back and the Big Blackfoot is certainly the most famous recovering trout stream in the West. When Robert Redford's film of Maclean's novella, *A River Runs Through It*, premiered in New York City, he donated the proceeds to start a river recovery fund. As the film showed around the country, the Orvis Company, Inc. helped gather money for a major effort to revitalize this famous, but ailing, stretch of Montana trout water. As Montana rivers go, the Blackfoot is terribly polluted by the West's three classic river scourges: mine drainage, siltation (from logging and roads), and dewatering for irrigation.

"That movie," as Montanans sometimes sneer, has helped other Western trout waters rebound by luring new fly-fishing adherents who soon found that the West's rivers—many transformed into sewers, irrigation ditches, and mine drains—are insufficient to the demand for good fishing.

Though not nearly as widespread as nuclear leftovers, another military waste pollutes the West: thousands of rockets and bombs, containing tons of poison gas and nerve agents, lie leaking in three chemical weapon depots, near Tooele, Utah; Pueblo, Colorado; and Hermiston, Oregon. Any one of the depots holds enough chemical agents to kill everybody in America several times over. The Army just started incinerating the weapons at the Tooele depot,

Spectacles of the Ugly West

Perhaps hundreds of toxic spots exist for every "superfund" site mapped here, which concentrate near the West's larger cities. The leftovers of chemical and biological weapons are more contained, in just three Western depots: Hermiston, Oregon; Tooele, Utah; and Pueblo, Colorado —where the military faces a choice between letting the weapons slowly deteriorate and leak, or burning them on site —neither of which appeals to local citizens. Unexploded conventional ordinance litter the weapons test ranges. The American Rivers Council includes 15 Western rivers on its most endangered roster, including Montana's Blackfoot, setting for the movie A River Runs Through It, and Colorado's Animas, threatened by what might be the last big Western water project.

Spectacles of the Ugly West

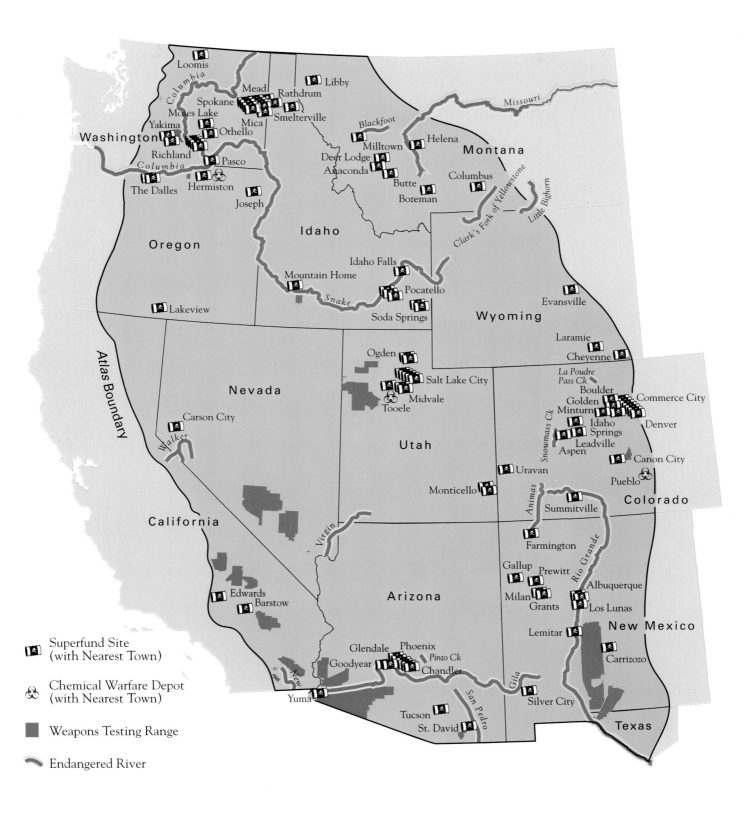

Loomis
Libby
Mead
Rathdrum
Spokane
Moses Lake
Smelterville
Mica
Yakima
Othello
Washington
Richland
Pasco
Columbia
The Dalles
Hermiston
Joseph

Blackfoot
Milltown
Helena
Deer Lodge
Anaconda
Columbus
Butte
Bozeman
Montana

Columbia

Missouri

Clark's Fork of Yellowstone

Little Bighorn

Oregon

Idaho

Idaho Falls
Mountain Home
Pocatello
Snake
Soda Springs

Evansville

Lakeview

Wyoming

Laramie
Cheyenne

Nevada

Ogden
Salt Lake City
Midvale
Tooele

La Poudre Pass Ck
Boulder
Golden
Commerce City
Minturn
Idaho Springs
Denver
Leadville
Aspen
Canon City
Pueblo

Snowmass Ck

Carson City

Walker

Utah

Uravan
Monticello

Colorado

Animas
Summitville

California

Virgin

Farmington
Gallup
Prewitt
Milan
Grants

Rio Grande

Albuquerque
Los Lunas

Edwards
Barstow

Arizona

Lemitar

New Mexico

Glendale
Phoenix
Goodyear
Pinto Ck
Chandler

Carrizozo

New

Gila

Yuma

San Pedro

Silver City

Texas

Tucson
St. David

Superfund Site
(with Nearest Town)

Chemical Warfare Depot
(with Nearest Town)

Weapons Testing Range

Endangered River

probably the only reasonable disposal method since they were forced to stop dumping chemical weapons into the ocean in the 1960s. But the state of Utah retains a right to halt the burning should any problems arise. Similar incinerators are ready at Pueblo, but here the process is even more controversial because the depot is close to a city of 100,000 people. At least Tooele lies in a more classic Western landscape of thinly populated, sagebrush valleys.

Other pervasive environmental problems in the West include a regional pall of haze and smog that limits the view into the Grand Canyon. The Grand Canyon Visibility Transport Commission's 1996 report revealed the difficulty of cleansing the Colorado Plateau's air.[3] Much of the haze drifts in from southern California, while the rest comes from dispersed sources that will be hard to curb: road construction and winter sanding, eroding soil, and fires. California is reducing its contribution through regulation, but interior sources of dust and smoke are likely to worsen. Most ecologists say that the West's forest and shrublands need more burning; they want fires lit purposefully to get the system back into some natural balance. Early explorers routinely reported reduced visibility due to smoke, but a century of successful fire suppression means that modern Westerners have, except during the Yellowstone fires in 1988, rarely known the region's naturally smoky skies. Ecosystem health may demand poorer views.

The region's success in attracting recreationists makes more problems for the environment. Trails throughout the West show the wear and tear of three decades of booming wilderness use. Even trout streams suffer from too many fly-fishers in neoprene waders disturbing the stream bottom. The national parks decay under the feet and tires of millions of visitors annually—the parking lot at Old Faithful seems as large as the geyser basin itself. Development around the parks—especially the ticky-tacky tourist traps at their entrances, called "gateway towns"—further degrades them, and endangers every animal that strays out of bounds.

Bison

(Bison bison)

Current Range

Natural Range

No Home on the Range

The Old and New Wests divide most decisively on wildlife policy, especially what to do about predators like wolves and the grizzly bear. Some paleontologists believe that Native Americans hunted a few species to extinction (perhaps the wild horse, mammoth, and giant beaver),[4] but the really dramatic wildlife declines followed the European invasion. Settlers not only hunted animals, but also built the farms, dams, and cities that ruined their habitat. Some species were killed because they threatened or competed with people (wolves, grizzlies, and coyotes), others provided food (bison), and some simply disappeared from the map as people invaded and transformed their living space. Wildlife in the West nowadays, even animals that kill livestock and, occasionally, people, are protected and many species are recovering.

The first European visitors to the West marveled at the wildlife. They wrote home about it, especially the buffalo. Lewis and Clark, crossing Montana on their way back from the Pacific in 1806, came on a large herd and wrote that "if it not be impossible to calculate the moving multitude, which darkened the whole plains, we are convinced that twenty-thousand would be no exaggerated number."[5] Moving herds held up wagon trains and railroads. A single herd took days to move past a fixed point. The West was home to some 50 to 75 million buffalo at the time of Lewis and Clark's expedition. Then Western immigrants began killing them *en masse*: as sport, for hides, to feed the calvary and rail workers, and even to subdue the Indians. A scorched earth policy would weaken the warrior Plains tribes, whose buffalo hunting skills made them strong combatants.

The bison's tale nicely joins Old and New West. The great kill-off hurt the ecology and hastened the decline of Indian cultures, but fixing this ecological hurt has helped rekindle Native pride and care for Western ecosystems. A few hundred bison survived in hideouts like the Yellowstone country, and a few were kept in zoos or corralled on private ranches. Then a new spirit—conservation—emerged at the turn of the century and Americans wanted the remaining buffalo protected. Congress created the National Bison Range on the Flathead River north of Missoula, Montana, in 1908, and buffalo were set loose to roam the plains of South Dakota's Custer State Park. Bison ranching limped along as an oddity until the 1980s, when American taste for leaner meats grew: now over a thousand Western ranches raise buffalo, including Ted Turner's Flying D Ranch on the Gallatin River south of Bozeman, Montana, where he replaced the cattle with 3,000 bison. Now the Inter-Tribal Bison Cooperative is working to add bison to Indian lands throughout the West, reinserting them into living Indian cultures. Unfortunately, not every place welcomes buffalo back: Montana officials force the Park Service to kill bison wandering out of Yellowstone during the winter, claiming that the buffalo transmit disease to cattle.

In less than a century we all but annihilated predators like the bald eagle, grizzly bear, and wolf, and did in fact kill off dozens of lesser known plant and animal species in the push for Western development. Many of these are recovering in the West—the bald eagle is coming back under federal endangered species protection, and game species like elk, big horn sheep, and moose recovered with help from hunters. Other creatures, for whom humans harbor more animosity, like the grizzly, and those in the way of progress, like the salmon, are still at risk.

Grizzlies, which roamed the entire West, were first exterminated in California—though the beast still graces the state flag; a few hundred now barely hold on in the Northern Rockies, occasionally exciting tourists in Yellowstone National Park or frightening hikers in Montana's Bob Marshall Wilderness. Grizzlies need large wild spaces; a single male may range over 300 square miles, and likes his own space. This is one reason only a few hundred grizzlies exist in the lower 48 states—too much of their space has been turned into farms, suburbs, and cities. Even Yellowstone National Park, covering 3,472 square miles, is insufficient space for the 200–300 grizzlies that call it home. The great bear's survival in the New West remains uncertain.

The salmon may be the West's most poignant tribute to human folly. Blocked by dams producing cheap electricity, the Salmon runs in the Columbia Basin, which once made rivers and lakes glow red with the spawn, dwindled to the trickle of a few lonely fish struggling back to the stream of their birth. Many areas of the

Bald Eagle
(Haliaeetus leucocephalus)

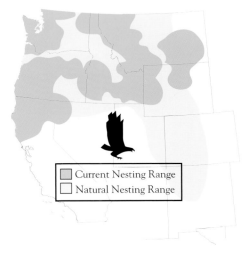

Current Nesting Range
Natural Nesting Range

Grizzly
(Ursus horribilis)

Current Range
Natural Range

Salmon

(Salmonidae)

Current Range < 50% Extinct
Current Range > 50% Extinct
Natural Range

Mountain Lion

(Felis concolor)

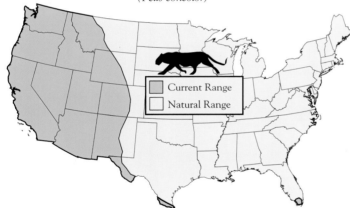

Current Range
Natural Range

basin were simply put off limits to the salmon by dams, in others the streams are too polluted. Half of the Northwest's salmon runs are gone and most of the remaining half are threatened.

The mountain West is outlined by the mountain lion's remaining range. Except for small, endangered populations in extreme southern Florida and Texas, mountain lions have made their stand in the West, from the Rocky Mountain foothills to the Pacific Coast. Numbers of the big cats are increasing because they feed on the growing smorgasbord of deer and elk. Mountain lions also patrol the wildland fringe of human settlement, taking the occasional pet and killing at least three people in the 1990s.

Coyotes are also doing fine just about everywhere, despite intense hunting. They seem to thrive on persecution in ways that wolves and grizzlies cannot. Skunk, raccoon, and other suburban species also do well as their artificial habitats expand. Several introduced plants are also spreading, like the cheat grass that now blankets southern Utah's canyonlands, and that icon of movie Westerns, brought from the Russian steppe, the tumbleweed. More deer, elk, and moose, which are simultaneously charismatic, tolerant of humans, and lucrative (in tourist and hunter dollars) roam the West than probably ever before.

The wolf is the New West's most recent and captivating wildlife success story. The last wolves in the West were killed by government hunters in the 1930s, not only to appease ranchers but also to increase the region's elk herd, a great source of appreciation. A few wolves slipped back and forth across the Canadian border into the Northern Rockies. Helped along by legal protection and recovering herds of good things to eat, some of these wolves were tentatively recolonizing parts of Montana and Idaho when federal wildlife officials decided to help: they would physically reintroduce the wolves to Yellowstone and central Idaho. In 1995, after 25 years of planning, research, and political maneuvering—overcoming ranchers' lawsuits and a Congress that turned, in 1994, decidedly antienvironmental—the first batch of wolves were captured in Canada and flown eight hundred miles to release points in the Idaho wilderness and Yellowstone National Park.

At just after 8 a.m. on January 12, 1995, protected by a Park Service SWAT team, accompanied by Secretary of Interior Bruce Babbitt, and cheered by local schoolchildren and wolf enthusiasts lining the highway, 14 jet-set wolves were trucked through Yellowstone National Park's northern gate.[6] A last-minute lawsuit filed by the Wyoming Farm Bureau kept them in the cages an extra 12 hours, but by 7 p.m. they were released into acclimation pens in the Park's Lamar Valley. The wolves were declared an "experimental population," thus receiving less protection under the Endangered Species Act than had they recolonized these great hunting grounds on their own, as some biologists expected them to do eventually. Still, on release from the holding pens they quickly made themselves at home, forming packs, eating elk, and, most importantly, breeding. They also became the Park's biggest tourist draw, chasing elk and bison, playing, and digging dens in easy view of thousands of visitors, including a bevy of dedicated amateur wolf watchers who saw, from roadside pull-outs during that first summer, the secret life of wolves rarely glimpsed even by professional wolf researchers.[7]

Wolf

(Canus lupus)

☐ Natural Re-colonization
☒ Reintroduced Range
☐ Natural Range
☐ Disputed Natural Range

In fact, most New Westerners appreciate wildlife, even the dangerous kind; though people consume wildlife habitat as they crowd into the rural West, they also bring political support for species—lawyers from the National Wildlife Federation and Defenders of Wildlife now represent wolves, grizzlies, and salmon and the habitats they need. Can increasing numbers of New Westerners share their home on the range with often dangerous animals (even elk and bison injure and kill tourists in the national parks)? The two population trends—more people and more wildlife—are on a collision course.

Death in Yellowstone: Endangered Wolves

Thirty-one gray wolves from Canada were released into Yellowstone National Park during 1995 and 1996. The last indigenous Yellowstone wolves had been killed by government hunters in the 1920s. Though legally protected as an endangered species, and happily producing pups, the wolves still face mortal dangers, both human and natural:

Male #10, Rose Creek Pack: The radio collar on this pack's "alpha" or dominant male sent out its mortality signal on April 26, 1995—the first death among the wolves reintroduced just three months earlier. Wildlife officials found the skinned carcass near Red Lodge, Montana, and a week later arrested carpenter Chad McKittrick, who was tried and convicted for the shooting. The wolf's mate, who would find it difficult to feed her three cubs without the father's hunting, was located by her radio collar and moved, with cubs, back to the acclimatization pen.

Male #22, Rose Creek Pack: The first wolf born in Yellowstone to die, this pup ran smack into the rear fender of a delivery van traveling Yellowstone's northeast entrance road.

Male #3, Crystal Creek Pack: Killed by federal agents for eating sheep near Emigrant, Montana.

Male #12, Soda Butte Pack: Illegally shot near Daniels, Wyoming.; the killer has not been identified.

Female #11, Soda Butte Pack: Shot by a Deseret Ranch hand near Meeteetse, Wyoming., who thought she was a coyote and quickly reported his mistake—thus avoiding criminal charges.

Female #36, Lone Star Pack: The pack's alpha female apparently fell into a geyser pool and died of scalding. Out of the acclimatization pen only a few days, she was pregnant with six pups.

Male #4, Crystal Creek Pack: The pack's original alpha male was killed in a fight with the neighboring Druid Peak Pack.

Male #20, Rose Creek Pack: This yearling also got into a fight with the Druid Peak Pack, who are obviously the Park's bullies.

Female #32, Chief Joseph Pack: The pack's alpha female was killed by an 18-wheeler on U.S. Highway 191, which skirts the Park's northwest corner.

Female #45, Soda Butte Pack: Died of natural causes inside the acclimatization pen.

Chapter 7: Visions for the Next West

The New West was built on both happenstance and vision. Nobody planned the energy boom and bust, and few could predict the crashes in copper or beef prices or imagine that Americans would pick up and move in droves to a region often considered a wasteland—or that they would come to regret, quite profoundly, killing off the wolf, grizzly, buffalo, and salmon. A tincture of vision also played a role in the region's postindustrial reincarnation. Certainly the developers made rich by the boom in downhill skiing and resort real estate had vision, as did the protectors of wilderness and wildlife.

The twenty-first century West will, no doubt, also reflect large measures of luck and historical contingency: Will the global oil glut dry up? What price are people willing to pay for a ski lift ticket? Will ranching die out? Will the Yellowstone wolves or Grand Canyon condors survive? The region's future will also be shaped by its contemporary visionaries: Indian tribes working for the return of the buffalo and salmon and a further strengthening of their cultural identity and political power; federal land managers seeking a more holistic, consensus-based land management instead of law suits; developers and property rights advocates demanding reduced federal regulation and maybe even privatization of public lands; and environmentalists who envision a region-wide ecosystem recovery.

The next West is already being mapped by today's visionaries, though they cannot expect to escape historical contingency any more than their predecessors.

War and Peace in the New West

On the Fourth of July, 1994, Dick Carver piloted a bulldozer toward a federal forest ranger trying to stop Carver from scraping an illegal road across national forest land. The Nye County, Nevada, commissioner and self-described "sagebrush rebel" not only ended up on the cover of *Time* magazine,[1] but also followed a long tradition that he and other Westerners, unhappy with the federal government's big presence and power over Western land, say goes back to the Boston Tea Party. Carver's 'dozer escapades, cheered on by a heavily armed group of antigovernment protestors, was almost an exact replay of a July 4, 1980, scene in Utah: Grand County commissioners sent a bulldozer into a BLM roadless area to protest federal wilderness designations, which they claimed locked up resources and hurt local economies. Instead of an armed federal agent, a lone environmentalist stood in front of the Utah bulldozer; he judiciously stepped aside as the commissioners ended their antifederal speeches and fired up the big cat's engine.

Antifederal protesters and property rights advocates speak of a growing "War on the West" in which an oppressive federal government puts ranchers, miners, and loggers out of business for no good reason. The Sagebrush Rebels took succor from Presidents Ronald Reagan and George Bush, and their interior secretaries—especially the outspoken James Watt—who tilted federal policy in favor of extractive industries and property rights. Most of the protests, though, stay short of true rebellion: even Grand County relented, under court order, and eventually obliterated the 'dozed road. Still, these powerful interests managed to parry most of the Clinton administration's land and environmental initiatives in the early 1990s. Interior Secretary Bruce Babbitt wanted ranchers to pay more for grazing cattle on the federal range and he pushed for better protection of endangered species. Range policies changed little, and the new National Biological Service—established to study declining species—was savaged by congressional appropriations committees. Babbitt bemoaned the 1872 law that required him to hand over lucrative leases to mining companies for little or no payment—holding showy press conferences reminiscent of sweepstakes awards ceremonies, with outsized lease documents displayed behind him. Congress, though, retained the mining law.

Declaring "County Supremacy" and "Custom and Culture"

Many Westerners are fed up with the federal government protecting species and ecosystems at the expense, they say, of local communities. County governments are fighting back, through "county supremacy" and "custom and culture" resolutions or ordinances; some even claim that federal land ownership is unconstitutional and assert their own land management authority. Utah's Uintah County land use plan declares:

> *We, the people of Uintah County, State of Utah, accept, support and sustain the Constitutions of the United States and of the State of Utah. We have demanded through our elected legislature and governor that the federal government comply with the Constitution, Article One, Section Eight, which limits the authority of the federal government to specific lands. We hereby reaffirm our demand that all lands in Uintah County not so specifically designated be relinquished to the citizens thereof . . . We declare that all natural resource and land use planning decisions affecting Uintah County shall be guided by the principles of protecting private property rights, sustaining valuable natural resources, protecting local custom and culture, maintaining traditional economic structures . . . and opening new economic opportunities though reliance on free markets.*

Catron County, New Mexico, not only asserted local control of public lands but also vowed to protect its "custom and culture," defined as ranching and logging on the national forests.

Clinton's and Babbitt's modest successes—wolf reintroduction, some crack-down on grazing, reduced federal subsidies for water and electricity, and a tilt toward "ecosystems management"—upset development forces and fueled the movement to protect the old, extractive economy. Babbitt frequently referred to a "New West" whose economy and urbane politics had moved beyond slash-and-burn resource practices, but this New West appears also to have evoked an antienvironmental backlash. A Utah congressman called for transfer of all BLM lands to the Western states, and House Republicans introduced legislation to protect grazing and logging on federal lands and proposed a commission to close down "unneeded" national parks. In response, Sierra Club members passed a resolution demanding an end to all timber cutting on the national forests. A few months later its board of directors voted to have Glen Canyon Dam, the second biggest in the West, torn down.

The crusade against the federal government and environmentalism is loosely termed the "Wise Use" movement; its adherents want environmental

War and Peace in the West

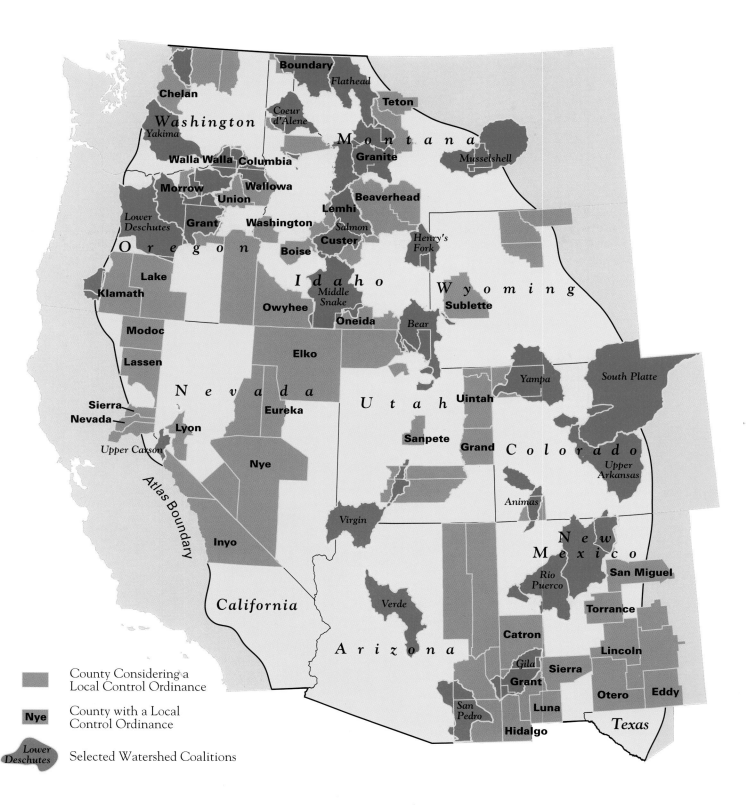

County Considering a
Local Control Ordinance

Nye County with a Local
Control Ordinance

*Lower
Deschutes* Selected Watershed Coalitions

laws revoked, federal lands privatized or transferred to states, and extractive uses subsidized. One widespread campaign of the Wise Use movement (teamed with the Sagebrush Rebels) emerged in Western places with the largest public land holdings. Under the banner of "county supremacy," some local officials and sympathetic lawyers, frustrated over federal decision making that appeared to hurt local economies, latched onto the U.S. constitution's "equal footing" clause. It guaranteed new states entering the union equal status with the original states, and the rebels argued that federal lands, so concentrated in the West, violated equal footing, as did public land management actions such as limiting how many cows can graze a particular area or whether ski areas can expand.

The county supremacy campaign, spearheaded by Dick Carver's Nye County, Nevada, spawned several types of ordinances asserting control over federal lands, or at least requiring federal consultation with counties on all land use decisions. Others seek specifically to protect an area's "custom and culture," a Wise Use phrase for mining, grazing, logging, and such. A few county ordinances make some federal actions illegal, requiring that sheriffs arrest federal officials making locally unpopular land use choices—like fencing cattle out of streams, designating wilderness areas, or, worse of all, reintroducing endangered species like wolves. So far, such threats have been mostly talk, and the Nye County, Nevada, ordinance asserting county right-of-way across all federal lands was struck down in U.S. District Court. It does reveal, however, that the Old West will not fade quietly into the New.

As standoffs between county and federal officials and the bombing of Forest Service offices in Nevada made news, some of the combatants wisely called a truce. In fact, people in several places around the West decided to work for a different kind of land management before the battle escalated to armed confrontations. A few ranchers invited environmentalists to look over their operations; Doc and Connie Hatfield in eastern Oregon, the Sun family in southern Wyoming, and the Tiptons in central Nevada even asked outsiders to join "Coordinated Resource Management" teams that help make land use decisions on their ranches.[2]

The most widespread type of New Western problem-solving is the "watershed coalition." Some are formally charted, by federal, state, or local government, to grapple with land, resource, and even economic problems that defy bureaucratic solutions. Others are almost subversive coalitions of individuals—environmentalists and Sagebrush Rebels sometimes questioning the logic of their own interest groups—seeking an alternative land management regime at a scale that avoids federal-local tensions.

Most of the coalitions come together out of frustration with government. The Henry's Fork Watershed Council formed when the state couldn't settle water fights between irrigation interests and the recreational and environmental communities. Watershed residents have reason to feel dumped on. In 1992, engineers building a hydroelectric project near Marysville let a canal burst: 17,000 tons of sediment went into the Fall River, choking it for miles. That fall, the Bureau of Reclamation tried to kill unwanted fish by draining Island Park Reservoir, inadvertently sending up to 100,000 tons of sediment into the Henry's Fork, perhaps the nation's best-known trout stream.

War and Peace in the West

Many Western county commissioners are "Sagebrush Rebels" claiming that the federal land management is unconstitutional. They claim "county supremacy" and pass local ordinances asserting authority over federal land management and demanding protection of "custom and culture," code words for traditional land uses like mining, ranching, and logging. We map counties having adopted, or are seriously considering, local control ordinances. Some of these make federal land management actions—like reintroducing an endangered species—illegal, and threaten agency personnel with arrest. If the county supremacy movement is a sign of polarization in the West, the watershed coalitions point to the potential for consensus and common ground. Many start up after the interests groups—ranchers, miners, environmentalists, recreationists—stalemate each other's land use desires with lawsuits and appeals. Here we map the most well-established watershed coalitions; many, like the Gila, Middle Snake, and Walla Walla, work despite the bad blood of the county-led sagebrush rebellion.

When they are not shouting at the Bureau of Reclamation—or one of the other 24 governmental entities with some authority over the watershed—members of the Henry's Fork coalition occasionally get on each other's nerves, especially environmentalists and irrigators. But they all agree to try to bridge their differences and to work by consensus, as do most of the coalitions. Up in northern Idaho, the Coeur d'Alene group has managed, by most reports, to make good progress cleaning up the mess of the nation's second largest superfund site, the Bunker Hill silver mining area. The citizen advisory council can be found in hip waders restoring wetlands, and even the mining companies contributed money and effort beyond superfund requirements. But peace does not come easy to all coalition activities. The Coeur d'Alene tribe is still suing the mining companies for downriver clean-up costs.

Almost universally the watershed coalitions consciously seek to incorporate ideals of both Old and the New West into solutions of longstanding land and water resource battles. Despite philosophical differences, coalition members often agree that bureaucratic government seems inept at managing the West's complicated ecosystems. Indeed, the simple reality is that many Westerners simply don't trust the federal government. When the Condor Recovery Team met with residents of the Utah canyon country where the birds were to be released into the wild, they ran into long-festering hostilities. Residents even reminded the federal biologists that they had been mistreated and lied to by the government during above-ground nuclear tests in the 1950s! Everything the government does seems to hurt locals and local economies, they said. The condors were released in 1996, but only after a judge denied a lawsuit brought by San Juan County claiming that condor reintroduction would ruin its rural economy.

A Wild Future

In 1993 environmentalist solidarity in the West appeared to be unraveling: Montana chapters of the Sierra Club tried to secede from the national organization because the national board withheld support of the Northern Rockies Ecosystem Protection Act (NREPA), legislation the Montanans helped create to radically change how the region's public lands were managed. Montana environmentalists, and eventually the national Sierra Club, wanted integrated protection of all federal lands in the region, and application of ecosystems principles to all land uses. When he introduced the bill, NREPA co-sponsor Gerry Sikorski (D-MN) said:

> We have to remember that all Americans own these lands. . . . They don't belong to the timber companies, or the miners, or the politicians. If the American people saw what I saw from a helicopter and a plane, the endless draglines that have eroded into gully washes, the hundreds and hundreds of acres of clearcuts over the past 20 years that have never been replanted . . . they would go absolutely ballistic. If the American public knew that their taxpayer dollars are subsidizing this destruction, they'd go thermonuclear.

A Wild Future

Environmental visionaries want the New West to look more like the primeval West, with all its species and ecosystems intact. This map shows public lands that still contain large, intact blocks of habitat. Conservationists see existing preserved lands and roadless areas—like national parks and wilderness areas—and currently unprotected habitats as building blocks for ecosystem reserve plans. Regionwide conservation schemes include wild cores, potential buffer areas, and landscape linkages that together can maintain a full range of native species and ecosystems into the future. Human presence in these areas would be muted, giving natural processes like animal migration and wildfire the space to play out in the landscape as they did before settlement.

A Wild Future

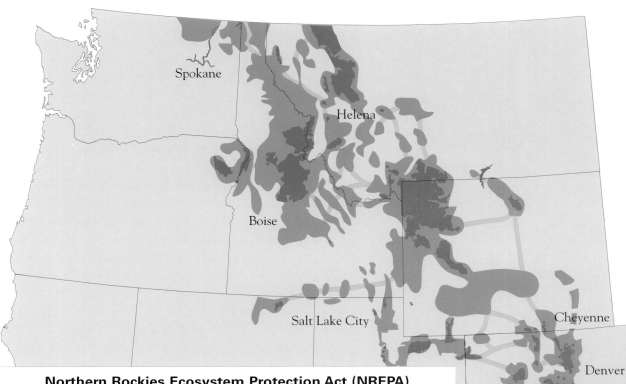

Northern Rockies Ecosystem Protection Act (NREPA)

Introduced into congress during 1993 as H.R. 2638, NREPA proposes a radical change in public land management for an entire bioregion. It would:

- *protect some 20 million acres of public lands in the Northern Rockies;*
- *designate five major "core" ecosystems like Glacier and Yellowstone National Parks;*
- *create additional wilderness areas and at least two new national parks: Hells Canyon on the Snake River and Flathead on the west side of Glacier National Park;*
- *create a new system of "biological linkage corridors" to reduce habitat fragmentation;*
- *initiate a program of "wildland recovery areas" where degraded land would be improved by planting trees, removing facilities that hurt wildlife, like roads and campgrounds, and reintroducing endangered species;*
- *create a new branch of the U.S. Forest Service, the Wildlands Recovery Corps, to manage the recovery areas;*
- *create an interagency, intergovernmental team to oversee the entire ecoregion.*

The region still contains most of its natural species, but many are endangered by development that fragments and reduces their natural habitat. NREPA supporters, like the Alliance for the Wild Rockies, estimate that the Northern Rockies could support 2,000 grizzlies if all their habitat in the region were protected. Western wildland advocates support similar plans for all of the Rocky Mountains and other Western regions rich in open land.

 Protected Core Areas

 Potential Location for Buffer Areas

 Potential Landscape Linkages

The Montanan ecosystem advocates had two special skills needed by all vision-aries. They could extrapolate current trends to logical, often horrendous, conse-quences, and they could picture a future different than historical currents por-tend. The trends discussed in this book, extended out a few decades, imply a West more crowded, more developed, and more economically vital. But, one person's job-creating ski area or factory outlet mall is another person's eyesore or ecologi-cal wound, and few Westerners can seriously contemplate the current develop-ment rush without worrying that the region will be smothered in subdivisions and shopping malls, parking lots and resorts, with only a few remaining natural spaces crowded by people fleeing the subdivisions and malls.

Environmentalists committed to keeping nature whole are mapping a vision for the West based on protected ecosystems and landscapes. Their vision-ary landscape is tethered to the few remaining truly wild parts of the West—con-gressionally designated wilderness areas and national parks—plus less protected, but not yet developed, public tracts that harbor many indigenous species. But even these remaining wildlands are not big enough to function as healthy, biot-ic refuges: animals and plants must migrate, share genes, and adjust to patterns of drought, fire, or even global warming. Yes, grizzly bears hold on in Yellowstone

Utah Wildlands

Bioregional visionaries in southern Utah are less concerned than their Rocky Mountain counterparts with ecosystem connections than with simply preserving large tracts of remaining wildland. Utah encompasses more undeveloped public land than any state other than Alaska, but little of it is set aside for preservation. So organizations like the Southern Utah Wilderness Alliance went around the seem-ingly endless formality of federal wilderness studies and cre-ated a fully integrated proposal of their own—mapping out huge swaths of land they want congress to list under the National Wilderness System. Their map calls for 5.7 million acres of wilderness, four times the amount proposed by the federal agencies.[3]

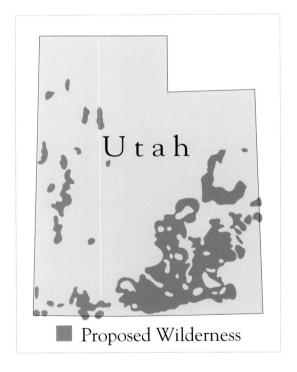

■ Proposed Wilderness

National Park, but they are separated from grizzlies elsewhere and slowly, degrad-ing as does any small, isolated gene pool.

New environmental visionaries are working on grand schemes to reduce ecological fragmentation. The Wildlands Project, an assemblage of bioregional-ists, applies the principles of conservation biology and latest geographic informa-tion systems to map ways to keep whole ecosystems going. Their goal is "nothing less than the rewilding of North America, nothing less than the renegotiation of the human covenant with the land."[4]

In the Rocky Mountains these environmental visionaries draw expanded boundaries around the remaining wild cores—the Yellowstone country, Central Idaho, and pockets of wilderness in the Southern Rockies—and link them via fragments of undisturbed forests and grassland. Thus was born the Northern Rockies Ecosystem Protection Act, and similar plans for the Southern Rockies. Landscape linkages, to be used by migrating animals and plants, could reconnect the entire Rocky Mountain ecosystem from north to south. Dozens of Western environmental organizations seek a wilder vision for the region. According to these big-think conservationists we must change the West from a landscape of development surrounding remaining pockets of naturalness into the reverse: limited development embedded in a geography of wildness. A radical vision, bucking the tide of western history and threatening to many people, but one offering a new form of regional development and a new way for people to live in the Western landscape.

I went back and reread *Beyond the Hundredth Meridian* the week after I took office and thought, Yes, it's as true now as it was then, the outcome is still very much in the balance, the forces are the same. Not much has changed in a hundred years. The stakes have gotten higher, because there aren't as many empty spaces, there are more people, more pressure, more demand for resources. But in that one book, and in his way of looking at the West, Stegner leaves us a message that the duality, the tensions have never been resolved. Each generation is once again given the chance to see if it can't somehow find that balance and realign its view of the land, its relationship with the land, and the way that our institutions can be put into the mix, not as adversaries, but as part of a broader community.

Interior Secretary Bruce Babbitt eulogizing Wallace Stegner
The Geography of Hope: A Tribute to Wallace Stegner (1996)

Consider your birthright, Stegner tells us, when fatigue or laziness threatens to slow our hungry slurping of culture, think who you are. Perhaps the greatest legacy that Wally has taught us is that our birthright is found in the land, in wilderness, in the geography of hope. . . . His life, his words, bind us together as a community of friends and family engaged in a vision. Let us regard the land as holy. Let us regard the land as sacred. They are our sacrament. Blood, body, sage. Let us breathe deeply.

Terry Tempest Williams eulogizing Wallace Stegner
The Geography of Hope: A Tribute to Wallace Stegner (1996)

The Shadows of Heaven Itself

by

Patricia Nelson Limerick

The shadows of the Rockies which fall across the Front Range every evening are more than a picturesque backdrop to our daily routine; they are the shadows of heaven itself.

Archbishop Francis Stafford
Pastoral Letter, November 24, 1994

Reliable information concerning the New West is of so recent date that the mass of the people in the East are not posted as to the actual facts. Were some well-posted citizen of the New West to present the actual facts about that domain to the inhabitants of the Eastern States, a multitude would denounce him as a liar, or pity him for possessing more imagination than judgment. . . . This book does not contain all the marvels of the New West, by any means.

William Thayer
Marvels of the New West, 1890

The "New West" is a phrase with a history. In 1869, excited by opportunities presented by the completion of the transcontinental railroad, the reporter Samuel Bowles called his book *Our New West*. "Nature, weary of repetitions," Bowles wrote, "has, in the New West, created originally, freshly, uniquely, majestically. . . . Nowhere are broader and higher mountains; nowhere, climates more propitious; nowhere broods an atmosphere so pure and exhilarating."

Nineteenth- and twentieth-century observers of their respective New Wests share an exhilaration brought to life by the novelty and power of Western nature. But twentieth century writers have an advantage: they have every opportunity to recognize that human nature, in its dreams, visions, and ambitions, has turned out to be just as "weary of repetition," just as original, just as astonishing, as anything nature itself ever cooked up.

Consider Denver's winter Stock Show. One of the oldest and biggest livestock markets and rodeos in the West, this annual event, a bastion of tradition, celebrates Old Western rural values. Men—briefly—ride bucking horses and bulls; merchandisers sell corral equipment and bull semen; and even apparent novelties, like the blow-driers used to primp cattle, serve the traditional goal of securing the best price possible for protein-on-the-hoof. And yet, for all the weight of the past, the Stock Show shows the passage of time in a thousand ways.

In January of 1996, the *New York Times* carried a story about the Stock Show. The reporter called me. What did I think about the rise of Western ranches devoted to emus and ostriches, llamas, and alpacas? I said that the history of the West has hinged on the introduction of exotic species; in that sense, the

(facing page) Saguaro at Eagle Mountain residential and golf development, east of Phoenix, Arizona.

ostrich and the emu were just the latest successors to cows and horses. But another comment, quoted at the end of the article, sticks more firmly in the mind. There is a world of difference in the amount of dignity and stature conveyed by the terms cowboy and cattleman, in comparison to emuboy and ostrichman.

The Newest New West calls itself to our attention in all sorts of ways, though this particular occasion of recognition is my favorite. It raises one's hopes for a new brand of Western literature, in which tall, silent ostrichboys, with their characteristic stiff-legged gait, face off against each other in showdowns on Main Street and then rejoin their Montessori schoolmarms for a debriefing and a capuccino, while the townspeople gather to watch anxiously from the mountain bike stores and the aromatherapy shop. At the turn of the century, Owen Wister published *The Virginian* and created the archetypal Westerner, despite his oddly southern name. The 1990s present a comparable opportunity, for an ambitious writer to make her authorial reputation with the publication of *The Californian*, symbol of the New West of emus and ostriches, espressos and utility vehicles.

"The rapid increase of [the New West's] population is as great a marvel as a canon," William Thayer wrote in 1890. To Thayer and his contemporaries, population growth was a wonderful phenomenon, an occasion for celebration. A century later, while some still celebrate growth, many others respond with laments and resistance. One thinks that one has seen all the possible variations on the injuries, costs, and disadvantages of uncontrolled human settlement, and reliably, one turns out to be wrong.

"Growth Hard on Rodents," announced a 1996 headline in the *Denver Post*. In the long-running battle pitting American enterprise against prairie dogs, the rodents had picked up unexpected allies. "Hated, hunted, and otherwise disposed of by ranchers and farmers, who considered them a menace to crops and livestock," prairie dogs now had advocates who recognized that the rodents provide food "vital to numerous animals," including eagles. Others simply found the animals "cute." The collision between expanding human settlements and established prairie dog villages had thus become a "public relations nightmare for developers, businesses, or cities."

What to do? Another headline hinted at the answer. "Dream Led to Prairie-Dog Vacuum": a man named Gay Balfour, in desperate circumstances, received inspiration in a dream. He "saw an enormous yellow truck with a green hose sticking out it, sucking prairie dogs out of the ground." A few days later, he came upon a yellow truck, used for suctioning out sewers, and, at a supply store, he found green hoses of exactly the right diameter. The dream took concrete form: a vacuum called "Dog-Gone." Inserted into a hole, Dog-Gone pulled out the rodent, rocketed it through the tube, and shot it out, "into a big tank on the back of the truck, slamming it into a wall of thick foam rubber," where it dropped onto a similarly padded floor.

The rapid pace of change in this region has made a lot of its longtime residents feel that they have been on the equivalent of the prairie dog's trip through the Dog-Gone, though without the benefit of the foam-rubber landing. Dreams drove the New West of the nineteenth century, and though they have taken a beating, dreams persist—even thrive—in our New West, familiar dreams of a new beginning in a new place, new dreams of humane vacuums for prairie dogs or dreams of open ranges of ostriches. Human nature has met and matched nature

"At the turn of the century, Owen Wister published The Virginian *and created the archetypal Westerner, despite his oddly southern name. The 1990s present a comparable opportunity, for an ambitious writer to make her authorial reputation with the publication of* The Californian, *symbol of the New West of emus and ostriches, espressos and utility vehicles."*

in wildness and novelty. William Thayer's phrase of 1890 has new resonance: "This book does not contain all the marvels of the New West, by any means."

The West as Remedy

Once there was a fellow in Missouri whose health reached a point of collapse. "I can't do anything more for you," his doctor told him. "Your only hope is to move as soon as you can to a place with a healthier climate."

Racing against frailty, the man packed up and left for Santa Fe. But the opportunity to breathe dry, pure air came too late, and his decline continued. In a matter of weeks, his body was returned for burial in Missouri. At the funeral, two of his pals stood contemplating the attractively presented corpse.

"Don't he look nice?" one of them said.

"He sure does," the other said. "It looks like Santa Fe done him a world of good."

Neither of them, however, thought to ask the follow-up question: what had their friend—and the many others who shared his hopes—done to Santa Fe?

Square at the center of the dreams directed at the American West has been the hope that the West will prove therapeutic, medicinal, restorative, and reinvigorating. Name the affliction, and the West seems to offer the remedy: dry air to cure respiratory problems; open spaces to relieve the pressures that weigh down the soul in teeming cities; freedom and independence to provide a restorative alternative to mass society's regimentation and standardization. As the story of the Missouri oldtimer indicates, the American West has defaulted as often as it has delivered on its promise to cure. And yet the a belief in the West as remedy persists. We stand currently on another one of its peaks.

In the nineteenth century, finding themselves afflicted with ill-defined diseases, a variety of influential Americans convinced themselves that their road to recovery ran westward. From Francis Parkman to Theodore Roosevelt, these men wrote vividly of their experiences, formalizing and codifying an image of the West as a place where purity of air, inspiring landscapes, and general vigor and heartiness brought weakened men back to strength. For a number of these health-seekers, luckier in their timing than the late-arriving fellow from Missouri, the American West did indeed do them a world of good, and they were ardent in passing on the news.

By the late nineteenth century, the West had a well-established reputation as an open-air pharmacy stocked with antidotes for the afflictions of conventional life. A century later, the faith that defines the West as remedy for the malaise of conventional life claims a multitude of believers. Life in the centers of power—in New York, in Los Angeles, in Washington, D.C.—wears down the soul; the spirit of rebellion flares. The powers-that-be need not, however, tremble. Before malaise can even begin to whisper the call to resist or rebel, the West will provide a remedy: a vacation, a second home, a skiing trip, an Indian painting, a New Age workshop, a sculpture of a coyote, a visit to a dude ranch. The movie *City Slickers* provided the best recent example of the pattern: the discontented businessman can't take the city and the rat race anymore; he and his friends head west to a ranch where they take a herd on the trail and find inner strength and peace; the businessman returns, in good spirits, to take up his burdens in the city. The West works him over and sends him back to the rat race, a restored and revitalized rat.

"Square at the center of the dreams directed at the American West has been the hope that the West will prove therapeutic, medicinal, restorative, and reinvigorating. Name the affliction, and the West seems to offer the remedy: dry air to cure respiratory problems; open spaces to relieve the pressures that weigh down the soul in teeming cities; freedom and independence to provide a restorative alternative to mass society's regimentation and standardization."

In the 1990s, the West is very popular indeed: popular as a remedy for social and personal discontent; popular as a setting for movies, documentaries, novels, essays, and memoirs; popular as a source of imagery for commercially appealing clothing, jewelry, furniture, buildings, and interiors; popular as a place of inspiration for seekers after spiritual connection in a disconnected world; and, perhaps most consequentially, popular as a residential sanctuary for prosperous emigrants from the East and West Coasts.

This is a heavy burden to bear. Consider what effort it takes that the city of Santa Fe remains properly quaint. In the late nineteenth century, Santa Fe's buildings represented a range of building types. Emotionally drawn to the style of Pueblo and Spanish colonial buildings, an Anglo elite in the city pushed for adobe construction. They encouraged use of the "Santa Fe Style," even if that meant covering brick or wooden buildings with a veneer of adobe-simulating stucco. In 1957, a city ordinance expanded the means of persuasion, beyond exhortation to mandate.

Today's visitors to Santa Fe may feel themselves in the company of the spirits of the distant Indian and Spanish past. They are, however, in more direct contact with the spirits of a group of twentieth-century Anglo boosters, determined to make Santa Fe look right. Santa Fe would fulfill the newcomers' dreams, even if it took a considerable exercise of regulatory power to bring the town into compliance. Santa Fe became one of a number of settings designed and built to convince visitors that they are having an authentic and genuine Western experience.

The processing and refining of Western places into marketable commodities is an old and established custom. The impact of television and movies surely added wagonloads of grist to this mill. Consider the opportunity presented to tourists to visit the home of the Cartwright Family. For people of a certain age, the Cartwrights remain a touchstone of the Real West—Pa, Adam, Hoss, and Little Joe, and their Ponderosa Ranch. At the beginning of each "Bonanza" episode, a branding iron descended on a map of northern Nevada, and as it seared into the paper, the brand—theoretically—marked the location of the Ponderosa Ranch. But there was no ranch, Ponderosa or otherwise, on the site where the brand hit the paper, and there wasn't even a stage set. This situation called out for correction.

Thanks to Western entrepreneurial energy, the fictional Ponderosa Ranch stands now where it should have been all along, where the branding iron hit the map. The ranch buildings are recreated (or, rather, created), the irrepressible spirit of the family lives again. Admission is charged and paid, in the proper New West manner, giving access to "the Cartwright ranch house, a museum, general store, frontier town, and stables." Years after they vanished from prime-time TV, the Cartwright Family—and the dreams and adventures of that independent and hearty, exclusively male family—finally have a home.

Viewed with detachment, the popularity of these places seems profoundly silly. In P. T. Barnum's times, there was a sucker born every minute, and the birth rate in this particular sector of the population has certainly not declined. These prove, moreover, to be very consenting suckers who regard any effort to

Ponderosa Ranch

N E V A D A

rescue them from error as an attack on a deeply held faith. Any effort to point out the fakeness of the "Real West" will unleash from its enthusiasts many cries of injury. Try to write realistically about the "Old West," and what you write will be condemned as "gloomy," "dark," or "disillusioning."

Is there anything surprising in this? Remember the West's emotional role as the antidote, the remedy, the painkiller, the refuge, the space where the soul recuperates from a multitude of injuries. At the end of the last century, John Muir referred to his treasured places in the Sierras as "temples," sacred places that commerce would desecrate and dishonor. At the end of this century, Muir's extension of the religious metaphor has kicked off the traces and run wild. Belief bordering on religious faith has been heavily invested in the most unlikely sites and situations. Commerce still devotes some of its time to its old habits of invading and trashing Muir's sacred natural settings. But commerce has also created a range of new Western sites, icons, and images that are, to their believers, equally sacred concerns. Among its other marvels and wonders, the New West offers shrines to the Old West, places where faith and profit making prosper together.

Babyboomers Home Alone

> [*American Demographics*] reports that, as the babyboomers turn 50, publications targeting older readers are using such euphemisms as "mature" and "prime" and coming up with upbeat titles such as "Looking Forward," "New Horizons," "Now Is the Time," and "Young at Heart."
>
> *Denver Post*, December 1996

> People blame New York when their relationships don't work out. They think if they just lived someplace else it would be better. But they don't want to go to Iowa. They want to go to Colorado. . . . It's so beautiful. It's like Shangri-La. It's a place to go where people never age.
>
> Interview with Candace Bushnell,
> author of *Sex and the City*

Why is the West currently so popular? What is it about the 1990s that brought Western dreaming to one of its all-time peaks?

There are any number of good answers. The most paradoxical of them rests on the fact that the 1990s are a time when so many things—entertainment, public debate, political conventions, commercial products—seem manipulated and manufactured. When reality appears in a state so unmistakably simulated, designed, and virtual, the Old West gains heightened appeal as the place where people who have had enough of falsity go to find authenticity—even if that Old Western authenticity is itself a theme-park creation.

These are, moreover, times in which no one wants to cast herself—or admit herself to be—an insider to power. Everyone running for office, for instance, struggles to claim the image of the outsider, free of the taint of Washington "Beltway" insiderness. There is no better stage set on which to play the role of the rugged outsider than the American West. Here, of course, is another sizable paradox: because the West is very much associated with individualism, it thereby attracts floods and herds and hordes of people sharing the identical ambition to play the part of rugged individualists, too.

"Any effort to point out the fakeness of the 'Real West' will unleash from its enthusiasts many cries of injury. Try to write realistically about the 'Old West,' and what you write will be condemned as 'gloomy,' 'dark,' or 'disillusioning.'"

Anxiety about gender is also at stake here. The enthusiasm for nature and for the Old West in the 1990s bears a noticeable correlation to a rejection of and retreat from the transformed gender roles of our times, whether in the presence of women in occupational areas formerly forbidden to them or in the androgynous self-presentation of stars like Michael Jackson. In peculiar times like these, some enthusiasts may well be thinking, best to retreat to the mythic region where men are men and women recognize and celebrate the maleness of men.

If this seems an overstretched interpretation, think of Edward Abbey, one of the New West's most popular writers, the writer frequently celebrated as representing—indeed, launching—a whole new attitude toward Western nature. There is reason to be moderate in finding originality or novelty in Abbey's thinking. Although Abbey is "usually portrayed as an outrageous iconoclast," the historian Elliott West has noted, Abbey's "refrain would ring familiar and true to thousands before him." Many European and Euro-American men before Abbey "have pictured themselves standing alone in the West's big spaces." Quite the opposite of a radical break in American attitudes toward nature, "nothing could be more traditional—more hidebound—than Abbey's old, longing dream." In West's memorable phrase, Abbey was the "the modern master of the adolescent male escape fantasy." However different their constituencies of fans may have been in politics and in attitudes toward extractive industries, John Wayne and Edward Abbey stood united in their warm feelings toward masculinity.

The environmental movement has, of course, done a great deal to persuade the American public that life lived in the presence of nature is life with a heightened opportunity for balance and sanity. Here, too, paradox works with a heavy hand: environmentalists spoke so persuasively of the attractions of nature that they recruited many visitors and new residents, who then, by their sheer numbers, jeopardized the natural attractions that the environmentalists had set out to protect in the first place.

White flight has also been a powerful factor in this story. Along with traffic, congestion, pollution, an uneven economy, and high real estate taxes, the racial and ethnic complexity of the West Coast and the East Coast was one of the principal "push" factors recruiting new arrivals to the interior; in much of the Rocky Mountain West, Whites were an undisputed majority. It was no coincidence that environmentalists like Edward Abbey and former Colorado governor Richard Lamm have been fierce in their condemnations of Mexican immigration. We should meet the immigrants at the border, Abbey was given to saying, "and then arm them. They can go back to Mexico and start their own revolution." When environmentalists targeted Mexican immigrants, strong emotion was giving reason a run for its money. Claiming that their concern is the overuse of natural resources and an excessively heavy human impact on the land, Western environmentalists who take up the cause of immigration restriction target Mexican immigrants, the people who are in the weakest position as consumers, the least likely to crowd into the national parks or into the newest subdivision. While the human diversity of the Interior West is considerable, for White Americans troubled by the ethnic complexity that is unmistakable and unavoidable on the East and West Coasts, areas like the Northern Rockies can still look like the place of remedy and refuge. When Los Angeles Police Department officer Mark Fuhrman, the man who, thanks to the O. J. Simpson

"Everyone running for office, for instance, struggles to claim the image of the outsider, free of the taint of Washington 'Beltway' insiderness. There is no better stage set on which to play the role of the rugged outsider than the American West. Here, of course, is another sizable paradox: because the West is very much associated with individualism, it thereby attracts floods and herds and hordes of people sharing the identical ambition to play the part of rugged individualists, too."

(facing page) Top: Old West shoot-out at the Ponderosa Ranch, Nevada, where 300,000 visitors annually commune with the spirits of TV's Cartwright family. Bottom: Lori Johnson, a college student from North Dakota, robs the Ponderosa Ranch breakfast haywagons every fifteen minutes.

trial, was for a time America's most famous racist, chose to relocate to northern Idaho, it was an unhappy reminder of the degree to which the 1990s enthusiasm for things Western coincides with a white retreat from other races.

An equally important, and much more frequently addressed, explanation for the West's popularity involves technology: the emergence of the FAX machines and computers and Internet ties that make it possible to detach the workers from the office, and let the workers choose their place of residence by its amenities and attractions, especially its scenic appeal. As telecommuters in places like Telluride report, their working day is invigorated and enriched by the chance to punctuate it with snowboarding or a hike. "It's great," reported one young woman, a writer of reports on focus groups, describing the pleasant working experiences she and her boss were able to achieve: "We ride up the chairlift with our red pens and edit reports."

Popular attitudes and tax policies of the 1980s are another important determinant. The 1980s took many of the restraints off the accumulation of wealth, wealth which would then head off in search of novel and satisfying ways to exercise purchasing power. One target of that quest would be real estate in handsome Western settings. And that real estate would carry particular attractions precisely because of the conglomeration of factors that had reduced its attractions in earlier times—isolation, aridity, altitude, heavy snow, or general ruggedness, particularly if there was a good airport a short distance away.

These answers are all surely clues to a puzzle that may be too immediate for solution in our times. But the answer that impresses me as the most important of all comes, compactly, in one word, and the word is "babyboomers."

In the middle of the twentieth century, when babyboomers were babies and toddlers, two trends of influence coincided: the rise of television and the popularity of Roy Rogers, Gene Autry, and Hopalong Cassidy. Hoppy was a particular marketing success. "Every product that adopted his name (at a fat fee to Hoppy)," *Time* magazine reported, "was sucked instantly into the maw of an insatiable demand. Badgered by their resourceful children, the parents of the babyboomers invested heavily in Hoppy items. Hoppy was a good guy who nonetheless wore black clothes (though symbol systems could only be stretched so far, and so he held on to his white hat). In one year during Hoppy's glory days, so many children wanted clothes modeled on his that the United States ran short of black dye.

In regular television episodes, Hopalong behaved admirably, with impeccable bravery, and reliably and regularly brought bad guys to justice. Hoppy's fictional virtue proved to be a powerful force in actuality. William Boyd, the actor who played the part, had been a profligate and unsteady fellow; after a year or two in the job, swept away by the admiration of his youthful fans, Boyd got his own life in order, refusing to let Hopalong be tainted by his impersonator's flaws. As Jane and Michael Stern summed it up, "He quit drinking; he quit smoking; he stopped going to wild parties; and he is reported to have stayed faithful to his wife until the day he died. William Boyd had been transformed into a good guy by his role as white-hatted Hoppy. As in all things Western, image and reality traveled, not as distant strangers, but as close companions and certainly as business partners.

William Boyd took to talking about himself—which is to say, about

"The 1980s took many of the restraints off the accumulation of wealth, wealth which would then head off in search of novel and satisfying ways to exercise purchasing power. One target of that quest would be real estate in handsome Western settings. And that real estate would carry particular attractions precisely because of the conglomeration of factors that had reduced its attractions in earlier times— isolation, aridity, altitude, heavy snow, or general ruggedness, particularly if there was a good airport a short distance away."

Hoppy—in the third person. "Look at the way these crowds act," he said. "They want to touch Hoppy . . . Crowds never pull at Hoppy or try to tear his clothing. If they start pushing I just say, 'Now kids . . . be good kids'—I call them all kids, grown-ups and all—and they settle down." Under his powerful influence, "children with impressively styled cap guns and bejeweled double holsters . . . were so commonplace that those without them seemed a little underdressed, and those who still carried such outmoded armament as X-ray Guns or Atomic Disintegrators, hopelessly old-fashioned."

Roy Rogers matched and even exceeded Hopalong Cassidy's marketing energy. At his peak, Jane and Michael Stern have written, "the only celebrity name on more things than Roy's was Walt Disney." Consider a partial listing from a recent collector's inventory of Roy Rogers memorabilia: alarm clocks, archery sets, badges, bandannas, savings banks, basketballs, beds, bedspreads, belts, binoculars, boots, briefs, bubble gum, calendars, cameras, canteens, cards games, cereal bowls, chaps, charm bracelets, chinaware, clay modeling sets, coats, coloring sets, combs, cups, curtains, dartboards, dolls, flashlights, footballs, furniture, milk glasses (marked, at different stages of emptiness, tenderfoot, posse leader, deputy, sheriff), gloves, guitars, guns, harmonicas, hats, holster outfits, rocking horses, horseshoes, jackets, jeans, jewelry, key cases, chains, and rings, knifes, lamps, lanterns, lariats, lassos, lunch-box sets, masks, mittens, moccasins, mugs, napkins, outfits, pajamas, pants, pens and pencils, pistols, plates, playing cards, playsuits, puppets, puzzles, raincoats, ranch sets, rifles, rings, robes, saddles, scarves, school bags, scrapbooks, shirts, shoes, shorts, slacks, sleepers, slippers, soap, socks, spurs, suits, suspenders, sweaters, sweatshirts, swim trunks, T-shirts, tables, writing tablets, telephones, telescopes, tents, ties, toothbrushes, tops, Trigger toys, TV chairs, vests, viewmasters, wall plaques, wallets, washcloths, watches, watercolor sets, and yo-yos, as well as toy buckboards, chuck wagons, covered wagons, horse wagons, jeeps, and stagecoaches. Roy Rogers's own children tested the products he endorsed, and thus they spent their childhood carrying items emblazoned with their father's name and face. Years later, Dusty (Roy, Jr.) poignantly "confided" that "one of his fondest dreams was to have a Gene Autry or Hopalong Cassidy lunchbox."

While one might, appropriately, accent the ways in which the TV cowboys shaped the consuming habits of the babyboomers, the influences may have been, at least temporarily, moral and political as well. The cowboys, as Jane and Michael Stern put it, "provided young babyboomers with unconfusing heroes and a clear sense of right and wrong." Everyone knows that a significant percentage of the people coming of age in the 1960s were driven by a hope for racial justice, effective social welfare policies, and meaningful individual action. Contemplate, then, a few items from the various "creeds" or "rules" or statements of belief offered by the 1950s Western TV heroes to guide and sustain their loyal fans. Here lies one point of origin for the activism of the 1960s in the picture of little 1950s cowboys and cowgirls pledging their faith to these various declarations of True Western behavior.

I believe that all men are created equal and that everyone has within himself the power to make a better world. (The Lone Ranger's Creed)

"Consider a partial listing from a recent collector's inventory of Roy Rogers memorabilia: alarm clocks, archery sets, badges, bandannas, savings banks, basketballs, beds, bedspreads, belts, binoculars, boots, briefs, bubble gum, calendars, cameras, canteens, cards games, cereal bowls, chaps, charm bracelets, chinaware, clay modeling sets, coats, coloring sets, combs, cups, curtains, dartboards, dolls, flashlights, footballs, furniture, milk glasses (marked, at different stages of emptiness, tenderfoot, posse leader, deputy, sheriff)…"

[The cowboy] must not advocate or possess racially intolerant ideas. He must help people in distress. (Gene Autry's Cowboys' Code)

Protect the weak and help them. (Roy Rogers Riders Club Rules to Live By)

No one knows what might or might not connect the cowboys' creeds to the Port Huron Statement of the Students for a Democratic Society and other inspirational statements of the 1960s New Left, but there is no question that the cowboy stars of the 1950s were very much aware of the particular bonds tying them to a certain demographic segment of babyboomer kids.

"What you have to understand, about Westerns and the people who were part of them," Gene Autry said, "is that it was a great way not to grow up." An interviewer of Hopalong Cassidy (speaking, as usual, through William Boyd) reported that Hoppy "seems to feel that he has tapped the same deep vein of American character which made the Old West, and that it is both his fate and his duty to strengthen the fiber of U.S. youth." "We were put in a position to be role models for many American boys and girls," Roy Rogers said, "and believe me, we have taken that job seriously." "It always happens," Rogers said of his encounters with middle-aged fans: "when people see me, they become kids again. I think some of them would crawl right into my lap if I let them." "I believed then, as I do now," testified one fan of mature years, "that if Roy Rogers knew that I needed him, he would come."

Cowboys were at their peak of popularity in the movies and on TV in the 1950s and early 1960s. Those years were the formative years for the hearts and minds of the babyboomers. Put those two facts together, and it is easy to see the New West coming. As children, a significant percentage of the babyboomers imprinted on the heroes of the open range. Cowboys trained them in consumerism; cowboys gave them purchasing desires that left them with two choices: buy or be miserable (in which case, make sure your parents hear plenty about, and finally come to share in, your misery). As adults, reaching the peak of their spending power and reaching the midpoint of their lives, assessing their achievements and assessing their disappointments, planning their vacations and planning their retirements, furnishing their homes and furnishing their clothes closets, buying movie tickets and buying novels, many of the more prosperous among the babyboomers would, predictably, be drawn back to the landscapes of their childhood yearnings, back to the mountains, deserts, and grasslands where Hopalong Cassidy and Roy Rogers and Gene Autry once rode free. With goals as clear and hands as steady as their one-time heroes, the babyboomers would reach for and draw their checkbooks and credit cards, and the New West would be the result. They no longer had to ask their parents; without having to waste time in pleading and wheedling, they could go direct to spending.

In the outdoor sports of the New West, the dreams of babyboomer childhood and the dreams of babyboomer middle age coincide. Performed in the landscape associated with televised western adventure, the vigorous outdoor exercise associated with the New West seemed to promise a postponement of aging and an extension of life itself. In a pattern familiar to several thousands of generations before them, the babyboomers have been getting clues that aging is itself a rough

"Cowboys were at their peak of popularity in the movies and on TV in the 1950s and early 1960s. Those years were the formative years for the hearts and minds of the babyboomers. Put those two facts together, and it is easy to see the New West coming."

(facing page) Coyote howls at Old Divide Trading Post, Colorado.

ride. This lesson, however, comes as a particular shock to the cohort of people who had the bad judgment to coin a slogan like "Don't trust anyone over thirty," a slogan that would not, over the long haul, be conducive to self-esteem. Thus, even if their years are going to add up anyway, babyboomers hold on to the option of behaving as if they are not over thirty, an option for which the New West provides an essential setting to play hide-and-go-seek with time. As much as they provide the center of the New West's economy, hiking, mountain biking, skiing, rock climbing, and rafting provide the rituals by which people of a certain age have been putting up a determined battle against aging.

An important indicator of the likely victor in the battle comes from members of the ski industry, who have recently developed a lively interest in demography. Ski resort operators are full subscribers to the babyboom theory of the New West, and they are, appropriately, starting to panic. The babyboom created the ski boom, and now "the problem for the ski business is that babyboomers, while numerous, are getting less physical." As one writer put it, "their knees hurt when it gets cold and that sleek snow suit doesn't fit the way it used to." The next five years, the editor of *American Demographics* magazine reported to a ski industry convention in 1996, are "the last years when you can rely on babyboomers as your core market. . . . Prepare for the departure of the baby boom now." Unhappily the 76.5 million, born between 1946 and 1964, would be followed by the comparatively paltry Generation X. But looming on the horizon was the Echo Boom, 78 million between the ages of 0 and 19 in 1996. While this group had a great enthusiasm for snowboarding, they had a much more limited interest in skiing. "How can teenagers relate to an industry that's run mostly by babyboomers?" one young person on a ski industry panel asked, indicating that this notion of "youth culture" was all too transportable over time. "Why should [teens] relate to a sport that's meant for their parents?"

For New Western babyboomers, *Mad Magazine*'s Alfred E. Newman's "What, me worry?" had been translated into "What, me age?" The eager attention that ski industry representatives gave to demographers suggested, however, that time held the winning hand. And yet the very term "New West" remains a babyboomer's dream come true. It is, elsewhere, pretty much the pattern that the passage of time transforms young things into old things. Years pass, and a young tree becomes an old tree; a new town becomes an old town; a young person becomes an old person. But the West has received a special dispensation, an option to reverse the rules of the universe. Time passes; ordinary logic reverses; and the Old West ages into the New West. This, any babyboomer would have to agree, is a heck of a good deal.

Salvation by Sage

On one count, the basic pattern behind the New West is very old: the late twentieth century provides another chapter in the long story of Americans wanting the West to be a remedy, a cure, and a restorative, wanting the West to make them feel young, vigorous, clean, and replenished again. And yet other patterns at work here make quite a break from the past.

If you want a contrast between the nineteenth-century West and the twentieth-century West, consider attitudes toward sagebrush. White people in the West in the mid-nineteenth century hated sagebrush. Mark Twain spoke for

"In the outdoor sports of the New West, the dreams of babyboomer childhood and the dreams of babyboomer middle age coincide. Performed in the landscape associated with televised Western adventure, the vigorous outdoor exercise associated with the New West seemed to promise a postponement of aging and an extension of life itself. In a pattern familiar to several thousands of generations before them, the babyboomers have been getting clues that aging is itself a rough ride."

many of his fellow white Americans when he described the botanical setting of Carson City. In this "infernal soil nothing but the fag-end of vegetable creation, 'sage-brush,' is mean enough to grow." Since few writers have directed more strong emotion at a plant, Twain is worth quoting at length:

> If you will take a lilliputian cedar tree for a model, and build a dozen imitations of it with the stiffest article of telegraph wire—set them one foot apart and then try to walk through them—you will understand, (provided the floor is covered twelve inches deep with sand) what it is to walk through a sage-brush desert. When crushed, sage-brush emits an odor which isn't exactly magnolia, and isn't exactly polecat, but a sort of compromise between the two. It looks a good deal like greasewood, and is probably the ugliest plant that was ever conceived of.

Twain, in other words, would have preferred a plant in a softer and greener model, a model which the deserts and plains of the West did not have in stock.

In the 1860s, the famed British traveler Richard Burton crossed the plains and matched Twain's feelings. He called sagebrush "this hideous growth," and that was one of his kinder remarks. "When used for cooking," Burton said, "it taints the food with a taste between camphor and turpentine." In its "gnarled, crooked, rough-barked deformity," sagebrush has "no pretensions to beauty," and "its constant presence in the worst and most desert tracks teaches one to regard it . . . with aversion." Here we have the judgment of the nineteenth century: other, better favored areas of the earth have trees and forests, and much of the West, in a draw of cosmic, botanical bad luck, got sagebrush.

Now try this act of the imagination: place Twain and Burton in a time machine and deposit them in Santa Fe, at the New Age fair and festival held there each summer. Before bewilderment can overwhelm them entirely, introduce the two time travelers to Wendy Whiteman, author of the pamphlet, *Sacred Sage: How It Heals*, on sale at the New Age fair.

In occupational terms, Whiteman describes herself as a "Wounded Healer," a term that asks for wide adoption and application: "Wounded Stockbroker," "Wounded Software-Designer," "Wounded Professor." In the 1980s, unaware of the full scale of her psychic injuries, Whiteman seemed to have everything she could want: a "secure, comfortable" East Coast world of "Cadillacs, fine jewelry, marriage, tennis, and society." But contentment moved out of her reach. "A still, small voice inside" was beginning to make itself heard, crying, "'Hear me, find me, heal me . . .'" The voice, she knew, was her "very own soul," and ignoring its call left her "listless and unmotivated." And then, "like a snake shedding layer after layer of skin," she left her marriage and her business and launched an uncertain effort to respond to the inner voice's urgings.

"By 1988," Whiteman reported, "Divine Grace saw that I needed some extra help to get grounded on my newfound path, and batted me to Second Base—the American West." When she arrived in Taos, New Mexico, "a remembrance eons old opened up within—I knew Taos, though I had never previously seen or heard of it." She had arrived, like so many drawn to the New West, at home. Walking in the Sangre de Cristo Mountains, Whiteman had her full epiphany. She was "introduced" to the "Spirit of the sagebrush": "I respectfully

"On one count, the basic pattern behind the New West is very old: the late twentieth century provides another chapter in the long story of Americans wanting the West to be a remedy, a cure, and a restorative, wanting the West to make them feel young, vigorous, clean, and replenished again."

asked the Spirit of the sage to share its knowledge of healing with me when the time was right."

Now imagine Mark Twain and Richard Burton listening to Wendy Whiteman speak in praise of that "hideous growth," that "fag-end of botanical creation." The smoke of burning sage, Whiteman believes, offers a means of "cleansing energy fields." "Our bodies," she explained, "can have astral entities 'sticking' to them."

> Have you ever had people come into and out of your space, and afterwards had it feel like they've left something behind? They could have dumped something on you: low emotions, illness, astral garbage.

What to do if you find yourself in the role of astral garbage dump? Smudging or smoking with sage proves to be the way to remove "unwanted astral beings" and "dead orgone energy" both from rooms and from people. When smudging people, it is important to pay "special attention to the chakra areas," or "the parts of humans and animals that are maximum energy intakers."

You would have had to cover Mark Twain's and Richard Burton's chakras with clouds of sage smoke to remove all of their unwanted astral beings and bring them to an understanding of Wendy Whiteman's vision of the West as a place of distinctive spiritual advantages. As the source of supply for sagebrush, and as the location of many land formations judged sacred by New Age practitioners, the old theme of the West as remedy has taken a curious new twist. The New Agers' celebration of sagebrush finds value where previous Westerners found only irritation. Conversely, many of the West's present emigrants reject the traditional forms of economic development that, for quite a long time, fueled and directed the West's development.

At its most disorienting, this rejection of earlier practices manifests itself as a direct and clear intention to reverse history, a determination to take the West and swing it around in an abrupt U-turn. Take, as one concrete example, what one might call the West's changeover in Turners. For many years, the famed historian Frederick Jackson Turner dominated interpretations of the American West, thanks to his influential 1893 essay, "The Significance of the Frontier in American History." Turner was also the author of a book called *The Rise of the New West*. Lest this title seem prophetic, note the dates of this particular "New West" in the full title: 1819–1829. Add one hundred and eighty years to the dates, though, and it is easy to imagine *The Rise of the New West* with an author of the same surname.

The West of the 1990s is, more than ever, a Turnerian West, but "Ted" has replaced "Frederick Jackson." As one of the bellwether moments in the coming of the New West, media mogul Ted Turner bought a ranch in Montana, and then flummoxed local ranchers by announcing that he was going to sell off the cattle on his range and replace them with buffalo. He wanted to make this change, first, because the buffalo were the emblematic animals of the Old West and especially of the days before the white American conquest (he was going to turn the clock back at the ranch, he said, nearly two hundred years), and second, because cattle prices were falling and buffalo prices were rising ("I also intend," Turner told his neighbors," to make twice as much from bison as you would make

"As the source of supply for sagebrush, and as the location of many land formations judged sacred by New Age practitioners, the old theme of the West as remedy has taken a curious new twist. The New Agers' celebration of sagebrush finds value where previous Westerners found only irritation. Conversely, many of the West's present emigrants reject the traditional forms of economic development that, for quite a long time, fueled and directed the West's development."

(facing page) Sagebrush fire, Colorado.

from cattle."). And the custom of casting the West as remedy was surely at work here: "In case I don't like being Vice Chairman of Time Warner," Turner said, "I can always come back here." By 1996, Turner owned nearly 1.3 million acres of western ranch land, and owned it with a "total control" that meant, in contrast to the more congested world of broadcasting, he "never has to make compromises."

Of all the people who could bear vivid witness to the changing times in the West, surely one of the best pieces of testimony would come from Bud Griffith, who had been manager of Turner's main ranch. After thirty years of managing a cattle ranch, Griffith found himself instructed by his new boss to oversee the "removal of all the outbuildings, corrals, cattle pens, and barbed wire fences that Griffith himself had put up over the past three decades," while also eliminating all the overhead power lines and utility poles. The achievements of the Old West had become the obstacles and impediments of the New West; the reversed direction of Ranch Manager Griffith's tasks embodied this surprising about-face. In one era, Griffith built corrals and fences; in the next era, he demolishes corrals and fences; and, while it does seem to add up to full employment for ranch managers, it does seem as if Griffith's life is some sort of regional capsule-version of the alienated labor of the army private who digs holes in order to fill them up.

The combination of sentiment and romance (Turner's dream of the lost West, restored) with economic ambition (Turner's recognition of the pleasant rise in buffalo prices) characterizes the New West. As Ted Turner once said, "If I want to save the West, I'll have to buy it." Far from states of opposition, commerce and sentiment weave between and around each other in a maypole dance, with the Western landscape playing the role of the maypole. Consider, for instance, the Arizona town of Sedona and its two namesake magazines. Located in handsome redrock country, with mountain and deserts in a riveting landscape dialogue, Sedona is one of the principal boom towns of the New West, with recreationists, retirees, and New Age seekers increasing the population dramatically.

One of the magazines named *Sedona* celebrates the town's abundant offerings in real estate deals, tourist entertainment, art galleries, and clothing and jewelry shops. This very glossy magazine, by all appearances, does not struggle against a shortage of advertising income. Housing developments in handsome redrock landscapes dominate the pages. "In the shadow of ruins from ancient Native American civilizations," to cite the description of one typical development, Enchantment Resort "combine[s] the tranquility of nature with all the amenities of sophisticated living." Mystic Hills is "Sedona's most beautiful and environmentally sensitive master planned residential community"—"so desirable that a great many of Mystic Hills homesite owners are Presidents or CEOs of Leading Corporations."

All this is very familiar, classic Western boosterism cast into a modern lingo. And then one turns to the second magazine named *Sedona*. This one, as a clue to its distinctiveness, carries the subtitle *Journal of Emergence!* If real estate dominates the other *Sedona*, somewhat less real states are the topic here. The cover promises "Past Lives of a Being from Neptune! Channeling from YHWH, Zoosh, Lazaris, Ramtha, Vywamus, Hilarion and Others! Features on Crop Circles,

"The West of the 1990s is, more than ever, a Turnerian West, but 'Ted' has replaced 'Frederick Jackson.' As one of the bellwether moments in the coming of the New West, media mogul Ted Turner bought a ranch in Montana, and then flummoxed local ranchers by announcing that he was going to sell off the cattle on his range and replace them with buffalo. He wanted to make this change, first, because the buffalo were the emblematic animals of the Old West and especially of the days before the white American conquest (he was going to turn the clock back at the ranch, he said, nearly two hundred years), and second, because cattle prices were falling and buffalo prices were rising ('I also intend,' Turner told his neighbors, 'to make twice as much from bison as you would make from cattle.')."

Mayan Calendar, Reincarnation, Healing and Astrology! Predictions on Earth Changes, the Weather, Human Energy, and More!" As a literary journal, *Sedona: Journal of Emergence!* has a very distinctive feature. Most of the articles are, one might say, coauthored, with a regular human being and a cosmic being in channeling partnership: "How Your Thought Affects Every Living Thing," by YHWH through Arthur Fanning; "You Are Creating the Changes," by Ramses through Brent Powell; "July Predictions," by Peter and the Beings of Light through Ruth Ryden; "The Great Infusion," by Archangel Michael through Ronna Herman; "Empowering Your Imagination," by Lazaris through Jack Pursel. In one of the few variations from the norm of cross-entity collaboration, the author of "Cosmic Astrology," Scott Amun of Cottonwood, Arizona, "writes through his present self," though lest this seem too conventional, note that he does this by "resonating from his past in ancient Sumeria."

A picture of the channeler, though never of the coauthor, accompanies each article, and the most astonishing element of the whole periodical is the utterly normal appearance of these people. They are the neighbors next door; they appear to be more likely voices for Tupperware and Avon products than for celestial beings. And yet they have struck up very comfortable partnerships with ancient and alien beings. "It is a pleasure to be connecting with you once again," Lazaris remarks to us through Jack Pursel, sounding as much at ease as a luncheon speaker at a Rotary or Elks Club meeting.

The "End-Time Historian" Zoosh and his channeler, Sedona resident Robert Shapiro, are a particularly comfortable and prolific pair. Shapiro "grew up with the experience of ET contact. Throughout his life there have been communications with beings from several star systems and dimensions." A channeler for "over sixteen years," Shapiro "can channel almost anyone or anything with an exceptionally clear and profound connection," but he "most often channels Zoosh." Zoosh and Shapiro are now at work on the third volume of *The Explorer Race*, immersed in a writing process quite different from more terrestrial forms of composition. Every Tuesday night in Sedona, Zoosh dictates through Shapiro; for a $10 admission fee, one can "be a part of this historic process as Zoosh goes deeper into the history and the future of the Explorer Race—the human race."

Thus, two seemingly very different, actually very compatible Sedona magazines. Neither magazine is, finally, any more or less commercial than the other. Both are full of advertisements, and hearty and earnest suggestions for the spending of money. However much time channelers might spend in the company of the extraterrestrials, they remain themselves material beings, with material desires and needs. Thus, books and tapes and workshops and healing sessions come with an appropriate fee schedule. Sedona is, in New Age belief, a vortex—a place where cosmic energies accumulate. Places where cosmic energies congregate are, in the 1990s, places where real estate agents congregate. More often than not, these two congregations prove capable of interfaith services.

Home on the Page

Once upon a time, there was a region whose stories fell into a trap. While life was as varied in this region as it was anywhere else on the planet, writers

"This very glossy magazine, [Sedona,] by all appearances, does not struggle against a shortage of advertising income. Housing developments in handsome redrock landscapes dominate the pages. 'In the shadow of ruins from ancient Native American civilizations,' to cite the description of one typical development, Enchantment Resort 'combine[s] the tranquility of nature with all the amenities of sophisticated living.' Mystic Hills is 'Sedona's most beautiful and environmentally sensitive master planned residential community'—'so desirable that a great many of Mystic Hills homesite owners are Presidents or CEOs of Leading Corporations.'"

found themselves stuck with two choices. By the first choice, they could write stories about white men riding horses in wide open spaces and sometimes shooting at each other. These stories would sell, but they would be recognized by everyone as unoriginal and formulaic Westerns. Or, by the second choice, they could write stories that reflected the actual human complexity of the region—stories about towns and cities, mines and boarding houses, ethnic barrios and Indian reservations, missile silos and sheep ranches. These stories would probably not sell well, and might not even get published; moreover, by virtue of the absence of white men on horseback, they would be disqualified from the category of Western literature.

This was a disheartening pair of choices. For a time, only a few writers gave the second choice a try, and even those who succeeded received only stingy praise and recognition. Western American literature had been backed into a corner: ride with the cowboys or don't ride at all. In the 1970s, Norman Maclean tried to find a publisher for his Montana stories, and the publishers found them commercially unpromising and told Maclean "No." "These stories have trees in them," one editor explained his decision. About the same time, twelve publishers said an equally emphatic "No" to Ivan Doig and his Montana memoir. They liked his writing, but they were certain that the manuscript had no commercial appeal.

And then the fairy-tale moment in this story about stories arrived. The Ugly Duckling turned into a swan; the prince proposed to Cinderella; the University of Chicago Press published Maclean's *A River Runs Through It*, and sold thousands and thousands of copies; the thirteenth publisher took Doig's *This House of Sky*, with comparable success. The more trees—and mesas and mountains and arroyos and streams and canyons—that one could get into a book, the better the chance of its publication. As peak moments go in the annals of regional vengeance and vindication, no one ever topped Norman Maclean's on a certain day in 1981. The letter he wrote was published twelve years later in *Harpers*, under the very apt title, "A Grudge Runs Through It." Maclean had been corresponding with an editor at Alfred A. Knopf about the prospect of publishing his second book, *Young Men and Fire*. He abruptly remembered that "Alfred A. Knopf turned down [the soon-to-be-bestselling *A River Runs Though It*] after playing games with it, or at least the game of cat's-paw, now rolling it over and saying they were going to publish it and then rolling it on its back when the president of the company announced it wouldn't sell." And now Knopf had expressed interest in his next book. Finding it likely that some of the "finest fuck-you prose in the English language" had been written under similar circumstances, Maclean added a memorable entry: "If the situation ever arose when Alfred A. Knopf was the only publishing house remaining in the world and I was the sole surviving author, that would mark the end of the world of books. Very sincerely, Norman Maclean."

The spillways were open, and a great flood of Western books poured through. Readers, who had found "keeping up" with Western American literature to be one of the easier projects in the literary world, were inundated. Norman Maclean, Ivan Doig, William Kittredge, James Welch, Mary Clearman Blew, Simon Ortiz, Rudolfo Anaya, Teresa Jordan, Leslie Marmon Silko, N. Scott Momaday, Terry Tempest Williams, Sherman Alexie, Judith Freeman, Levi Peterson, Luci Tapahonso, Dierdre McNamer, Linda Hogan, Barbara Kingsolver,

"Western American literature had been backed into a corner: ride with the cowboys or don't ride at all. In the 1970s, Norman Maclean tried to find a publisher for his Montana stories, and the publishers found them commercially unpromising and told Maclean 'No.' 'These stories have trees in them,' one editor explained his decision. About the same time, twelve publishers said an equally emphatic 'No' to Ivan Doig and his Montana memoir. They liked his writing, but they were certain that the manuscript had no commercial appeal."

(facing page) Sun sculpture along Baca Grant Way North, in the Crestone community of spiritual followers, Colorado.

Joy Harjo, C. L. Rawlins: the bookshelves began bending under the weight of their work.

Many of the reasons for the general popularity of the West worked equally well as explanations for this regional literary bonanza. But there was an added dimension here, one connected to the fact that many of these writers were born and raised in the West and now spoke explicitly of writing about "home." For more than a century, the pattern of the most influential writing about the West had been of the "visit from outside" tradition. Easterners or Europeans traveled to the West and found it exotic and unsettling; their perception of Western difference set their writings in the vein of discovery and surprise. In the late twentieth century, writing about the West underwent a basic reorientation; instead of unsettled outsiders writing from their position as strangers, literature about the West was, more and more, the product of people who had grown up in the West, who did not see it as exotic, but who saw it as home. While Indian people were leading participants in the Western literary renaissance, many of those now claiming status as insiders were the descendants of the white invaders.

Having so many people who were born and raised in the West writing well-received novels, short stories, poems, essays, and memoirs has been tremendously beneficial. Their writing has improved our chances for regional self-understanding; it has given interested non-Westerners a much more grounded and complicated picture of the West to contemplate; it has done a great deal to lessen the regional inferiority complex that has, for so long, been an element of the Western intellectual scene.

And yet, in the 1990s, one begins to wonder about some aspects of this celebration of the nativeness of white writers. Isn't there a good chance that this will, in the judgment of future historians, register as a predictable phase for a settler society? Begin with a place occupied by aboriginal people; they may have migrated and shifted location, but they were native to North America over centuries and millennia. Then an invading population appears on the scene and takes control of the place, generating all the moral discomfort and unease that comes with conquest. At a certain point, the descendants of those invaders could be expected to make a great show of settling down, nestling in, cocooning, declaring and demonstrating their credentials as indigenous folk, referring to their places of origin as home. It is a movement in which I was an enthusiastic participant, and it was exactly the movement that one would expect from a settler society now entering into its fifth or sixth generation. Whatever might be in the minds of individual writers, the audience enthusiasm for this school of writing suggests that the idea of whites at home in the West relieves some of the inherited tensions of conquest. Tired of being the invaders and the intruders, whites now find a way of claiming pedigree, a line of descent, a status of legitimacy.

The struggle to claim legitimacy is, of course, the oldest story in the region: one group of people gets settled in, and then another group of people appears on the scene and challenges the standing and power of the group who arrived earlier, and then everyone struggles and pushes and shoves to try to get possession of the title, "Legitimate and Authentic Resident of the West." Sometimes the locals, who are defending themselves ardently against the newest wave of emigrants and settlers, are people who only established their own stand-

"The spillways were open, and a great flood of Western books poured through. Readers, who had found 'keeping up' with Western American literature to be one of the easier projects in the literary world, were inundated. Norman Maclean, Ivan Doig, William Kittredge, James Welch, Mary Clearman Blew, Simon Ortiz, Rudolfo Anaya, Teresa Jordan, Leslie Marmon Silko, N. Scott Momaday, Terry Tempest Williams, Sherman Alexie, Judith Freeman, Levi Peterson, Luci Tapahonso, Dierdre McNamer, Linda Hogan, Barbara Kingsolver, Joy Harjo, C. L. Rawlins: the bookshelves began bending under the weight of their work."

ing as locals in the very recent past. Thus, the movement among writers to claim the West as "home" and to stake their claims to the status of Western insiders, natives, and indigenes becomes the most recent episode in a long-running contest to claim legitimacy, a contest for which there have never been any agreed-upon ground rules.

Have we gone overboard in celebrating the insights of insiders? Have we, by sanctifying line or descent or birthplace or pedigree, mystified the process of understanding a place, and condemned new arrivals to a permanent condition of folly and ignorance? Have we, at the same time, discounted the value of the insights and impressions that newcomers, outsiders, and visitors have been known to have from time to time? While the knowledge that comes from being at home is often deep and valuable, the observations of visitors do not, by that recognition, surrender their value. One thinks of the pleasure and surprise still triggered by a reading of Meriwether Lewis's and William Clark's journals; one thinks of the heightened appreciation of one's home territory to be gained by reading travelers like Isabella Bird; one thinks, especially, of Lord James Bryce's observations in *The American Commonwealth*. Touring the West in the 1880s, the British aristocrat and ultimate outsider found the behavior of Western boosters to be a marvel and puzzle. In his book, Bryce wrote down a speech he wished he had the occasion to give to Western men. These remarks carry undiminished relevance for the New West, and they also reawaken respect for outsiders as interpreters of the West:

> Gentlemen, why in heaven's name this haste? You have time enough. No enemy threatens you. No volcano will rise from beneath you. Ages and ages lie before you. Why sacrifice the present to the future, fancying that you will be happier when your fields teem with wealth and your cities with people? In Europe we have cities wealthier and more populous than yours, and we are not happy. You dream of your posterity, but your posterity will look back to yours as the golden age, and envy those who first burst into this silent splendid Nature, who first lifted up their axes upon these tall trees. . . . Why, then, seek to complete in a few decades what the other nations of the world took thousands of years over in the older continents? Why do things rudely and ill which need to be done well, seeing that the welfare of your descendants may turn upon them? Why in your hurry to subdue and utilize Nature, squander her splendid gifts? . . . Why hasten the advent of that threatening day when the vacant spaces of the continent shall have been filled, and the poverty or discontent of the older States shall find no outlet? You have opportunities such as mankind has never had before, and may never have again. Your work is great and noble; it is done for a future longer and vaster than our conceptions can embrace. Why not make its outlines and beginnings worthy of these destinies the thought of which gilds your hopes and elevates your purposes?

Why not, indeed?

Region, Heal Thyself

In the 1990s, the idea of the West as the remedy for individual and national ills was running head on into a visible and unmistakable fact: the West

"The struggle to claim legitimacy is, of course, the oldest story in the region: one group of people gets settled in, and then another group of people appears on the scene and challenges the standing and power of the group who arrived earlier, and then everyone struggles and pushes and shoves to try to get possession of the title, 'Legitimate and Authentic Resident of the West.' Sometimes the locals, who are defending themselves ardently against the newest wave of emigrants and settlers, are people who only established their own standing as locals in the very recent past."

(facing page) Top: Debris from above-ground nuclear bomb blast, Frenchman Flat, Nevada. These aluminum domes were tested as community shelters; the area may become a tourist attraction. Bottom: "Ground Zero"—outsider art by DeWayne Williams at Dooby Lane, Black Rock Desert, Nevada. The site includes rocks inscribed with excepts from the Bible, Koran, Beat Poetry, and vernacular stories.

was badly in need of remedies itself. The social conflicts over growth, the wounds inflicted by the decline of rural enterprises, the overstretched infrastructure of roads and water systems, and very familiar American dilemmas of inequality by race and class all served as reminders that the West's shelf life as a remedy was reaching its expiration date.

Most compelling—and most expensive—of the situations calling for remedy were the nuclear weapons production and testing sites, places like Hanford, Rocky Flats, and the Nevada Test Site. In the 1980s, reporters and community groups dug out the hidden stories of these places, stories of shortcuts, expedient and risky waste disposal, compromises on safety, and knowingly misleading reassurances to the public. The terrible paradox finally came to light: during the years of the Cold War, American atomic weapons were never used to injure an enemy population; the only people whose well-being was jeopardized by these weapons were American citizens—uranium miners working in unventilated mines in the Four Corners region; production plant workers exposed to worrisome doses of radiation; people living downwind from the Nevada Test Site, and downwind and downriver from the Hanford Nuclear Reservation.

The end of the Cold War made these revelations all the more unsettling, since the unravelling of the Soviet Union carried a particular blow for the American West. Without an evil empire to oppose, the mandate for preparedness in defense lost much of its punch. Base closing, downsizing, and the termination of weapons production shook many local Western economies. Without an evil empire of communism to serve as external threat, the West lost one of its principal claims on federal money. The Cold War had provided the reason to continue the defense-spending party begun in World War II; indeed, the party went on so long it gained the status of a normal, taken-for-granted, and even reliable element of regional prosperity. Western towns and cities with military bases as neighbors benefitted most directly; patriotism merged pleasantly with the advantages flowing from the presence of a larger workforce with paychecks to spend.

Thus, there were double, even triple, reasons for a Western sense of resentment at the end of the Cold War. Lost access to federal money was the clearest and most direct inspiration for injury. Tangled together with that was the recognition of the Cold War's legacy to the West of radioactivity and toxic chemicals. Muddling this already complicated situation was the ideological disorientation brought on by the loss of the Soviet Union. The Cold War had established a mandate for a patriotic telling of Western American history. The struggle with Communism required the United States to be the innocent and honorable party; with American identity so thoroughly tied to the images of the frontier, the cowboy, and the pioneer, Western American history was the perfect piece of turf for a tug-of-war between those who insisted on American innocence and honor and those who saw human nature, wherever it operated, as complex and mixed. With the end of the Cold War, the rope pulling for a patriotic and proud version of the development of the American West suddenly snapped. The pattern presented by this tug-of-war is a common one: when the rope on one side breaks, the forces on both sides lose their footing; no one knows quite which way to pull; and thus the pulls come from all directions at once, in a pattern almost beyond discerning.

The question at issue was an impossible one: How had the West turned out? No one could deny that the development of Western resources had exacted

high social and environmental costs. But was the outcome nonetheless one to be celebrated? Assessing the degree, direction, and quality of recent change in the West has not been an easy task for anyone. The national press has not been of great help in the task.

Various Western states observed their statehood centennials in 1989, and *Newsweek* used that occasion to appraise the condition of Wyoming, Montana, Idaho, Washington, and North and South Dakota. Rhetorically, this article was its own marvel of writing about the West, a high achievement in prose drenched with doom and gloom. "America's Outback," the article was called: "Amid scarcity and broken dreams, six western states mark 100 hard years at the end of the cracked whip." A flood of "d-words"—decline, destitution, desolation, desperation—cast the hundred-year birthday party for these states in shades of black: "the commemoration," *Newsweek* said, "is pocked by scarcity and stillborn dreams."

Thus was the curtain drawn down upon the West: "the frontier's precious vein of promise and possibility is running out." The Rocky Mountain West—or at least its northern half—was a battered, smashed, wrecked, and ruined place. If there were a Dr. Jack Kevorkian for regions, it was time to get his pager and lodge an urgent request.

And then a few years passed.

Now it was *Time* magazine weighing in for an appraisal, and it took a keen eye to recognize the dilapidated and drained region of four years before. "Boom Time in The Rockies," the cover of *Time* said: "More jobs and fewer hassles have Americans heading for the hills." "These are sustainable economies, absolutely," *Time* quoted former Colorado governor Richard Lamm, belying his nickname "Governor Gloom." It's not just another cycle but a permanent, historic shift." With a series of portraits of refugees fleeing from both coasts, *Time* declared the states from Montana to New Mexico to be "the good news-belt," with a higher growth rate and a lower unemployment rate than any other region of the country.

For a reader trying to be attentive to these various expert reports, bewilderment was the only sensible response. When was the West in a bust and when was it in a boom, and how on earth was one to tell the difference? If the national media at one moment told you that you were living in a moribund region and, at the next moment told you that you were living in one of the most vital regions of the nation, in what sort of region did you actually live? If one sector—the traditional rural, extractive industries—of a local economy was declining sadly, and another sector—recreation and the relocation of prosperous, amenity-seeking settlers—was growing exuberantly, was the economy in a boom or a bust? And, if the prosperity, cheer, comfort, and good times of the privileged rested on the hard work and low pay of the poor, how widely distributed was the "good" in this "good news-belt"?

On Thanksgiving Day, 1994, one of the most powerful statements on the dilemmas of the New West appeared. "The Heights of the Mountains Are His: The Development of God's Country" was a pastoral letter from J. Francis Stafford, Archbishop of Denver. If the New Agers devoted any thought or attention to the distribution of wealth in the New West, such concern seldom works its way into magazines, books, newsletters, leaflets, or transcripts of channelling.

"The Cold War had provided the reason to continue the defense-spending party begun in World War II; indeed, the party went on so long it gained the status of a normal, taken-for-granted, and even reliable element of regional prosperity. Western towns and cities with military bases as neighbors benefitted most directly; patriotism merged pleasantly with the advantages flowing from the presence of a larger workforce with paychecks to spend."

(facing page) Highway deconstructed to be rebuilt, Las Vegas, Nevada.

In contrast to New Age comfort and complacency, in this remarkable pastoral letter, the Catholic Church took readers on an unsettling journey to the foundation of the New West.

Colorado's mountain and West Slope communities are in the midst of a boom, the Archbishop's letter noted, focused on recreation. This episode of growth exposes these small towns to particular peril:

> In the last century the Western Slope functioned as a resource colony for timber and mining interests. Those scars will be with us for generations. We cannot afford to stand by now as the culture of a leisure colony, like the walled communities which dominate so many American suburbs, takes its place.

Resort communities like Breckenridge rely on the labor of women and men who cannot afford to live in these islands of privilege; they are forced to live at some distance in less ritzy towns, often in trailers or tents, enduring "long commutes on highways that, especially during the winter months, cannot safely or adequately handle the traffic flow." Confronted with the needs of the working poor, "the basic social infrastructure is simply being overwhelmed," with churches, public schools, utilities, courts, and social services swamped by more demands than they can handle.

"The New West's Servant Economy," *High Country News* headlined an article in 1995. Among the preparers and servers of food and the cleaners of rooms, the writer Ray Ring found "all sorts of people who came a long way to earn treadmill wages here and get tucked away in the trailer-park ghettos or low-income apartments or behind some pretty mountain, where their problems are mostly invisible to the skiers and vacation-homesteaders." Ring even found a group of West African immigrants, dispatched by an employment agency in New York to Colorado, where they made a daily 120-mile commute from Kremmling to their jobs at the Breckenridge Hilton.

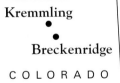

As an Immigration and Naturalization Service raid in Jackson, Wyoming, in 1996 showed, Mexican immigrants are an increasingly important part of the New West labor force. That pre–Labor Day raid seized one hundred twenty undocumented Mexican workers and sent them home; a little over a week later, one hundred and sixteen had returned. As working class residents were squeezed out of the mountain boom towns, as ski bums aged and sought more rewarding jobs, "into this vacuum came the Latinos." "El Nuevo West," *High Country News* labeled the situation in late 1996, pointing out the continuity between the past and the present: "The gruntwork in the West has always been done by the foreign born. El Nuevo West is also the old West."

These stark differences in wealth and privilege in the New West, the Archbishop's Pastoral Letter said, must be understood "in the wider moral ecology of our lives." "We are moral as well as economic creatures"; "authentic growth can never be merely economic; it is always primarily moral." Thus, in New Western towns where the privileged ignore the dilemmas of the poor, "we may legitimately speak of economic 'structures of sin,' constructed stone by stone from many acts of indifference and other personal sins over time."

"When was the West in a bust and when was it in a boom, and how on earth was one to tell the difference? If the national media at one moment told you that you were living in a moribund region and, at the next moment, told you that you were living in one of the most vital regions of the nation, in what sort of region did you actually live? If one sector—the traditional rural, extractive industries—of a local economy was declining sadly, and another sector— recreation and the relocation of prosperous, amenity-seeking settlers—was growing exuberantly, was the economy in a boom or a bust?"

(facing page) The Las Vegas Strip was officially designated a Scenic Route on March 21, 1996. View from in front of the Frontier Casino.

"In the most memorable warning in the Pastoral Letter, Archbishop Stafford spoke to the biggest social, economic, moral, and cultural problem of the New West: 'What we risk creating, then, is a theme-park 'alternative reality' for those who have the money to purchase entrance. Around this Rocky Mountain theme park will sprawl a growing buffer zone of the working poor.' The dreams of people of privilege would design the theme park, and the hopes of the poor would recruit the workforce to build and maintain it."

(facing page) Top: Moonrise over the Black Rock Desert. The desert, in Nevada's Basin and Range topography, encompasses a huge dry lake bed or playa, home to the world land speed record. Bottom: Winter fog from hot springs, The Needles, Pyramid Lake, Nevada.

In the most memorable warning in the Pastoral Letter, Archbishop Stafford spoke to the biggest social, economic, moral, and cultural problem of the New West: "What we risk creating, then, is a theme-park 'alternative reality' for those who have the money to purchase entrance. Around this Rocky Mountain theme park will sprawl a growing buffer zone of the working poor." The dreams of people of privilege would design the theme park, and the hopes of the poor would recruit the workforce to build and maintain it.

The dream is unending, even if it changes its shape like Proteus. Through sagebrush smoke or affordable real estate, through novel workplaces or novel vacations, through every variation on the theme of newness, the West will make us whole. It will separate us from the familiar and the wearying; it will return us to bedrock; it will reassure us that we are people who matter. In a region so dominated by mountains, the West lies, as the Archbishop's Pastoral Letter said, in the "shadows of heaven itself." Heaven's shade both shelters and darkens our lives.

Notes

Chapter 1
A Region Defined

1. Joel Garreau, *The Nine Nations of North America* (New York: Avon Books, 1981), 287–327.

2. "Boom Time in the Rockies: More Jobs and Fewer Hassles Have Americans Heading for the Hills," *Time*, September 6, 1993, 20–27.

3. Donald Snow, "As the Mirage Begins to Fade," *Northern Lights*, Fall, 1994, 3.

4. Ed Marston, "This Boom Will End Like All the Others—In a Deep, Deep Recession," *High Country News*, September 5, 1994, 22–23.

5. "Unrest in the West." *Time*, October 23, 1995, 52–66.

6. Ibid., 64.

7. Sharman Apt Russell, *Kill the Cowboy: A Battle of Mythology in the New West* (Reading, Mass.: Addison-Wesley, 1993), 2.

8. Judy Blunt, "The Good and Bad of Ranching," in Karl Hess and John Baden, eds., *Writers on the Range* (Niwot, Colo.: University Press of Colorado, in press).

9. William Kittredge, *Owning it All* (St. Paul: Graywolf Press, 1987), 61.

Chapter 2
Infrastructure for the New West

1. "Boom Time in the Rockies," *Time*.

2. Ed Marston, "An Ersatz Democracy Gets what it Deserves." *High County News,* January 23, 1995, 20.

3. Enos Mills, "Touring in our National Parks." *Country Life in America,* January, 1913, 36.

4. Wallace Stegner, "The Rediscovery of America: 1946," *The Sound of Mountain Water: The Changing American West* (New York: E.P. Dutton, 1980) 46–76.

5. "Boom Time in the Rockies," *Time*.

6. Bernard DeVoto, "The West: A Plundered Province," *Harper's*, August, 1934, 355–364.

Chapter 3
Water for the New West

1. John Wesley Powell, *Report on the Lands of the Arid Region of the United States* (Washington, D.C.: Government Printing Office, 1879); see also Wallace Stegner, *Beyond the Hundredth Meridian: John Wesley Powell and the Second Opening of the West* (Boston, Mass.: Houghton Mifflin Company, 1953).

2. Sandy Tolan, "The Central Arizona Project is Designed to Water Homes," *High Country News*, February 20, 1984.

3. William Graves, "When the Well's Dry, We Know the Worth of Water," *National Geographic*, November, 1993, 1.

4. Thomas S. Maddock and Walter G. Hines, "Meeting Future Public Water Supply Needs: A Southwest Perspective," *Water Resources Bulletin,* 31(2), 1995, 319, 325.

5. U.S. Geological Survey, "Estimated Use of Water in the United States in 1990," *National Circular,* 1081, 1991.

6. Mohamed T. El-Ashry and Diana C. Gibbons, *Water and Arid Lands of the Western United States* (New York: Cambridge University Press, 1988), 12; US Geological Survey, "Estimated Use of Water in the United States in 1990."

7. Richard Conniff, "California: Desert in Disguise," *National Geographic*, November, 1993, 38.

8. Philip L. Fradkin, *A River No More: The Colorado River and the West* (New York: Alfred A. Knopf, 1981).

9. Wallace Stegner, *Beyond the Hundredth Meridian*.

10. Marc Reisner, *Cadillac Desert: The American West and Its Disappearing Water* (New York: Penguin Books, 1986), 117.

11. Ibid.

12. Ibid., 167–70; Paul Koberstein, "Northwest is Asked to Give Up 18 Dams," *High Country News*, February 7, 1994.

13. Charles F. Wilkinson, *Crossing the Next Meridian: Land, Water, and the Future of the West* (Washington, D.C.: Island Press, 1992).

14. Pat Ford, "How the Basin's Salmon-Killing System Works," *High Country News*, April 22, 1991.

15. Charles F. Wilkinson, *Crossing the Next Meridian*, 200.

16. Mary Wood, "A Comparison: Lessons from the Columbia Basin and the Upper Colorado Basin Fish Recovery Efforts," *Proceedings of a Conference on Biodiversity and the Endangered Species Act* (Natural Resources Law Center, University of Colorado, Boulder, 1996).

17. Paul Koberstein, "Northwest is Asked to Give Up 18 Dams"; Pat Ford, "How the Basin's Salmon-Killing System Works."

18. Northwest Power Planning Council, *1994 Columbia River Basin Fish and Wildlife Program Overview*; Paul Koberstein, "Northwest is Asked to Give Up 18 Dams."

19. Paul Koberstein, "Northwest is Asked to Give Up 18 Dams."

20. Charles F. Wilkinson, *Crossing the Next Meridian*.

21. Reisner, *Cadillac Desert*, 194–98; Wilkinson, *Crossing the Next Meridian*.

22. Fradkin, *A River No More*, 155.

23. Fact sheets from the Colorado Rivers Alliance, Durango, Colo.

24. Steve Hinchman, "Animas-La Plata: The Last Big Dam in the West," *High Country News*, March 22, 1993.

25. Ed Marston, "Cease-Fire Called on the Animas-La Plata Front," *High Country News*, November 11, 1996.

26. Bryan Foster, "Some Dams Self-Destruct," *High Country News*, February 7, 1994.

27. Barry Noreen, "Dam Opponents Boil Over at Conifer Hearing," *High Country News*, May 9, 1988.

Chapter 4
People in the New West

1. Stan Steiner, *The Waning of the West* (New York: St. Martin's Press, 1989), 199.

2. Joel Garreau, *The Nine Nations of North America*.

3. Timothy Egan, "Eastward Ho! Disenchanted, Californians Turn to the Interior West," *New York Times*, May 30, 1993, 1, 12.

4. William Kittredge, "The Last Safe Place," *Time*, September 6, 1993, 27.

5. John Sedgwick, "The Californication of Montana," *GQ*, December, 1995, 243.

6. Quoted in Ray Ring and Alexie Rubenstein, "Resort Towns Battle Monsters," *High Country News*, September 5, 1994, 8.

7. Ed Marston, "This Boom Will End Like All the Others."

8. Ray Ring, "The New West's Servant Economy," *High Country News*, April 17, 1995, 1, 8–14.

9. Gundars Rudzitis, John Hintz, and Christy Watrous, "Snapshots of a Changing Northwest" (Department of Geography, University of Idaho, Moscow, 1996).

10. Raymond Rasker, "Rural Development, Conservation, and Public Policy in the Greater Yellowstone Ecosystem," *Society and Natural Resources*, 6, 1993, 109–126.

11. Thomas M. Power, *Lost Landscapes and Failed Economies* (Washington, D.C.: Island Press, 1996).

12. Gundars Rudzitis, John Hintz, and Christy Watrous, "Snapshots of a Changing Northwest."

13. Thomas M. Power, *Lost Landscapes and Failed Economies*.

Chapter 5
New West Lifestyles

1. Timothy Egan, "Picking up the Vibes in Sedona," *New York Times*, July 7, 1996, Travel Section, 11, 17.

2. Listings of New Age, alternative lifestyle, and transformative vacation centers in the West appear in: *New Consciousness Sourcebook: Spiritual Community Guide*, Sixth Edition (Pomona, Calif.: Arcline Publications, 1985); Ellen Lederman, *Vacations That Can Change Your Life* (Naperville, Ill.: Sourcebooks, Inc., 1996); Roger Housden, *Retreat: Time Apart for Silence and Solitude* (New York: Harper Collins, 1995), 174–181.

3. Patricia Stokoski, *Riches and Regrets: Gambling in Two Colorado Mountain Towns* (Niwot, Colo.: University Press of Colorado, 1996).

4. Pro Rodeo Cowboy Association Media Guide (Colorado Springs, Colo.: Pro Rodeo Cowboy Association, 1996).

5. Kurt Rhody, *Rendezvous: Reliving the Fur Trading Era of 1750–1840* (Mariposa, Calif.: The Sierra Press, 1996).

6. Quoted in Philip L. Fradkin, *A River No More*, 181.

7. Lauren Lucas, "A Synopsis of the History of Recreational River Running on the Colorado River in Grand Canyon National Park," *Glen Canyon Environmental Studies*, February 4, 1987.

8. Edward Abbey, *The Monkey Wrench Gang* (New York: Avon Books, 1975), 53.

9. Wallace Stegner, "Coda: Wilderness Letter," in *The Sound of Mountain Water: The Changing American West* (New York: E.P. Dutton, 1980), 153.

10. Steve Bonowski, "Colorado 14er Initiative," *Trail and Timberline*, May, 1996, 410.

11. "Separation of Rock and State," *Newsweek*, May 20, 1996, 8; "An Excellent Effort: Climbers Comply with Devil's Tower Voluntary Closure," *Access Notes*, Fall, 1995.

12. Richard Boyer and David Savageau, *Places Rated Almanac: Your Guide to Finding the Best Places to Live in America* (Chicago: Rand McNally and Co., 1981). The latest edition is: David Savageau and Richard Boyer, *Places Rated Almanac* (New York: Macmillan, 1993).

13. John Villani, *The 100 Best Small Art Towns in America* (Santa Fe: John Muir Publications, 1996).

Chapter 6:
The Ugly West

1. Terry Tempest Williams, *Refuge: An Unnatural History of Family and Place* (New York: Vintage Books, 1991).

2. Raye Ringholz, *Uranium Frenzy: Boom and Bust on the Colorado Plateau* (Albuquerque: University of New Mexico Press, 1989), 11.

3. Grand Canyon Visibility Transport Commission, *Improving Western Vistas* (Denver, Colo.: Western Governors Association, 1996).

4. Paul S. Martin, "Pleistocene Overkill," *Natural History Magazine*, December, 1967, 32–38.

5. Quoted in David A. Dary, *The Buffalo Book: The Full Saga of the American Animal* (Columbus: Swallow Press/Ohio University Press, 1974), 21.

6. Hank Fischer, *Wolf Wars* (Helena, Mont.: Falcon Press, 1995).

7. Gary Ferguson, *The Yellowstone Wolves: The First Year* (Helena, Mont.: Falcon Press, 1996).

Chapter 7
Visions for the Next West

1. Erik Larson, "Unrest in the West," *Time*, October 23, 1995, 52–66.

2. Dan Dagget, *Beyond the Rangeland Conflict: Toward a West that Works* (Layton, Utah: Gibbs Smith, 1995).

3. Information on conservationists' proposals for wilderness in southern Utah can be obtained from the Southern Utah Wilderness Alliance, 1471 South 1100 East, Salt Lake City, Utah, 84105–2423.

4. The Wildlands Project, special issue of *Wild Earth* (1992). Information on the Northern Rockies Ecosystem Protection Act, and related efforts to protect large swaths of Rocky Mountain Ecosystems can be obtained from the Alliance for the Wild Rockies, Box 8731, Missoula, Mont., 59807.

Map Source Notes

Base Maps

Base maps for the *Atlas of the New West* are derived from U.S. Geological Survey (USGS) Digital Cartographic Data (DCD) and Digital Elevation Model (DEM). Some of this data was downloaded directly from the USGS, and we also used ArcUSA™ 1:2 million, a product of the Environmental Systems Research Institute, Inc., which provides a convenient compilation of these and other map data for the U.S. We updated and checked places and features using other sources, including USGS and other government agency specialty maps (digital and hard copy) and official road maps of the Western states. We cross-referenced these to various sources, including National Geographic Society maps and atlases, American Automobile Association maps, DeLorme Mapping's *Atlas and Gazetteer™* for selected Western states, and the *New Mexico Road and Recreation Atlas*, by Benchmark Maps.

The American West, page 11, Lay of the Land, page 48, and Damming the West, page 85

Land cover coloration for The American West from Advanced Very High Resolution Radiometer (AVHRR) imagery for July, 1992, downloaded from the USGS. GRASS, a U.S. Army Corps of Engineers geographic information system, and EdWare™ from Computer Terrain Mapping, Inc. (CTM), Boulder, Colo., were used for color selections, projections, and rendering.

Places on the Land, page 50

A selection of towns and cities from USGS place names file.

The Bureaucratic West, page 52

Information from each agency applied to base map with USGS DCD state and county boundaries.

The Region Compared, page 54

Overlaid base maps with constant scale.

A Blank Space, page 55

Data are 1995 county population estimates from the Population Distribution and Population Estimates Branches, U.S. Census Bureau, divided by county area in square miles.

Black Hole, page 56

Map from the International Dark-Sky Association, Tucson, Ariz.

Filling the Void, page 57

Calculated from 1990 and 1995 county population estimates, Population Distribution and Population Estimates Branches, U.S. Census Bureau.

Public West, Private East, page 58

Data from U.S. Department of the Interior, Bureau of Land Management.

A Wealth of Public Lands, page 60

Bureau of Land Management data compiled by the National Applied Resource Science Center, Denver, Colo. National Park and U.S. Forest Service lands taken from the *Atlas* base maps described above.

Sovereign Lands, page 63

Indian land areas from base maps described above checked against the Indian Claims Commission 1978 determination. Cross-checked against *A Map of American Indian Nations* (1993), copyright George L. Russell, Thunderbird Enterprises, Phoenix, Ariz., with additional data from the Council of Energy Resource Tribes, Denver, Colo. and the Native American Fish and Wildlife Society, Broomfield, Colo. Population and language information from the U.S. Census Bureau and Reddy Marlita, *Statistical Record of Native North Americans* (Detroit, Mich.: Gale Research, 1995). Tribal colleges from the American Indian Higher Education

Consortium, Alexandria, Va. Additional advice from the Native American Rights Fund, Boulder, Colo., with special thanks to Laura West.

Writing the New West, page 66

Selections by the *Atlas* team of writers and books that evoke western places.

Flying In and Out of the West, page 69

Airline commuter-sheds were determined by finding locations where the distance from an airport along a road and distance from the road to a point between roads is less than 60 miles. Road data are from ArcUSA™ 1:2 million, a product of the Environmental Systems Research Institute, Inc. Scheduled airline service is from individual airlines, and the *Official Airline Guide®*, North American Edition, Desktop Guide™ April 1, 1996, Vol. 22, No. 13, published by Reed Travel Group, Oak Brook, Ill., a division of Reed Elsevier Inc. Airline service changes over time, and this map is not meant as a travel planning tool but rather to provide a geographic impression of accessibility.

Jet-Setting the West, page 71

Airport data from 1995 *World Aeronautical Charts* and *U.S. Terminal Procedures*, Southwest and South Central volumes, published by the National Oceanic and Atmospheric Administration. Airports were chosen by the runway length needed for a Gates Learjet 25™ based on altitude and a standard weather day. This map is not for use by pilots.

A Road Runs Through It, page 73

Outbacks were plotted as areas of 5,000 acres and larger that are more than 10 miles from a paved road. Road data are USGS Digital Line Graph from ArcUSA™ 1:2 million, a product of the Environmental Systems Research Institute, Inc.

Connecting the West, page 76

The Internet backbone maps were compiled from data and maps found on the following World Wide Web sites:
http://www.westnet.net/Maps/sprint.html
http://www.agis.net/backbone.htm
http://www.uu.net/intlmap/
http://www.bbn.com/backbone.htm
http://www.ans.net/ANS/ANSnet.html
http://www.mci.net/bipp96.html
http://www.sni.net/sni/products/sncon.html#internet
http://www-1.okulski.com/rmii/rmii/bw
http://www.pawneenet.com/
WESTNET Inter-Regional Connectivity comes from: www.westnet.net. The cellular telephone service area is from the CellMaps™ *Cellular Coverage Map*, by Action Cellular: Rent a Phone, Inc., with thanks to Martin Gauthier. Any map of telecommunications data changes rapidly.

A Corporate Void, page 78, and Capital for the New West, page 79

Interior West corporate headquarters of firms listed in "The Forbes 500s Annual Directory," *Forbes*, April 22, 1996, 230-416.

Arid, Extra Dry, page 80

Adapted from a U.S. Water Resources Council map.

Quenching the Thirst, page 81, and Drenching the Fields, page 83

Data from US Geological Survey, "Estimated Use of Water in the U.S. in 1990," National Circular 1081 (U.S. Geological Survey: Reston, Va., 1991).

Damming the West, page 85

Dam sites from U.S. Bureau of Reclamation Dam Safety Office, Bureau of Reclamation *Project Data*, and the Bureau of Land Management's Interior Columbia Basin Ecosystem Management project office, checked against base map and other map sources described above.

"Jurassic Pork," page 90

U.S. Bureau of Reclamation information plotted on the *Atlas* base map.

Plumbing the Divide, page 92

Data from the Denver Water Board *Raw Water Supply System Map* and Office of the State Engineer, Denver, Colo.; additional data from USGS, *Water Resource Data, Colorado, Water Year 1994*, Vols. 1 and 2 (Reston, Va.: U.S. Geological Survey, 1995).

Peopling the New West, page 95

Migration data is based on "County-to-County Migration Flow Data," from Statistics of Income, Statistical Information Services, U.S. Internal Revenue Service, Washington, D.C.

Origins, page 98

Race and ethnicity data is from 1990 U.S. Census Bureau Summary Tape File 1 for: White; Black; American Indian, Eskimo, or Aleut; Asian or Pacific Islander; and Persons of Hispanic Origin—which can overlap with other classes depending on how people categorize themselves on census forms.

Tuning Into Diversity, page 100

We compiled the list of Hispanic and Native American newspapers and radio from several sources, including 1996 issues of *Editor and Publisher* (Editor and Publisher Co., New York, N.Y.), Gebbie Press's (New Paltz, N.Y.) World Wide Web media directory (www.gebbieinc.com), individual tribes, and the Native American Rights Fund, Boulder, Colo.. Gay newspapers are from Ferrari's *Places for Men: Worldwide Gay Guide 1993–1994* (Phoenix, Ariz.: Ferrari Publications), and help from the Gay Media Resource List on the World Wide Web as well as personal communications with friends across the West.

Electing Women, page 102

Data from the Center for the American Women and Politics, National Information Bank on Women in Public Office, 1996, Eagleton Institute of Politics, Rutgers University, New Brunswick, N.J.

Owning a Home on the Range, page 103

Median home value data are from 1990 U.S. Census Data Summary Tape File 1.

Ghost Houses, page 106

Proportion of second homes is calculated using 1990 U.S. Census Data Summary Tape File 1, data on Seasonal, Recreational, or Occasional home use (Vacancy Status-H5) divided by Occupied plus Vacant Units (Occupancy Status-H2).

Yellowstone's Service Economy, page 107, and Strongholds of the Traditional Economy, page 108

County-level employment data come from the Regional Economic Information System (1969-94), Full-Time and Part-Time Employees by Industry, Bureau of Economic Analysis, U.S. Department of Commerce, and U.S. Census Bureau *County Business Patterns*. Data for individual counties are sometimes estimated by the Department of Commerce or not reported if only one or two firms reside in that county, a condition holding for many Western resource counties. Thus, county comparisons are difficult. We enhanced the data with U.S. Forest Service information on timber-dependent counties. The "traditional economy" is defined here as the sum of agricultural services, forestry, fishing, and mining, plus lumber and wood products numbers from the manufacturing category for timber-dependent counties identified by the U.S. Forest Service. By mapping only counties with more than a third of their jobs in resource extraction we identify places

heavily dependent on commodities; resource-oriented jobs, though fewer, still exist in the other Western counties.

Retirement Hot Spots, page 111

A compilation of places appearing on recent list of preferred retirement sites, including: David Savageau, *Retirement Places Rated*, Fourth Edition (New York: Macmillan, 1995); Lee and Saralee Rosenberg, *50 Fabulous Places to Retire in America* (Hawthorne, N.J.: The Career Press, 1995); Elinor Craig, "The 20 Best Retirement Communities in America," *New Choices for Retirement Living*, July/August, 1995, 62-68; and Theresa Braine, "The Best College Towns for Retirees," *New Choices for Retirement Living*, October, 1994, 30–37.

The Cultured West, page 113

Information from: National Public Radio and the Pacifica Radio network (note that member stations serve many other Western towns via radio repeaters); *Peterson's Guide to Four Year Colleges* 26th Edition (Princeton, N.J.: Peterson's, 1997); *Musical America: International Directory of the Performing Arts* (Great Barrington, Mass.: ABC Leisure Magazines, 1995); "Gallery Guide" *Southwest Art*, January, 1996, 75–151; Lance S. Gudmundsen, "Out-Of-The-Way Arts Road Map to Music, Dance, Theatre, Opera, and Film" *The Salt Lake Tribune*, June 4, 1995.

New Age in the New West, page 114

Various sources, including: *New Consciousness Sourcebook: Spiritual Community Guide*, Sixth Edition (Pomona, Calif.: Arcline Publications, 1985); Ellen Lederman, *Vacations that Can Change Your Life* (Naperville, Ill.: Sourcebooks, Inc., 1996); Marcia and Jack Kelly, *Sanctuaries: The West Coast and Southwest: A Guide to Lodgings, Monasteries, Abbeys, and Retreats* (New York: Crown Publishing Group, 1993); Roger Housden, *Retreat: Time Apart for Silence and Solitude* (San Francisco: Harper San Francisco, 1995); and *Atlas* team personal experience.

Consuming in the New West, page 116

Coffee locations based on field work by the *Atlas* team looking for espresso in the small-town West, plus kind help and tips from Allegro Coffee Co.; Starbucks Coffee Co.; Peaberry Coffee Ltd. (thanks to Larry Jones); and Mill Creek Coffee Roasters. Because good coffee places come and go, travelers requiring espresso should check ahead. Other information from: Land Rover North America, Inc.; The Orvis Company, Inc., catalog list of full-line Orvis dealers (other fly-fishing shops may carry Orvis equipment); Patagonia Inc.'s dealer list, 1995 catalog; and kind help with distribution information from the New York Times Company. This information changes quickly.

What's Brewing in the New West? page 119

Institute for Brewing Studies, North American Brewery List, March 15, 1996; and "Homebrew Clubs," *Zymurgy* (1996), the American Homebrewers Association Registered Homebrew Club list.

The Old West Lives On, page 121

Thanks to Bobby Newton, editor of *Rope Burns* (Gene Autry, Okla.), for his list of the best cowboy poetry festivals; many other cowboy poetry gatherings exist. Michael Branson, National Muzzle Loaders Rifle Association, supplied the list of rendezvous locations. Dude ranches compiled from *The Dude Rancher*, The Dude Ranchers' Association (La Porte, Colo.) 1996 directory; with additions based on individual dude ranch brochures and *Atlas* team experience. Rodeos mapped from the Professional Rodeo Cowboys Association (Colorado Springs, Colo.) listing of approved rodeos by state as of October 30, 1996. Wild horse and burro management areas from: James Muir and R. Stuart Hanson, *Opportunity and Challenge: The Story of BLM* (Washington, D.C.: U.S. Government Printing Office, 1988), 146.

America's Playground, page 124

Atlas team favorites and well-known recreational sites compiled from conversations with assorted climbers, bikers, mountaineers, fly-fisherpeople, and whitewater boaters. Some off-road sites from "Offroad America," *Men's Journal*, November, 1994 and 1995.

Paying to Play, page 127

Ski areas compiled from several sources, including: ski area World Wide Web sites, state tourism brochures; *Powder, the Skier's Magazine, Ski,* and the *Western U.S.A. Ski Map* (New York: H.M. Gousha/Simon and Shuster, 1994). Rock gyms compiled from various issues of *Climbing*; Heli-skiing from the "Heli-Ski Directory," *Ski,* October, 1994; and elite golf courses from the *Golf Digest* World Wide Web site lists: "America's 100 Greatest Golf Courses" and "Top 75 Public Courses."

Places Rated, Places Raided, page 130

Ratings according to: *Money* magazine's list of the "300 Biggest Places in the U.S.," September, 1994 and 1995; *Money* magazine's "Top 50 Small Boom Towns in the U.S.," April ,1996; *Outside* magazine's "dreamtowns" (e.g., Mike Steere, "You Could be Living Here"); *Outside,* July, 1992, 77-82; David Savageau and Richard Boyer, *Places Rated Almanac* (New York: Macmillan, 1993); and John Villani, *The 100 Best Small Art Towns in America* (Santa Fe: John Muir Publications, 1996).

A Nuked Landscape, page 134

Information from the U.S. Department of Energy, Office of Environmental Management; see: *Closing the Circle on the Splitting of the Atom* (Washington, D.C.: U.S. Department of Energy, 1996), and the DOE Environmental Management Office World Wide Web site.

Spectacles of the Ugly West, page 137

Superfund sites from the U.S. Environmental Protection Agency, "National Superfund Priorities List," March, 1995, for each state. Endangered rivers according to American Rivers, Washington, D.C.: *Most Endangered Rivers of North America* and *Most Threatened Rivers of North America,* 1993, 1994, 1995, and 1996. Chemical weapons depots from Knight-Ridder Tribune news service and U.S. Army Chemical and Biological Defense Command. Weapons testing ranges from base maps described above.

No Home on the Range, maps on pages 138–141

Bison: H.W. Reynolds, R.D. Glaholt, and A.W.L. Hawley, "Bison," In Joseph A. Chapman and George A. Feldhamer, eds., *Wild Mammals of North America* (Baltimore, Md.: The Johns Hopkins University Press, 1982), 972–1007.

Bald Eagle: J. Price, S. Droege, and A. Price, *The Summer Atlas of North American Birds* (San Diego, Calif.: Academic Press, 1995); and the U.S. Fish and Wildlife Service Breeding Bird Survey, accessed through their World Wide Web page; J.R. Sauer, B.G. Peterjohn, S. Schwartz, and J.E. Hines, "The North American Breeding Bird Survey Home Page" Version 95.1, Patuxent Wildlife Research Center, Laurel, Md. Eagle nesting sites appear to be expanding in the U.S.

Grizzly: T. McNamee, *The Grizzly Bear* (New York: Knopf, 1995); David E. Brown, *The Grizzly in the Southwest* (Norman: University of Oklahoma Press).

Salmon: U.S. Department of Energy, Bonneville Power Administration, Portland, Oreg.; and *Areas of At-Risk or Extinct Salmon* map by The Wilderness Society, Washington, D.C.

Mountain Lion: Kenneth R. Dixon, "Mountain Lion," in Joseph A. Chapman and George A. Feldhamer, eds., *Wild Mammals of North America* (Baltimore, Md.: The Johns Hopkins University Press, 1982), 711–727.

Wolf: John L. Paradiso and Ronald M. Nowak, "Wolves," in Joseph A. Chapman and George A. Feldhamer, eds., *Wild Mammals of North America* (Baltimore, Md.: The Johns Hopkins University Press, 1982), 460–474. Reintroduction areas adapted from maps issued by the U.S. Fish and Wildlife Service, Washington, D.C.

War and Peace in the West, page 144

Information on county supremacy from the Clearinghouse on Environmental Advocacy and Research, Washington, D.C., and research by Nancy Nelson. Watershed coalitions from *The Watershed Sourcebook,* Natural Resources Law Center, University of Colorado at Boulder, with thanks to Teresa Rice.

A Wild Future, page 147

A compilation and interpretation of various large-scale ecosystem protection visions, plotted on the federal lands base map described above and drawing from mapping efforts of: the Wildlands Project, Tucson, Ariz.; the Northern Rockies Ecosystem Protection Act maps by the Wild Rockies Action Fund and the Alliance for the Wild Rockies, Missoula, Mont.; and, for the Southern Rockies, the Forest Conservation Council, Santa Fe, N.Mex., and the Southern Rockies Ecosystem Project, Boulder, Colo. Interpretations and errors on the map are ours and not those of the ecosystem protection organizations. Information on Rocky Mountain ecosystem protection efforts can be obtained from the Wildlands Project, 1955 West Grant Road, Suite 148, Tucson, Ariz., 85745: the Alliance for the Wild Rockies, Box 8731, Missoula, Mont., 59807; and the Southern Rockies Ecosystem Project, 1567 Twin Sisters Road, Nederland, Colo., 80466.

Map Index

Abbey, Edward, *Desert Solitaire*, 66
Absaroka Wilderness, WY, 73
Acoma Pueblo Reservation, NM, 63, 66
Agua Caliente Reservation, CA, 63
Ahora Spanish News, NV, 100
Alamo Navajo Reservation, NM, 63
Alamogordo, NM, 69, 111, 121, 134
Alamosa, CO, 69, 76, 113
Albertson's, CO, 79
Albuquerque, NM, 50, 52, 69, 73, 76, 85, 111, 113, 116, 121, 130, 137, 147
Alkali Lake, OR, 71
All American Canal, CA, 85
Alpine Meadows, CA, 127
Alpine, WY, 71
Alta, UT, 127
Alta, WY, 116
Alturas Rancheria Reservation, CA, 63
Alturas, CA, 50
Alva B. Adams Tunnel, CO, 92
American Fork Canyon, UT, 124
American Stores Corp., UT, 79
Anaconda, MT, 137
Anaya, Rudolfo, *Bless Me, Ultima*, 66
Angle Fire, NM, 71
Animas Coalition, CO, 144
Animas River, CO, 85, 90, 124, 137
Animas-La Plata River Project, CO, NM, 90
Arches National Park, UT, 60, 66
Arcosanti, AZ, 114
Arizona State University, 113
Arkansas River, CO, 48, 85, 92
Aspen, CO, 50, 69, 76, 113, 116, 127, 137
Atlanta, GA, 54
Atom Mashers, NM, 119
Augusta, MT, 121
Augustine Reservation, CA, 63
Austin, NV, 50, 71
Banning, CA, 121
Barstow, CA, 50, 121, 137
Battle Mtn. Reservation, NV, 63
Battlement Mesa, CO, 111
Bear Coalition, UT, 144
Bear River Wildlife Refuge, UT, 66
Bear River, ID, 85
Beaverhead County, MT, 144
Beaverhead, MT, 124
Belt, MT, 121
Bend, OR, 50, 111, 116, 121
Benton Paiute Reservation, CA, 63
Berthoud Pass Ditch, CO, 92
Big Blackfoot River, MT, 66
Big Fork, MT, 130
Big Hole River, MT, 124
Big Horn County News, MT, 100
Big Mountain, ID, 127
Big Pine Reservation, CA, 63
Big Sky, MT , 127
Bighorn River, MT, 85, 124
Billings, MT, 69, 76, 113, 121, 130
Bisbee, AZ, 130
Bishop Reservation, CA, 50, 63, 71, 116, 121
Blackfeet Reservation, MT, 63
Blackfoot River, MT, 124, 137
Blue River, CO, 85
Bob Marshall Wilderness, MT, 73
Bodio, Steve, *Querencia*, 66
Boise Cascade Corp., ID, 79
Boise County, ID, 144
Boise River, ID, 85
Boise, ID, 50, 52, 69, 73, 85, 113, 116, 121, 130, 147
Borah Peak, ID, 124
Boreas Pass Ditch, CO, 92
Boston, MA, 54
Boulder, CO, 50, 76, 92, 111, 113, 116, 130, 137
Boundary County, ID, 144
Box Canyon River, NM, 124
Bozeman, MT, 50, 69, 116, 121, 137
Brawley, CA, 121
Breckenridge, CO, 113
Bridgeport Colony Reservation, CA, 63
Bridger, MT, 121

Brigham Young University, UT, 113
Bryce Canyon National Park, UT, 60, 71
Buena Vista, CO, 76
Buffalo Bill Dam, WY, 85
Bullhead City, AZ, 50, 69, 111, 121
Burley, ID, 121
Burlington, CO, 76
Burns Paiute Reservation, OR, 63
Burns, OR, 50, 71, 116
Bush-Ivanhoe Tunnel, CO, 92
Butte, MT, 50, 69, 116, 121, 137
Cabazon Reservation, CA, 63
Caldwell, ID, 121
Cambio!, AZ, 100
Camp Verde Reservation, AZ, 63
Canada, 50
Canon City, CO, 76, 121, 137
Canoncito Navajo Reservation, NM, 63
Canyon Country Zephyr, 66
Canyonlands National Park, UT, 60, 124
Capitol Reef National Park, UT, 60
Carefree, AZ, 116
Carlsbad Caverns National Park, NM, 60
Carlsbad Test Site, NM, 134
Carlsbad, NM, 69
Carrizozo, NM, 137
Carson City, NV, 50, 111, 116, 121, 130, 137
Carson Colony Reservation, NV, 63
Carson River, NV, 85
Cascade Range, 48
Cascade, ID, 111
Casper, WY, 50, 69, 113, 116, 121
Castle Pines Golf Course, CO, 127
Castle Rock, CO, 76, 121
Cataract Canyon River, UT, 124
Catron County, NM, 144
Cave Creek, AZ, 121
Cedar City, UT, 69
Cedarville Reservation, CA, 63
Cedarville, CA, 121
Central Arizona Project, 85
Central Utah Project, UT, 85
Chaco Culture National Park, NM, 60
Chama, NM, 50, 116
Chandler, AZ, 137
Charles H. Boustead Tunnel, CO, 92
Chelan County, WA, 144
Chemehuevi Reservation, CA, 63
Cheney, WA, 121
Cherry Hills Country Club, CO, 127
Chewelah, WA, 111
Cheyenne, WY, 50, 69, 76, 85, 113, 116, 121, 137, 147
China Lake Weapons Center, CA, 134
Christmas Valley, OR, 71
Circle K Corp., AZ, 79
Circus Circus Corp., NV, 79
City of Rocks, ID, 124
Clark Fork River, MT, 85
Clark Fork, MT, 124
Clark's Fork of Yellowstone River, MT, WY, 137
Coachella Canal, CA, 85
Coalville, UT, 121
Coastal Ranges, 48
Cochiti Lake, NM, 127
Cochiti Pueblo Reservation, NM, 63
Cocopah Reservation, AZ, 63
Cody, WY, 50, 69, 116, 121
Coeur d'Alene Coalition, ID, 144
Coeur d'Alene Reservation, ID, 63
Coeur d'Alene, ID, 111, 121
Colorado Basin, 85
Colorado City, AZ, 71
Colorado College, CO, 113
Colorado Plateau, 48
Colorado River, 48, 85, 90 ,92, 124
Colorado River Aqueduct, CA, 85
Colorado River Reservation, AZ, CA, 63
Colorado Springs, CO, 50, 69, 76, 85, 92, 111, 113, 116, 119, 121, 130
Colorado State University, 113
Columbia Basin, 85
Columbia County, WA, 144

Columbia Plateau, 48
Columbia River, OR 48, 85, 137
Columbine Ditch, CO, 92
Columbus, MT, 137
Colville Reservation, WA, 63
Colville, WA, 121
Commerce City, CO, 137
Conejos River, CO, 85
Copper Mtn, CO, 76
Cortez, CO, 69, 121
Costilla, CO, 108
Cottonwood, AZ, 111
Coulee City, WA, 121
Crater Lake National Park, OR, 60
Crested Butte Brewskiers, CO, 119
Crested Butte, CO, 124
Crow Reservation, MT, 63
Crowheart, WY, 50, 116, 121
Cuchara Valley, CO, 71
Custer County, ID, 144
Cyprus Amax Minerals Corp., CO, 79
Dead Brewer's Society, AZ, 119
Death Valley National Park, CA, 60, 124
deBuys, Willaim, *Enchantment and Exploitation*, 66
Deer Lodge, MT, 137
Delta, CO, 111, 121
Delta, UT, 50, 121
Denver, CO, 50, 52, 69, 73, 76, 85, 90, 92, 113, 116, 121, 130, 137, 147
Deschutes River, OR, 85, 124
Desert Forest Golf Course, AZ , 127
Desolation and Gray Canyons River, UT, 124
Dhamma Dena, CA, 114
Dial Corp., AZ, 79
Dillon, MT, 71, 121, 130
Dinosaur, CO, 50
Diversity, ID, 100
Divide, CO, 130
Doig, Ivan, *This House of Sky*, 66
Dolores River, CO, 85
Douglas, WY, 116, 121
Dresslerville Colony Reservation, NV, 63
Driggs, ID, 50, 71, 116
Drummond, MT, 121
Dubois, WY, 50, 116, 121, 124
Duck Valley Reservation, ID, NV, 63
Duckwater Reservation, NV, 63
Durango, CO, 50, 69, 76, 90, 111, 113, 116, 121, 124, 130
Dutch John, UT, 71
Eagle, CO, 69, 92, 121
East Fork, Carson River, NV, 124
East Wenatchee, WA, 130
Eaton, CO, 76
Eddy County, NM, 144
Edgewood Tahoe, NV, 127
Edwards, CA, 137
El Continental, TX, 100
El Hispano News, NM, 100
El Paso, TX, 50, 52, 69, 85, 113, 116, 121
Eldorado Canyon, CO, 124
Elgin, OR, 121
Elko County, NV, 144
Elko, NV, 50, 69, 116, 121
Ellensburg, WA, 121
Ely Colony Reservation, NV, 50, 63, 69
Esmeralda, NV, 108
Estes Park, CO, 121
Eureka County, NV, 144
Eureka Ditch, CO, 92
Eureka, NV, 108
Evanston, WY, 121
Evansville, WY, 137
Evergreen, CO, 121
Ewing Ditch, CO, 92
Fairfield Snow Bowl, AZ, 127
Fallon Reservation, NV, 63
Fallon Test Site, NV, 134
Fallon, NV, 130
Farmington Test Site, NM, 134
Farmington, NM, 69, 116, 121, 137
Fernley, NV, 116

Filer, ID, 121
Finova Group Corp., AZ, 79
First Security Corp., UT, 79
Flagstaff, AZ, 50, 69, 113, 116, 121, 130
Flaming Gorge Dam, UT, 85
Flaming Gorge, WY, 124
Flathead (Salish) Reservation, MT, 63
Flathead Coalition, MT, 144
Flathead River, MT, 85
Foam on the Range, CO, 119
Forest Highlands Golf Course, AZ, 127
Fort Apache Reservation, AZ, 63
Fort Collins, CO, 50, 76, 92, 116, 121
Fort Hall Reservation, ID, 63
Fort Independence Reservation, CA, 63
Fort McDermitt Reservation, OR, NV, 63
Fort Mojave Reservation, AZ, 63
Fradkin, Philip, *A River No More*, 66
Frank Church River of No Return Wilderness, ID, 73
Freeman, Judith, *Set For Life*, 66
Frying Pan River, CO, 85, 124
Ft. Collins, CO, 69, 111, 113, 130
Ft. McDowell Reservation, AZ, 63
Ft. Yuma Reservation, CA, 63
Furnace Creek, CA, 71
Gallitan River, MT, 124
Gallup, NM, 50, 69, 116, 137
Gardenerville, NV, 130
Gardiner, MT, 50, 116
Gates of Lodore River, UT, 124
Gila Bend Reservation, AZ, 63
Gila Bend, AZ, 71
Gila Coalition, NM, 144
Gila River Reservation, AZ, 63
Gila River, AZ, NM, 85, 137
Glacier National Park, MT, 60
Glacier Peak, WA, 124
Glen Canyon Dam, AZ, 85
Glendale, AZ, 116, 137
Glenrock, WY, 116
Glenwood Springs, CO, 76, 130
Globe, AZ, 121
Golden, CO, 50 116, 137
Goodyear, AZ, 137
Goshute Reservation, NV, UT, 63
Grace, ID, 121
Grand Canyon, AZ, 69, 73, 124
Grand Coulee Dam, WA, 85
Grand Coulee, WA, 71
Grand County, UT, 144
Grand Junction, CO, 69, 111, 113, 116, 121
Grand River Ditch, CO, 92
Grand Staircase, UT, 73
Grand Teton National Park, WY, 60
Grand Teton, WY, 124
Granite County, MT, 144
Granite Mountain, AZ, 124
Granite Peak, MT, 124
Grant County, NM, 144
Grant County, OR, 144
Grants, NM, 137
Grass Valley, CA, 111
Grays Peak, CO, 124
Great Basin, 85
Great Basin National Park, NV, 60
Great Basin Range, 48
Great Falls, MT, 69, 113, 121
Great Salt Lake, 48
Great Salt Lake Desert, UT, 73
Greeley, CO, 76, 92, 121, 130
Green River, 48, 50, 85, 116, 124
Grey Bull, WY, 71
Guadalupe Mountains National Park, TX, 60
Gulf of California, 48
Gunnison River, CO, 85, 124
Gunnison, CO, 69, 76, 121
Haidakhandi Universal Ashram, CO, 114
Hamilton, MT, 111
Hanford Nuclear Site, WA, 134
Hardin, MT, 121
Harold D. Roberts Tunnel, CO, 92
Havasupai Reservation, AZ, 63

Hayden, CO, 76, 121
Heavenly, CA, 127
Heber City, UT, 121, 130
Hebgen Lake, MT, 71
Helena, MT, 50, 69, 85, 113, 116, 121, 130, 137, 147
Hells Canyon River, OR, 124
Henderson, NV, 116
Henry's Fork Coalition, ID, 144
Henry's Fork River, ID, 85
Henry's Fork, ID, 124
Heppner, OR , 121
Hermiston, OR, 121, 137
Hesperia, CA, 111
Hidalgo County, NM, 144
High Country News, 66
High Mountain Heli-Skiing, WY, 127
Holden Village, WA, 114
Homstake Tunnel, CO, 92
Hoosier Pass Tunnel, CO, 92
Hoover Dam, AZ, NV, 85
Hopi Reservation, AZ, 63, 90
Hopping Anarchists, MT, 119
Hualapai Reservation, AZ, 63
Hueco Tanks, NM, 124
Humboldt River, NV, 85
Humphreys Peak, TX, 124
Hurricane Cliffs, AZ ,73
Hyland Hills, CO, 127
Idaho Falls, ID, 50, 69, 116, 121, 130
Idaho National Engineering Laboratory, ID, 134
Idaho Springs, CO, 137
Incline Village, CA, 127
Indian Canyon, WA, 127
Indio, CA, 121
Inyo County, CA, 144
Inyokern, CA, 69
Iron Mountain, WY, 66
Island Park, ID, 50, 116
Isleta Pueblo Reservation, NM, 63
Jackson Hole, WY, 127
Jackson, WY, 50, 69, 113, 116, 121, 130
Jefferson River, MT, 85
Jefferson, MT, 108
Jemez Pueblo Reservation, NM, 63
Jicarilla Apache Reservation, NM, 63
Jordan, Teresa, *Riding the White Horse Home*, 66
Jornada del Muerto, NM, 73
Joseph, OR, 121, 130, 137
Joshua Tree National Park, CA, 60
Joshua Tree, CA, 124, 130
Kaibab Reservation, AZ, 63
Kaiparowits Plateau, UT, 73
Kalamath Falls, OR, 116
Kalispel Reservation, WA, 63
Kalispell, MT, 50, 69, 111, 116, 121
Kanab, UT, 50
Kaycee, WY, 121
Kayenta, AZ, 69
Kelly Creek River, ID, 124
Kennewick, WA, 121
Ketchum, ID, 50, 111, 113, 116
Kingman, AZ, 69, 111, 121
Kings Canyon National Park, CA, 60
Kingsolver, Barbara, *High Tide in Tucson*, 66
Kirkwood, CA, 127
Kittredge, William, *Owning it All*, 66
Klamath County, OR, 144
Klamath Falls, OR, 69, 121
Kootenai Reservation, ID, 63
Kootenai River, MT, 85
Kremmling, CO, 71
La Plata River, CO, 85, 90
La Poudre Pass Creek, CO, 137
La Voz de Idaho, ID, 100
LaBarge, WY, 124
Laguna Pueblo Reservation, NM, 63, 66
Lake County, OR, 144
Lake Havasu City, AZ, 69, 111
Lakeview, OR, 137
Lama Foundation, NM, 114
Lamoille, NV, 130
Lancaster, CA, 121

Lander, NV, 108
Lander, WY, 124
Laramie, WY, 50, 69, 92, 113, 116, 121, 137
Las Cruces, NM, 50, 69, 111, 113, 116, 130, 147
Las Vegas Colony Reservation, NV, 63
Las Vegas, NV, 50, 52, 69, 73, 76, 85, 111, 113, 116, 121, 130
Lassen County, CA, 144
Lassen Volcanic National Park, CA, 60
Laughlin, NV, 121
Leadville, CO, 76, 137
Leavenworth, WA, 124
Lee's Ferry, AZ, 124
Lehi, UT, 121
Lemhi County, ID, 144
Lemitar, NM, 137
Lewiston, ID, 50, 69, 116, 121
Libby, MT, 71, 137
Life Partners Group Corp., CO, 79
Likely Rancheria Reservation, CA, 63
Lincoln County, NM, 144
Little Bighorn River, MT, WY, 137
Little Colorado River, AZ, 85
Livingston, MT, 116, 121
Loa, UT, 71
Lochsa River, ID, 124
Lodge Grass, MT, 116
Logan, UT, 121
Logan, WY, 113
Logandale, NV, 121
Lone Pine Reservation, CA, 63
Longs Peak, CO, 124
Lookout Rancheria Reservation, CA, 63
Loomis, WA, 137
Los Alamos Laboratory, NM, 134
Los Alamos, NM, 116
Los Angeles, CA, 56, 76, 85
Los Lunas, NM, 137
Loveland, CO, 76, 121, 130
Lovelock Colony Reservation, NV, 63
Lover's Leap, CA, 124
Lower Deschutes Coalition, OR, 144
Lumpy Ridge, CO, 124
Luna County, NM, 144
Lyon County, NV, 144
Maclean, Norman, *A River Runs Through It*, 66
Mad Mountain Mashers, WY, 119
Madison River, MT, 85, 124
Madrid, NM, 130
Magdalena, NM, 66
Mammoth Lake, CA, 71
Mammoth Mountain, CA, 124
Mammoth, CA, 127
Manville Corp., CO, 79
Maricopa Akchin Reservation, AZ, 63
McCall, ID, 71, 111, 116
Mead, WA, 137
Meeker, CO, 116
Mesa Verde National Park, CO, 60
Mesa, AZ, 111, 116
Mescalero Apache Reservation, NM, 63
Metaline Falls, WA, 130
Metolius River, OR, 124
Mexican Hat, UT, 50
Mexico, 50
Mica, WA, 137
MicroAge Corp., AZ, 79
Micron Technology Corp., ID, 79
Middle Fork Salmon River, ID, 124
Middle Snake Coalition, ID, 144
Midvale, UT, 137
Milan, NM, 137
Milltown, MT, 50, 116, 137
Minturn, CO, 128, 137
Mirage Resorts Corp., NV, 79
Missoula, MT, 50, 66, 69, 116, 121
Missouri Basin, 85
Missouri River, 48, 85, 124, 137
Moab, UT, 50, 66, 69, 116, 121, 124, 130
Moapa River Reservation, NV, 63
Modoc County, CA, 144
Moffat Water Tunnel, CO, 92

Mojave Desert, 48
Monte Vista, CO, 121
Monticello, UT ,137
Montrose, CO, 69, 76, 111
Moose, WY, 66
Morongo Reservation, CA, 63
Morrow County, OR, 144
Moscow, ID, 50, 113, 116, 130
Moses Lake, WA, 69, 121, 137
Mountain Cloud Zen Center, NM, 114
Mountain Home, ID, 137
Mt. Baker, WA, 127
Mt. Adams, WA, 124
Mt. Batchelor, OR, 127
Mt. Elbert, CO, 124
Mt. Hood Ski Bowl, OR, 127
Mt. Hood, OR, 124
Mt. Lemmon, AZ, 124
Mt. Rainier National Park, WA, 60
Mt. Shasta Ski Park, CA, 127
Mt. Whitney, CA, 124
Muddy River, NV, 85
Musselshell Coalition, MT, 144
Nabhan, Gary, *The Desert Smells Like Rain*, 66
Nambe Pueblo Reservation, NM, 63
Nampa, ID, 121
Navajo Dam, NM, 85
Navajo Nation Reservation, 63, 66
Navajo Times, AZ, 100
Needles, CA, 50, 71, 116
Nephi, UT, 121
Nevada City, CA, 111
Nevada County, CA, 144
Nevada Test Site, NV, 134
New Mexico State University, 113
New River, CA, 137
New York, NY, 54, 56
Newmont Mining Corp., CO, 79
Nez Perce Reservation, ID, 63
North Cascade Heli-Skiing, WA, 127
North Cascades National Park, WA, 60
North Platte River, 48, 85, 124
Northern Arizona University, 113
Northern Cheyenne Reservation, MT, 63
Northern Lights, 66
Northern Utah Militia of Brewers, UT, 119
Novell Corp., UT, 79
Nye County, NV, 144
Nyingma Institute of Colorado, The, 114
Oakley, UT, 121
Ogden, UT, 113, 121, 137
Okanogan River, WA, 85
Omak, WA, 121
Oneida County, ID, 144
Ortiz, Simon, *Woven Stone*, 66
Otero County, NM, 144
Othello, WA, 121, 137
Otter Creek River, UT, 85
Ouray, CO, 124
Out Front, CO, 100
Owens River Gorge, CA, 124
Owens River, CA, 85
Owyhee County, ID, 124, 144
Owyhee River, OR, 85
Pacific Ocean, 48
Pack Creek Ranch, UT, 127
Page, AZ, 69
Pagosa Springs, CO, 111
Pahrump, NV, 111, 121
Palm Desert, CA, 116
Palm Springs, CA, 50, 69, 111, 116
Panguitch, UT ,50, 116, 121
Paonia, CO, 66
Park City, UT, 50, 116, 121, 127
Parleys River, UT, 85
Pasco, WA, 69, 121, 137
Pascua Yaqui Reservation, AZ, 63
Payette River, ID, 85, 124
Payson Comm. Reservation, AZ, 63
Payson, AZ, 71, 111, 121
Pendleton, OR, 50, 69, 116, 121
Pershing, NV, 108

Petrified Forest National Park, AZ, 60
Phelps Dodge Corp., AZ, 79
Philadelphia, PA, 54
Phoenix University, AZ, 113
Phoenix, AZ, 50, 52, 69, 73, 76, 85, 111, 113, 116,
   121, 130, 137
Piceance Test Site, CO, 134
Picture Rocks Retreat Desert House of Prayer, AZ,
   114
Picuris Pueblo Reservation, NM, 63
Pillar of the Gay, Lesbian, and Bi-Sexual Community,
   UT, 100
Pinedale, WY, 50, 71, 116
Pinnacle West Corp., AZ, 79
Pinto Creek, AZ, 137
Pittsburgh, PA, 54
Plains, MT, 121
Platte River, CO, 92
Pleasant Grove, UT, 121
Pocatello, ID, 69, 121, 137
Pojoaque Pueblo Reservation, NM, 63
Polson, MT, 111
Prescott, AZ, 69, 111, 113, 116, 121
Preston, ID, 121
Prewitt, NM, 137
Price River, UT, 85
Price, UT, 121
Priest River, ID, 111
Prineville, OR, 121
Provo River, UT, 85
Provo, UT, 50, 113, 116, 130
Public Service Corp., CO, 79
Pueblo, CO, 50, 69, 76, 92, 113, 121, 130, 137
Pullman, WA, 69
Pyramid Lake Reservation, NV, 63
Quincy, CA, 50
Raleigh, NC, 54
Ramah Navajo Reservation, NM, 63
Rathdrum, ID, 137
Raton, NM, 130
Rawlins, C. L., *Sky's Witness*, 66
Red Lodge, MT ,121
Red Rocks, NV, 124
Redmond, OR, 69
Reno, NV, 50, 69, 73, 85, 111, 113, 116, 121, 130
Reno-Sparks Community Reservation, NV, 63
Richland, WA, 137
Ridgecrest, CA, 121
Rio Chama, NM, 85
Rio Grande, 48, 85, 137
Rio Grande Basin, 85
Rio Puerco Coalition, NM, 144
Riverton, WY, 69, 121
Roaring Fork, CO, 85, 124
Rock Springs, WY, 50, 69, 121
Rocky Flats Laboratory, CO, 134
Rocky Mountain National Park, CO, 60
Ruby Mountain Heli-Ski Guides, NV, 127
Ruidoso, NM, 111
Rulison Test Site, CO, 134
Sacramento River, CA, 85
Sacramento-San Joaquin Basin, 85
Safford, AZ, 121
Saguaro National Park, AZ, 60
Salida, CO, 76, 130
Salmon Coalition, ID, 144
Salmon River, ID, 85
Salmon, ID, 50, 71, 121
Salt Lake City, UT, 50, 52, 56, 69, 73, 76, 85, 113,
   116, 121, 130, 137, 147
Salt River Reservation, AZ, 63
Salt River, AZ, 85
Salt, AZ, 124
Salton Sea, CA, 48
Saludos Hispanos, CA, 100
San Joaquin River, CA, 85
San Carlos Reservation, AZ, 63
San Felipe Pueblo Reservation, NM, 63
San Francisco, CA, 76
San Ildefonso Pueblo Reservation, NM, 63
San Juan Pueblo Reservation, NM, 63
San Juan River, 85, 90, 124

San Luis, CO, 50
San Manuel Reservation, CA, 63
San Miguel County, NM, 144
San Pedro Coalition, AZ, 144
San Pedro River, AZ, 137
San Xavier Reservation, AZ, 63
Sandia Laboratory, NM, 134
Sandia Pueblo Reservation, NM, 63
Sandpoint, ID, 50, 111, 116, 128
Sangre de Cristo Range, NM, 66
Sanpete County, UT, 144
Santa Ana Pueblo Reservation, NM, 63
Santa Clara Pueblo Reservation, NM, 63
Santa Fe, NM, 50, 69, 85, 90, 111, 113, 116, 121,
   130, 147
Santa Rosa, NM, 66
Santo Domingo Pueblo Reservation, NM, 63
Saratoga, WY, 71
Scottsdale, AZ, 111, 116, 121
Seattle, WA, 56, 76
Sedona, AZ, 50, 111, 113, 114, 116, 124
Selway River, ID, 124
Sequoia National Park, CA, 60
Sevier River, UT, 85
Shadow Creek Golf Course, NV, 127
Sheridan, WY, 50, 69, 116, 121, 130
Shivwits Reservation, UT, 63
Shoshone National Forest, WY, 124
Shoshone Reservation, NV, 63
Shoshone River, WY, 85
Show Low, AZ, 69
Sierra County, CA, 144
Sierra County, NM, 144
Sierra Nevada, 48
Sierra Vista, AZ, 69
Silko, Leslie Marmon, *The Delicacy and Strength of
   Lace*, 66
Silver City, NM, 69, 111, 116, 121, 137
Silver Creek River, ID, 124
Sisters, OR, 121
Skull Valley Reservation, UT, 63
Smelterville, ID, 137
Smith Rock, OR, 124
Smith's Food and Drug Corp., UT, 79
Snake River, 48, 85, 124, 137
Snow Bird, UT, 127
Snowflake, AZ, 71
Snowmass Creek, CO, 137
Socorro, NM, 116
Soda Springs, ID, 137
Sonoran Desert, AZ, 48, 66
South Fork Boise River, ID, 124
South Fork, ID, 124
South Platte Coalition, CO, 144
South Platte River, CO, 48, 85, 92, 124
Southern Ute Reservation, CO, 63, 90
Spanish Fork, UT, 121
Sparks, NV, 111
Spokane Reservation, WA, 63
Spokane River, WA, 85
Spokane, WA, 50, 69, 73, 85, 113, 116, 121, 130,
   137, 147
Springville, UT, 130
Squaw Valley USA, CA, 127
St. David, AZ, 137
St. George, UT, 50, 69, 111, 116, 121
Stanford, MT, 121
Steamboat Springs, CO, 50, 69, 76, 92, 116, 121, 127
Stegner, Wallace, *Where the Bluebird Sings to the
   Lemonade Springs*, 66
Sterling, CO, 76
Stonewall News, WA, 100
Strawberry River, UT, 85
Sublette County, WY, 144
Summit Lake Reservation, NV, 63
Summitville, CO, 137
Sun Valley Helicopter Ski Guides, ID, 127
Sun Valley, ID, 50, 69, 111, 113, 116, 127
Sundance, UT, 127
Sunriver, OR, 71
Susanville Rancheria Reservation, CA, 63
Taos Pueblo Reservation, NM, 63

Taos Ski Valley, NM ,127
Taos, NM, 50, 71, 111, 113, 116, 130
Tapahonso, Luci, *A Breeze Swept Through*, 66
Taylor Fork, CO, 85
TCI Corp., CO, 79
Te-moak Reservation, NV, 63
Tehachipi, CA, 121
TeleCom-Liberty Media Corp., CO ,79
Telluride Helitrax, CO ,127
Telluride, CO ,50, 69, 71, 76, 113, 116, 121, 127,
    130
Tesuque Pueblo Reservation, NM, 63
Teton County, MT, 144
Teton River, ID ,85
The Bottom Line, CA, 100
The Dalles Dam, OR, 85
The Dalles, OR, 121, 137
The Grainful Heads, NM, 119
Thompson Falls, MT, 71
Timbi-Sha Shoshone Reservation, CA, 63
Tohono O'Odham Reservation, AZ, 63, 66
Tombstone, AZ, 50, 121
Tonasket, WA, 121
Tonopah, NV, 50
Tooele, UT, 130, 137
Toppenish, WA, 121
Torrance County, NM, 144
Torres Martinez Reservation, CA, 63
Torreys Peak, CO, 124
Tremonton, UT, 121
Trinity Test Site, NM, 134
Truckee River, NV, 85
Truckee, CA, 71, 116, 121
Truth or Consequences, NM, 50, 71
Tuba City, AZ, 71
Tucson, AZ, 50, 66, 69, 85, 111, 113, 116,
    121, 130, 137
Turner, Jack, *The Abstract Wild*, 66
Twentynine Palms, CA, 71, 121
Twentynine Palms Reservation, CA, 63
Twin Falls, ID, 50, 69, 116
Twin Lakes Tunnel, CO, 92
Uintah and Ouray Reservation, UT, 63
Uintah County, UT, 144
Umatilla Reservation, OR, 63
Union County, OR, 144
Union, OR, 121

University of Arizona, 113
University of Colorado–Boulder, 113
University of Denver, 113
University of Nevada–Las Vegas, 113
University of New Mexico, 113
University of Texas–El Paso, 113
University of Utah, 113
University of Wyoming, 113
Upaya Foundation, NM, 114
Upper Arkansas Coalition, CO, 144
Upper Arkansas River, CO, 124
Upper Carson Coalition, CA, 144
Uravan, CO, 137
U.S. Air Force Academy, CO, 113
U.S. West Communications Corp., CO, 79
U.S. West Media Corp., CO, 79
Utah State University, 113
Ute Mountain Reservation, UT, 63, 90
Vail, CO, 50, 69, 92, 113, 116, 127
Vedauwoo, WY, 124
Verde Coalition, AZ, 144
Verde River, AZ, 85
Vernal, UT, 69, 121
Victorville, CA, 111
Vidler Tunnel, CO, 92
Virgin Coalition, UT, 144
Virginia City, NV, 116, 130
Voz Hispano de Colorado, CO, 100
Walden, CO, 71
Walker River Reservation, NV, 63
Walker River, CA, NV, 137
Walla Walla County, WA, 144
Walla Walla, WA, 50, 69, 116, 121, 130
Wallowa County, WA, 144
Warm Springs Reservation, OR, 63
Warm Springs, OR, 116
Warm Springs, WA, 50
Warner Mountains, OR, 66
Wasatch Powderbird Guides, UT, 127
Washington County, ID, 144
Washington, D.C., 54
Washoe Reservation, NV, 63
Weber River, UT, 85
Welch, James, *Killing Custer*, 66
Wells, NV, 71
Wenatchee, WA, 69, 111
West Jordan, UT, 121

Westwater Canyon River, UT, 124
Wheeler Peak, NM, 124
Wheeler Peak, NV, 124
White River, CO, 85
White Sands, NM, 134
White Sulphur Springs, MT, 66
Wickenburg, AZ, 111
Willcox, AZ, 121
Williams, Terry Tempest, *Refuge*, 66
Wind River Range, WY, 66
Wind River Reservation, WY, 63
Window Rock, AZ, 50, 121
Winnemucca, NV, 50, 71, 121, 130
Winslow, AZ, 50, 116
Winthrop, WA, 71
Wise River, MT, 130
Worland, WY, 69
Wort First!, AZ, 119
Wray, CO, 76
Wurtz Ditch, CO, 92
Wyoming Basin, 48
XL Ranch Reservation, CA, 63
Yakama Nation Reservation, WA, 63
Yakama Nation Review, WA, 100
Yakima Coalition, WA, 144
Yakima River, WA, 85
Yakima, WA, 50, 69, 116, 121, 137
Yampa Coalition, CO, 144
Yampa River, CO, 85, 124
Yampa Valley Yeast Ranchers, CO, 119
Yavapai Reservation, AZ, 63
Yellowstone National Park, WY, 60, 107
Yellowstone River, 48, 85, 124
Yerington Reservation, NV, 63
Yomba Reservation, NV, 63
Yosemite National Park, CA, 60
Ysleta Del Sur Pueblo Reservation, TX, 63
Yucca Mountain, NV, 134
Yucca Valley, CA, 121
Yuma Desalting Plant, AZ, 85
Yuma, AZ, 50, 69, 111, 116, 121, 130, 137
Zia Pueblo Reservation, NM, 63
Zion National Park, UT, 60
Zions Bancorporation, UT, 79
Zoo City Zymurgists, MT, 119
Zuni Mountain Citizen, NM, 100
Zuni Pueblo Reservation, NM, 63

General Index

100 Best Small Art Towns in America, The, 131
Abbey, Edward, 19–22, 49, 67, 126, 157
Absaroka, 51
Absaroka/Beartooth Wilderness, 74
Alamogordo, NM, 135
Alamosa, CO, 118
Alamosa River, 135
Albertson's, 79
Albuquerque, NM, 49, 56, 67, 99
Alexie, Sherman, 170
Alfred A. Knopf, 169
Alliance for the Wild Rockies, 147
Alternative Dispute Resolution (ADR), 90
American Commonwealth, The (Bryce), 171
American Demographics, 155, 162
American Stores, 79
Anaconda, MT, 49
Anaya, Rudolfo, 170
Angel Fire, NM, 51
Angel's Landing, 51
Angel Peak, 51
Angle of Repose (Stegner), 65
Animas–La Plata Project, 90–91
Antelope Retreat and Education Center, 114
Apache County, AZ, 99
Apache Junction, AZ, 117
Arches National Park, 19, 67
Arendt, Hannah, 38
Arizona, 26, 29, 105, 110
Arizona Cardinals, 32
Arizona Republican, 29
Arizona–Sonora Desert Museum, 32
Arkansas River, 44, 125, 136
Asian (census category), 97–101
Aspen, CO, 18, 53, 95, 102, 103, 106, 112, 117, 118
Aspen Highlands, 126
Aspen Mountain, 126
Aspen Music Festival, 112
Aspenization, 53
Associated Press, 122
Atlantic City, NJ, 105
Atomic City, ID, 135
Atomic Energy Commission, 132
Audubon Society, 23
Austin, NV, 24–25
Babbitt, Bruce, 26–27, 140, 143, 149
Back of Beyond Books, 117
Back to Methuselah (Shaw), 38
Badenoch, Geoff, 39
Badwater, CA, 47, 49
Baker v. Carr, 29
Baker, NV, 23
Bald Eagle (*Haliaeetus leucocephalus*), 139
Balfour, Gay, 152
Basin and Range, 25
Basque Museum, 32
Batatakin, 51
Bear Tooth Pass, MT, 72
Beartooth Peak, 53
Beaver Creek, CO, 126
Bend, OR, 96
Berthoud Pass, CO, 72
Beyond the Hundredth Meridian (Stegner), 26, 65, 149
Beyond the Rangeland Conflict (Dagget), 26
Big Blackfoot River, 135
Big Dam Era, 84
Big Sky, MT, 126
Big Rock Candy Mountain, The (Stegner), 42, 65
Big Timber, MT, 51
Bighorn County, MT, 99
Billings, MT, 51, 131
Bird, Isabella, 171
Bison (*Bison bison*), 138
Bitteroot National Forest, 19
Black (census category), 97–101
Black Cowboy Rodeo, 123

Black Rock Desert, 172, 178
Blaine County, ID, 107
Blew, Mary Clearman, 169
Bob Marshall/Scapegoat/Great Bear Wilderness, 74, 139
Bobcat Pass, NM, 72
Boise, ID, 30, 32, 49, 56, 68, 79, 80, 95, 102, 131
Boise Cascade, 79
Bolle, Arnold, 19
Bolle Report, 19
Bonneville Dam, 86–89
Bonneville Power Administration, 88–89
Booker, Bill, 23
Boston, MA, 80
Boulder, CO, 67, 131
Boyd, William, 158–161
Bozeman, MT, 139
Breckenridge, CO, 126
Bridger/Fitzpatrick/Popo Agie Wilderness, 74
Bright Angel, 51
Brower, David, 84, 128
Brown Cloud, the, 15
Brown, Dee, 64
Brown's Canyon, 125
Bryce, James, 171
Buck's Lake Wilderness, 42
Budweiser, 118
Buena Vista, CO, 15
Buffalo, NY, 110
Burton, Richard, 163, 165
Bury My Heart at Wounded Knee (Brown), 64
Bush, George, 142
Bushnell, Candace, 155
Butte, MT, 51, 135, 136
California, 15, 30, 41, 42, 51, 57, 68, 72, 78, 82, 95, 96, 99, 138
California's Central Valley, 84
California Trail, 68
Camelot, 120
Campbell, Ben Nighthorse, 91
Canadian Lakota Tribe, 115
Canine Cowboy, The, 117
Canyon Country Zephyr, 21, 67
Canyonlands National Park, 125
Cape Cod, 105
Cappucino Cowboy Coffee House, 117
Carlin, NV, 114
Carlsbad, NM, 132
Carson City, NV, 23
Carter, Jimmy, 91
Cartwright Family, 154
Carver, Dick, 62, 142, 145
Cascade Range, 34, 46, 49
Casper, WY, 131
Catron County, NM, 23, 143
CBS, 41
Central Arizona Project, 81, 84
Central City, CO, 120
Ceremony (Silko), 65
Chama, NM, 23
Chase, Alston, 67
Cheyenne, WY, 123, 131
Chicago, IL, 22
Chinook Pass, WA, 72
City Slickers, 122, 153
Clappe, Amelia, 41
Clark, William, 138–139, 171
Clark's Fork of the Yellowstone River, 136
Clearwater County, ID, 109
Clinton, William, 72, 79, 91, 143
Clovis, NM, 120
Coca–Cola, 122
Coeur d'Alene River, 146
Coeur d'Alene Tribe, 146
Colorado, 49, 51, 53, 54, 55, 68, 70, 75, 77, 79, 82, 88, 90, 93, 95, 99, 101, 102, 104, 110, 118, 125, 126, 128, 129, 132, 134, 136, 155, 157, 175, 177

Colorado–Big Thompson Project, 88, 93
Colorado Front Range, 53, 80, 93, 95
Colorado Mountain Club, 128
Colorado Plateau, 18, 31, 46, 49, 95, 109–110, 111, 133, 138
Colorado River, 49, 53, 82, 125
Colorado River Basin, 93
Colorado Rockies, 32
Colorado Springs, CO, 49, 110, 131
Colstrip, MT, 53
Columbia Basin, 139
Columbia Plateau, 47, 49
Columbia River, 31, 62, 86–89
Colville Reservation, 62
Community and the Politics of Place (Kemmis), 38–39
Conejos County, CO, 99
Confederated Tribes of the Warm Springs Reservation, 34–38
Connors Pass, NV, 72
Coordinated Resource Management, 145
Coors, 118, 120
Coors, Adolf, 118
Costilla County, CO, 99
Council of Energy Resource Tribes, 62
Cowboy Aviation, 117
Cowboy Blues Diner, 117
Cowboy Coffee Co., 117
Cowboy Computer Corp., 117
Cowboy Computers, 117
Cowboy Cooking and Supply, 117
Cowboy Heaven, 117
Cowboy Logic, 117
Cowboy Pest Control, 117
Cowboy Snowmobiles, 117
Cowboys and Lace Antiques, 117
Crested Butte, CO, 103, 128
Crestone, CO, 112, 169
Cripple Creek, CO, 131
Crow Reservation, 62
Crystal, Billy, 122
Crystal Mountain, WA, 126
Cumbres Pass, NM, 72
Cunningham, John, 43
Custer Battlefield National Monument, 64
Custer, George Armstrong, 51, 64
Custer State Park, 139
Custer Died for Your Sins (Deloria), 33, 64
Cyprus Amax, 79
Dagget, Dan, 26
Daniels, Wy, 141
Dante's View, 51
Death Valley, 47, 49, 80
Death Valley National Park, 61
deBuys, William, 67
Defenders of Wildlife, 141
Delicate Arch, 21
Deloria, Vine, Jr., 33, 37, 64
Denver, CO, 15, 29, 30, 32, 49, 51, 54, 55, 56, 70, 79, 80, 91, 131, 132, 135, 151, 152, 174
Denver Broncos, 31–32
Denver Center for the Performing Arts, 31–32
Denver International Airport, 70, 72
Denver Post, 152, 155
Deschutes River, 34
Deseret Chemical Depot, 136
Desert Lands Act, 84
Desert Solitaire (Abbey), 21, 67
Detroit, MI, 110
Devil's Garden, 51
Devil's Golf Course, 51
Devil's Playground, 51
Devil's Punchbowl, 51
Devil's Slide, 51
Devil's Thumb, 51
Devil's Tower, 47
Devil's Tower National Monument, 129
DeVoto, Bernard, 78

Dillon, CO, 54
Divide, CO, 131
Doc Holliday, 120
Dodge, 122
Doe, Phil, 91
Dog–Gone prairie–dog vacuum, 152
Doig, Ivan, 169
Dominy, Floyd, 31
Dona Ana County, NM, 99
Donner Pass, CA, 53, 72
Donner Party, 68
Douglas County, CO, 57
Driggs, ID, 70
Dubois, WY, 117
Durango, CO, 51, 90
Durango Herald, 91
Eagle, CO, 15
Eagle River, 136
Eagles Nest Wilderness, 18
Eastern Oregon State College, 37
Eaton, Earl, 15, 23
Echo Summit, CA, 72
Egypt, 120
El Capitan, 75
El Paso, TX, 49, 56, 99
El Tovah Hotel, 70
Elko, NV, 120
Ely, NV, 31
Emigrant, MT, 141
Encampment, WY, 53
Encounters with the Archdruid, 31
End–Time Historian Zoosh, 167
Endangered Species Act, 26, 87, 128, 140
Escalante, UT, 117
ESPN, 122
Eureka County, NV, 55, 109
Even Cowgirls Get the Blues (Robbins), 65
Evil Knievel, 49
Explorer Race, The (Shapiro and Zoosh), 167
Extraterrestrial Highway, 115
Fall River, 145
Fallon, NV, 131, 133, 135
Fat Tire Ale, 118
Feather River, Middle Fork, 41, 43
Feathered Pipe Ranch, 114
Fifty Classic Climbs of North America (Steck and
    Roper), 128
Firehole River, 58
Flathead, 51
Flathead County, MT, 104
Flathead River, 139
FLPMA (Federal Land Policy Management Act),
    23
Fonda, Jane, 97
Forbes, 79
Fort Apache Reservation, 62
Fort Collins, CO, 131
Four Corners, 90
Fradkin, Phillip, 84, 90
Frank Church–River of No–Return Wilderness,
    74
Freeman, Judith, 170
Fremont, John C., 47, 68
Frenchman Flat, NV, 132, 172
Frisco, CO, 117
Frontier Days Rodeo, 123
Fuhrman, Mark, 157
Galena Summit, ID, 72
Gallatin River, 139
Gallatin Valley, 97
Garreau, Joel, 55, 94
Garrison Dam, 89
Gay Rodeo Association, 123
Gene Autry's Cowboy's Code, 161
Geography of Hope: A Tribute to Wallace Stegner,
    The, 149
Gibbon River, 58
Gila River, 145

Glacier Peak Wilderness, 74
Glen Canyon Dam, 82, 86, 90, 125
Gold Hill, CO, 55
Gold Rush, 29
Good City and the Good Life, The (Kemmis), 38
Gore Valley, 15
GoreTex, 123
Grand Canyon, 123–125, 132, 138
Grand Canyon National Park, 59, 61
Grand Canyon Visibility Transport Commission,
    138
Grand Coulee Dam, 86
Grand County, UT, 21, 142
Grand Junction, CO, 111, 133
Grand River, 53
Grand Staircase–Escalante National Monument,
    61
Grand Tetons, 46, 47
Grantsville, UT, 131
Great Basin, 47, 49, 95, 131
Great Plains, 46, 47
Great Plains, The (Webb), 22
Great Salt Lake, 49, 53, 112
Great Smoky Mountains, 105
Great Falls, MT, 131
Green River, 53
Grey, Zane, 64
Griffith, Bud, 166
Grizzly Bear (Ursus horribilis), 139
Guadalupe County, NM, 99
Gunnison, CO, 23
Gunnison River Valley, CO, 26
Guthrie, A.B., 65
Hanford Nuclear Reservation, 132, 135, 172
Harjo, Joy, 170
Harper's, 78
Hatfield, Doc and Connie, 145
Haxtun, CO, 117
Heard Museum, 32
Heart Seed Retreat Center, 114
Heart Mountain, WY, 94
Heath, Benny, 37
Heavenly Valley, CA, 126
Heber City, UT, 131
HeHe, OR, 37
Helena, MT, 114
Hell's Canyon, 47, 51
Hell's Half Acre, 51
Henderson, NV, 118
Henry's Fork of the Snake River, 125
Henry's Fork Watershed Council, 145–146
Hermiston, OR, 136
Hess, Karl, 62
Hidalgo County, NM, 99
High Country News, 57, 67, 70, 105, 177
High Uintas Wilderness, 74
Hispanic (census category), 97–101
Hogan, Linda, 37, 170
Holthaus, Gary, 43
Homestead Act, 84
Hoosier Pass, CO, 72
Hoover Dam, 82, 86
Hopalong Cassidy, 158–161
Hopi Reservation, 62
Hopi Tribe, 31
Hornby, Bill, 32
Hualapai, 51
Hubcap Ale, 118
Huckleberry Feast, 35–36
Hugo, Richard, 41
Hungry Horse Dam, 86
Idaho, 31, 42, 49, 51, 55, 79, 82, 86, 87, 94, 102,
    103, 105, 106, 107, 109, 110, 118, 132, 134,
    140, 144, 146, 175
Idaho National Engineering Laboratory, 132
Illinois, 95
Imperial County, CA, 99
Independence Pass, CO, 72

Indian Child Welfare Act, 33
INFOZONE, Telluride, CO, 77
Integrated Services Digital Network (ISDN), 77
International Conscious Breathing Center, 114
Internet, 77
Inter–Tribal Bison Cooperative, 139
Iron Mountain, WY, 67
Irwin v. Phillips, 30
Ishawooa, 51
Island Park Reservoir, 145
Ives, Lt. Joseph C., 123–124
Jackson, WY, 18, 70, 102, 106, 117, 155, 165, 177
Jackson County, CO, 109
Jackson Hole, WY, 104, 126
Jacob's Ladder, 51
Jaramillo, Debbie, 104
Java Monthly, 118
Jeep Safari, 18
Jefferson County, MT, 109
Jeffrey City, WY, 135
Jefferson, Thomas, 38
Jemez Mountains, 51
John Day River, 34
John Muir Wilderness, 74
Johnson, Lori, 157
Jordan, Teresa, 65, 67, 170
Joshua Tree, CA, 131
Joshua Tree National Monument, 125
Judge Flannery, 23
Kalispell, MT, 110
Kanab, UT, 117
Kaparich, Chuck, 38–41
Keet Seel, 51
Kemmis, Daniel, 38, 39
Kennecott, UT, 49–51
Kerr, Andy, 88
Ketchum, ID, 110
Kill the Cowboy: A Battle of Mythology (Russell), 65
Killington, VT, 126
Kingsolver, Barbara, 170
Kittredge, William, 18, 67, 96, 169
KWSO–FM, 35
L'Amour, Louis, 64
La Plata Valley, 90
La Sal Mountains, 46
Laguna Pueblo, 67
Lake Mead, 84
Lake Tahoe, 15, 41
Lake Tahoe ski area, CA, 104
Lake Havasu City, AZ, 110
Lake Powell, 86, 90
Lakota Tribe, 115
Lamm, Richard, 15–17, 57, 157, 175
Lamoille, NV, 131
Land Rover, 118
Lander, WY, 122
Laramie, WY, 51
Las Cruces, NM, 131
Las Vegas, NV, 32, 49, 51, 81, 110, 120, 131, 135,
    177
Last Settler Syndrome, 93
Last Stand at Little Bighorn (Welch), 64
Le Cowboy, 117
Leadville, CO, 53, 106, 136
Lee's Ferry, AZ, 125
Lewis, Meriwether, 138–139, 171
Lewiston, ID, 86
Lincoln County, MT, 77
Little America (Swigart), 65
Little Big Man, 64
Little Bighorn Battlefield National Monument, 64
Little Bighorn River, 53
Logan Pass, MT, 72
Lone Pine, CA, 70
Lone Ranger's Creed, 159
Los Alamos, NM, 135
Los Angeles, CA, 29, 54, 70, 93, 101, 153,
Los Angeles Police Department, 157

Lost Trail Pass, ID, 72
Loveland Pass, CO, 72
Luna Mesa, 115
MacKenzie Pass, OR, 72
MacLean, Norman, 128, 135, 136, 169, 170
Mad, 162
Mammoth Mountain, CA, 126
Manhasset, NY, 77
Manhattan, 120
Manifest Destiny, 30
Many Glacier Hotel, 70
Marston, Ed, 57, 70, 105
Marvels of the New West (Thayer), 151
McClosky, Michael, 27
McKinley County, NM, 99
McKittrick, Chad, 141
McNamer, Dierdre, 170
McPhee, John, 25, 31
McQuinn Strip, 34–35
Medicine Bow, WY, 47
Meeteetse, WY, 141
Menominee Restoration Act, 33
Mesa Verde National Park, 59
Meta Tantay, 114
Metaline Falls, WA, 131
Mill Creek Canyon, 19
Mills, Enos, 72
Minidoka, ID, 94
Missoula, MT. 38–41, 67, 139
Missoula Redevelopment Agency, 39
Missouri River, 18
Moab, UT, 18–22, 67, 111, 117, 120, 125,
    129, 133
Moab Rim, 19
Mojave Desert, 128
Momaday, N. Scott, 37, 170
Monarch Pass, CO, 72
Money, 77, 131
Monkey Wrench Gang, The (Abbey), 21, 49, 126
Mono Lake, 54
Montana, 38, 39, 46, 47, 51, 55, 67, 78, 86, 95, 96,
    102, 104, 107, 110, 118, 126, 132, 134, 136,
    138, 140, 165, 169, 175
Montgomery Pass, NV, 72
Mora County, NM, 99
Mormons, 102, 112
Mount Bachelor, WA, 126
Mount Jefferson, 34
Mountain Lion (*Felis concolor*), 140
Mountain of the Holy Cross, 47, 51
Mountains of the Moon National Monument, 49
Mt. Whitney, 75, 125
Muir, John, 17, 128
Mulholland, William, 29
Nakota Tribe, 115
Names on the Land (Stewart), 51
National Biological Service, 143
National Bison Range, 139
National Environmental Policy Act, 23
National Public Radio, 112, 117
National Western Stock Show, 151
National Wildlife Federation, 141
National Wildlife Refuges, 58
Native American (census category), 97–101
Natural Resources Defense Council, 23
Navajo County, AZ, 99
Navajo Dam, 90
Navajo Reservation, 62, 84, 128
Navajo Tribe, 22, 31, 33, 89, 128
NBC, 41
Negro Bill Canyon, 19
Nevada, 72, 80, 96, 102, 105, 115, 118, 120, 131,
    132, 154, 172
Nevada Test Site, 135, 172
New York, 29, 55, 59, 70, 75, 95, 104, 136, 153,
    155, 177
New York Times, 26, 41, 95, 112, 131, 151
New Age, 112, 114–115, 165–167

New Mexico, 23, 53, 54, 96, 99, 115, 128, 132,
    163, 175
Newlands, Francis (senator), 84
Newman, Alfred E., 162
Newsweek, 175
Nez Perce Tribe, 51, 89
Nine Nations of North America, The (Garreau), 55,
    94
Northern Lights, 27, 67
Northern Rockies Ecosystem Protection Act,
    146–48
Northwest Power Planning Council, 89
Novell, 79
Nye County, NV, 23, 25, 62, 142, 145
Ogden, UT, 102
Old Divide Trading Post, 161
Old Faithful, 53, 107, 138
Old Faithful Lodge, 70
Olgilvie, Jim, 91–93
Orange County, CA, 78
Oregon, 31, 34, 37, 59, 67, 78, 87, 95, 99, 105,
    136, 144
Oregon Natural Resources Council, 88
Ortiz, Simon, 37, 170
Orvis Company, Inc., 117, 136
Osgood, Charles, 41
Outside, 125, 131
Owens Valley, CA, 29
Owning it All (Kittredge), 67
Pacific Crest Trail, 42
Pacifica Radio, 112, 117
Paepcke, Elizabeth and Walter, 112
Pagosa Springs, CO, 111
Palm Springs, CA, 81, 110, 117
Palo Felchado Pass, NM, 72
Panther Creek, 136
Paonia, CO, 67
Park City, UT, 18, 77, 126
Parkman, Francis, 153
Pasayten/Stephen Mather Wilderness, 74
Patagonia, 118
Pendleton, OR, 123
Peterson, Roger, 41
Peterson, Levi, 170
Phelps Dodge, 79
Phoenix, AZ, 26, 29, 30, 32, 49, 56, 72, 79, 80–82,
    110, 151
Phoenix Gazette, 29
Phoenix Suns, 32
Pinchot, Gifford, 19, 59
Pinedale, WY, 31, 53, 70
Pitkin County, CO, 103
Places Rated Almanac (Savageau and Boyer),
    129–131
Platte River, 91
Playing God in Yellowstone (Chase), 67
Plumas County, CA, 42
Poison Spider Mesa, 19
Polson, MT, 111
Ponderosa Ranch, 154, 157
Portland, OR, 31
Poston, AZ, 94
Powder River Pass, WY, 72
Powell, John Wesley, 53, 84, 123
Power, Thomas, 111
Professional Rodeo Cowboy Association, 120, 122
Provo, UT, 111, 131
Pueblo, CO, 136
Pueblo Chemical Depot, 136
Psychic Cowboy–Tarot, The, 117
Pyramid Lake, 178
Quiet Crisis, The (Stewart), 17
Quillen, Ed, 32
Quincy, CA, 41–44
Quincy Library Group, 44
Rawlins, C.L., 67, 170
Reagan, Ronald, 61, 142
Reclamation Act, 29, 84,

Red Lodge, MT, 141
Red Lady Ale, 118
Red Mountain Pass, 72
Redfish Lake, 87
Redford, Robert, 112, 136
Reel Cowboys, 117
Refuge (Williams), 49, 132
Reno, NV, 30, 128, 131
Reopening the Western Frontier (Marston), 23
Resource Advisory Councils, 27
Richland, WA, 131, 135
Riding the White Horse Home (Jordan), 65–67
Ring, Ray, 177
Ringholz, Raye, 133
Rio Grand Basin, 93
Rio Grand National Forest, 79
Rio Arriba County, NM, 99
River No More: The Colorado River and the West, A
    (Fradkin), 90
River of No Return, 51
River of No Return Wilderness, 47
River Runs Through It, A (MacLean), 96, 128, 135,
    136, 169
Roaring Fork Valley, 95
Robbins, Royal, 128
Robbins, Tom, 65
Rock Creek, 42
Rocky Flats nuclear bomb plant, 132, 135, 172
Rocky Mountains, 15–18, 46–47, 95, 146–148,
Rocky Mountain National Park, 72
Rogers Pass, MT, 47
Rogers, Roy, 158–161
Romer, Roy, 26
Ronan, MT, 117
Roosevelt County, MT, 99
Roosevelt, Theodore, 19, 29, 59, 84, 128, 153
Roswell, NM, 117–119
Ruby Mountains, 131
Russell, Sharman Apt, 65
Sacred Sage: How It Heals (Whiteman), 163
Sagebrush Rebellion, 23, 25, 61, 145
Salmon (*Salmonidae*), 86–89, 140
Salt Lake City, UT, 29, 30, 32, 49, 130, 131, 133
Salt Lake Roasting Company, 32
San Carlos Reservation, 62
San Francisco, CA, 22
San Francisco Bay, 78
San Juan County, UT, 99
San Juan Mountains, 68
San Luis Valley, 46
San Rafael Triangle, 115
Sand Creek, CO, 53
Sand Point, ID, 118
Sandia National Labs, 135
Sangre de Cristo Range, 51, 67
Santa Cruz County, AZ, 99
Santa Fe, NM, 32, 51, 99, 102, 103–104, 114, 117,
    118, 131, 153, 154, 163
Santa Fe County, NM, 99
Santa Fe New Age Fair, 163
Santa Fe Style, 154
Saratoga, WY, 70, 105, 118
Sarin gas, 136
Savory, WY, 114
Sawtooth Mountains, 87
Scottsdale, AZ, 110, 117
Seattle, WA, 32
Sedona, AZ, 104, 112, 114, 117, 166–167
Sedona: Journal of Emergence!, 166–167
Self–Determination Act, 33
Selway–Bitteroot Wilderness, 74
Separation Rapids, 51, 123
Seven Hands, Seven Hearts (Woody), 37
Sex and the City (Bushnell), 155
Shapiro, Robert, 167
Shasta Dam, 86
Shaw, George Bernard, 38
Shiprock, NM, 128

Shirley Letters from the California Mines, The (Clappe), 41
Siebert, Pete, 15, 23
Sierra Club, 23, 27, 84, 143, 146
Sierra Nevada Range, 46–47, 49, 54, 68, 125
Sierraville, CA, 114
Sikorski, Gerry, 146
Silicon Valley, 78
Silko, Leslie Marmon, 37, 65, 67, 170
Silver Lake, CO, 47
Simpson, O.J., 157
Sinclair, WY, 51
Sitting Bull, 53
Slickrock Trail, 125
Slickrock Cafe, 117
Smelterville, MT, 53
Snake River, 86–87
Snow, Donald, 27, 57
Snowbird, UT, 126
Snowmass, CO, 126
Snowmass Mountain, 51
Snowy Range Pass, WY, 72
Sonora Pass, CA, 72
South Fork of the Coeur d'Alene River, 136
Southern Ute Tribe, 90
Southern Utah Wilderness Alliance, 148
Spokane, WA, 49, 51, 131, 135
Squaw Valley, CA, 15, 17
Stafford, Archbishop J. Francis, 151, 175–178
Steamboat Springs, CO, 104
Steamboat ski area, CO, 126
Stegner, Wallace, 26, 32, 41, 42, 65, 74, 126–128
Stekler, Paul, 64
Stewart, George, 51
Stiles, Jim, 21
Stillpoint Center, 114
Summit County, UT, 55, 96, 107
Summitville, CO, 135
Sun City, AZ, 110
Sun family, 145
Sun Valley, ID, 18, 70, 103, 112, 117, 126
Sundance Ski Resort, 112
Sweetwater County, WY, 109
Swigart, Rob, 65
Tamarack, CA, 47
Taos, NM, 18, 117, 163
Taos County, NM, 99
Taos Pueblo, 33
Tapahonso, Luci, 170
TCI, 79
Telluride, CO, 77, 106, 112, 126
Tempe, AZ, 117
Temple Square, 32
Testimony (Zwinger), 19
Teton County, WY, 103
Teton Pass, WY, 72, 106
Teton/Washakie Wilderness, 74
Thayer, William, 151, 153
This House of Sky (Doig), 169
Three Quarter Circle Ranch, 122

Time, 62, 70, 77, 96, 158, 175
Tioga Pass, CA, 72
Tipton, Tony and Jerrie, 25, 145
Togwotee, 51
Togwotee Pass, WY, 72
Tohono O'odham Reservation, 62
Toiyabe Range, 25
Tonto, 51
Tooele, UT, 131, 136
Topaz, UT, 94
Trail Ridge, CO, 72
Trans Montane Rod and Gun Club, 23
Trinity Alps Wilderness, 74
Trinity Site, NM, 53, 135
Truth or Consequences, NM, 51
Tucson, AZ, 30, 49, 56, 70, 75, 110
Turner, Frederick Jackson, 23
Turner, Ted, 97, 139, 165–166
Twain, Mark, 163, 165
Twin Falls, ID, 31, 49
Two Forks Dam, 54, 93
U.S. Army Corps of Engineers, 84–86
U.S. Bureau of Reclamation, 53–54, 87–93
U.S. Census Bureau, 97
U.S. Bureau of Indian Affairs, 33
U.S. Bureau of Land Management, 26, 59–61, 122, 142–143
U.S. Department of the Army, 136
U.S. Department of Energy, 133
U.S. Environmental Protection Agency, 54, 135
U.S. Forest Service, 22, 25, 42, 53, 59, 75, 107
U.S. Immigration and Naturalization Service, 177
U.S. National Park Service, 53, 75, 129
Udall, Stewart, 17, 133
UFO Museum and Research Center, 115–117
Uintah and Ouray Reservation, 62
Uintah County, UT, 143
Umatilla Tribe, 89
Umatilla Chemical Depot, 136
United States v. Winans, 35
University of Montana Law School, 38
Uranium Frenzy (Ringholz), 133
Uravan, CO, 135
Utah, 24, 49, 53, 55, 61, 67, 74, 77, 94, 102, 105, 107, 112, 117, 118, 132, 136, 138, 142, 146
Utah Jazz, 32
Ute Mountain Ute Tribe, 90–91
Vail, CO, 15–17, 38, 41, 103, 104–105, 106, 126
Vail Associates, 18
Vail Board of Realtors, 18
Vail Pass, CO, 72
Valenica County, NM, 99
Vibram, 123
Victor, ID, 117
Virginian, The, (Wister), 152
Volvos, 97
VX gas, 136
Wainanwit, Donna L., 37
Warm Springs Reservation, 34–38
Warm Springs Tribe, 34–38, 89

Warner Mountains, 67
Wasatch Front, 93
Wasatch Range, 32, 96
Wasco Tribe, 35
Washakie, 51
Washburn, Henry, 58
Washington, 31, 59, 78, 95, 102, 130, 132, 134, 175
Washington, DC, 31, 61, 153, 155
Waste Isolation Pilot Plant, 133–135
Watt, James, 59, 61, 142
Webb, Walter Prescott, 22
Welch, James, 37, 64, 169
Wells, NV, 120
Wenatchee, WA, 111
Wenminuche Wilderness, 74
West, Elliott, 157
Wetmore, CO, 114
White (census category), 97–101
White, Gilbert, 93
Whiteman, Wendy, 163
Who Owns the West (Kittredge), 18, 67
Wilderness Society. 23
Wildlands Project, 148
Williams, DeWayne, 172
Williams, Terry Tempest, 49, 132, 149, 170
Wilson, WY, 103
Wind River, 53
Wind River Mountains, 67
Wind River Reservation, 62
Winnemucca, NV, 131
Winter Olympics (1976), 15–17
Winter Park, CO, 126
Wise Use Movement, 23, 27, 104, 143–145
Wise River, MT, 131
Wister, Owen, 152
Wolf (*Canus lupus*), 141
Wolf Creek Pass, CO, 72
Woody, Elizabeth, 37
World Wide Web, 77
World War II, 29
Wrangler World of Rodeo, 122
Wyoming, 53, 70, 94, 101, 104, 107, 109, 118, 120, 125, 126, 134, 140, 144, 175, 177
Wyoming Farm Bureau, 140
Yakama Reservation, 62
Yakama Tribe, 89
Yankee Fork of the Salmon River, 136
Yellowstone National Park, 58, 61, 74–75, 77, 107, 125, 139, 141
Yosemite National Park, 58, 75
Young Men and Fire (MacLean), 169
Young, Brigham, 112
Yucca Mountain, NV, 75, 132, 133, 135
Yuma, AZ, 131
Zion Canyon, 47
Zion National Park, 61
Zwinger, Ann, 19